Teddy Bare

The following statement is authorized for publication by John Farrar, the skindiver who removed Mary Jo Kopechne's body from Senator Kennedy's car after the Chappaquiddick incident.

Having been directly involved in the recovery of the victim at Chappaquiddick, and the legal affairs which followed, I believe that this book, *Teddy Bare*, is the most dynamic and factual book ever published on this latest Kennedy tragedy.

The author, Zad Rust, and the publisher, Western Islands of Belmont, Massachusetts, should be complimented for bringing this information to the attention of the American people. I highly recommend it to everyone, both as an insight into what really happened that night, and more importantly, as a closer look at those friends of Senator Kennedy, in high places, who went to work to smother the real story of Chappaquiddick. It's a shocker!

John Farrar
At Edgartown, Massachusetts
August 12, 1971

TEDDY BARE
The Last Of The Kennedy Clan

by

Zad Rust

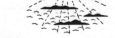

WESTERN ISLANDS

BOSTON   LOS ANGELES

Table Of Contents

PART THREE
Final Hocus Pocus

Prologue

This book follows the circumstances of the Chappaquiddick tragedy, from its mysterious beginning to its squalid conclusion in a top-secret inquest and before a terrorized grand jury, as they were allowed to come to the knowledge of the American public by official activity and inactivity.

This explains certain blanks and imprecisions in its first chapters, and explains also why the reader will be deprived, in the end, of what he probably hopes to be told: the story of what really happened to Mary Jo Kopechne on the night of July 18, 1969.

The fact that all the efforts of the police and judiciary authorities were directed, in this very special case, not toward the discovery of the truth but toward its burial, forever if possible, would be a sufficient reason for every just-minded person to denounce and expose this malfeasance. This certainly played a part in my decision to write the following pages, but I must confess that my principal motivation was less sentimental and more matter of fact.

The man for whose benefit so much legal and illegal manipulation has been practised is, as was each of his two brothers, one of the prominent operators chosen by the Hidden Forces that are hurling the countries of Western Civilization toward the Animal Farm world willed by Lenin and his successors — a world of which Soviet Russia and the eleven European countries handed over to Stalin at

Yalta; continental China, delivered to Mao Tse-tung by the Marshall Mission; and Cuba, given to Castro at the infamous Bay of Pigs, are the current models.

Only a regenerated United States can prevent this satanic Utopia from coming true. The conquest of the White House by still another Kennedy will create, on the contrary, the best possible conditions for its realization. And by the same token, what is now the Enslaved World will have lost the very last hope, faint and beyond reason as it may seem today, of seeing Teheran, Yalta, the Marshall Mission, and the Bay of Pigs redeemed by action of the very country that bears the responsibility for those gargantuan errors.

Introduction

In the case of President Kennedy's assassination, nobody but the persons directly responsible would be able to say today who the murderers were. But there is no one in the United States or anywhere else, with a normal thinking apparatus and normal curiosity and information, who believes that the explanation of this murder offered by the Warren Commission, with its accompanying procession of strangely disappearing witnesses, is the correct one. Thinking people are, on the contrary, convinced that this Commission had no other mission than to conceal the truth, and that it was relentlessly helped in this mission by many official agencies and by *some powerful organized Force of universal scope and character.*

An ugly vista had already been opened thereby — for those, both at home and abroad, who had not been alarmed long before — on the dark recesses of certain political activities in the United States. With the death of Mary Jo Kopechne, however, the collusion between that Force and official authorities, in the effort to bury the truth together with the body of Mary Jo, seems to have reached and stirred up the deepest and most pestilential strata of this country's political privy.

The identity of the person responsible for that young girl's death — the person whose reputation and political future this unholy collusion is trying to save — is known to everybody. He is a United States Senator who belongs to a prominent political clan and who is a proclaimed postulant for the Presidency.

He represents typically, as did his two brothers also, that

brand of political tycoons permanently in power since the Roosevelt era, under both Democrat and Republican administrations. To politicians of this sort the world owes the tacit alliance between the United States and Soviet Russia — between the only remaining Western great power and the Eastern conquerors — with all its disastrous military, political, social, intellectual, and spiritual consequences.

The activities of those operators and of the Force which they obey interest not only the United States but also, obviously, the entire world — the countries that have already lost their liberty, and those whose liberty is threatened. What happens in or to the United States, the last non-Communist big power, happens to all the non-Communist countries, large and small, but most especially to those countries in Europe, Asia, Africa, and Ibero-America that are already in Communist bondage or about to be conquered by the Communist Conspiracy.

This Force of Darkness has already brought the world very near to the point of no return on the road to total annihilation of the liberties of man and the independence of nations, and to the enthronement of the Antichrist. If they hasten, today, to protect the man responsible for the death of Mary Jo Kopechne, it is because, after the disappearance of his two brothers, they counted upon him for the last push.

That is why it is of the greatest importance that everyone in the United States and in other countries know and remember forever the true circumstances of the tragedy of the Dyke Bridge, and understand the true character of the man that this Force of Darkness was prepared to introduce into the White House. They may still put him there — or somebody else of the same description. The danger of such an enthronement will always exist as long as the U.S. electorate, both in the primaries and in the final elections, continues to vote for the *best-advertised* candidate, who is almost always the candidate of the Establishment, and not for the *best* candidate, who as President could only be its sworn enemy.

PART ONE

THE TRAGEDY

July 18, 1969 - July 25, 1969

CHAPTER I

Camelot

In one respect the newspapers were unfair to Senator Edward M. Kennedy after the Dyke Bridge tragedy. They reproached him with having, in this hour of trial, repudiated all the ways and traditions of the Kennedy family as personified in his two brothers, John and Robert: sincerity, altruism, courage, frankness, justice, and the drive toward excellence. He was accused, particularly, of having lost his wits under stress, whereas his brothers, who had jointly held the Presidency of the United States for nearly three years, were never at the end of theirs, even in the most complex or dangerous situations.

We, on the contrary, like Mrs. Rose Kennedy, his mother, are of the opinion that the Senator demonstrated, after the tragedy that took Mary Jo's life, that he knew as well as his brothers how to extricate himself from the most awkward and uncomfortable situations. We also think that on that occasion Senator Kennedy demonstrated that he was in full possession of all the other qualities characteristic of the Kennedy clan, as shown by universally known facts. These qualities are quite different from those suggested to the public mind by a relentless and formidable international publicity effort, comparable only to that exerted by the organs of public information of every country to kill, morally and politically, Senator Joe McCarthy, or to transform into an apostle of peace and non-violence Martin Luther King, Jr., the communistoid agent, provoker, and organizer of all the

1

violence that has disrupted the national life of the United States in the last decade and that will continue to disrupt it for years to come.

The qualities demonstrated by the Kennedys during their recent history, and especially during the John-Robert condominium, were principally: (1) boundless ambition; (2) readiness to get, by whatever means, what they have decided to get; (3) slavish obedience to the Force to which they have decided to adhere as the most likely to help them get and keep what they want; (4) a remarkable capacity of dissimulation; (5) an unabashed nepotism; (6) implacability in persecution of anyone who either deliberately or by chance stands in the way of their purpose; (7) a pachydermous skin, impervious to any denunciation or accusation, however justifiable; and (8) an imperturbable effrontery and histrionism — by which, in the case of Edward Kennedy's appearance on television, a lot of people, including even the family of the Poucha Pond victim, let themselves be fooled for a while.

What the first American generation of Kennedys very understandably wanted to get from their new country was money. The grandfather got it by selling booze. What the second generation wanted was more money, and power. Ambassador Joseph B. Kennedy got them by selling more and better booze and, chiefly, by bartering (at the proper price) his American attitude — identical with that of Herbert Hoover, Charles Lindbergh, and Congressman Hamilton Fish — in the face of the storm that was raging in Europe for a complete adherence to Roosevelt's alien-built policy.*
Backed by the enormous amount of money acquired through this last master stroke, the third generation could concentrate entirely on the pursuit of power, and they did it with a vengeance. Conquering and keeping the White House for the family was the supreme purpose. It was still the major worry

---

*We recommend on this subject the reading of James Forrestal's *Diary* and Curtis Dall's *F.D.R.: My Exploited Father-in-Law.*

of the last of the Kennedy brothers after the Dyke Bridge tragedy, as proved by his ignominious behavior while the body of Mary Jo was "swishing back and forth in the tides for over nine hours."

The White House having been conquered by the John-Robert team, thanks to a fraudulent majority of 122,700 votes out of 69 million cast, a guarantee had to be given by the Kennedys to the Powers that had chosen them definitely as their chief operators. This was done as in other cases by accepting imposed overseers, the Rostow brothers this time, and especially Walt W. Rostow, as the almighty controllers of United States foreign policy. A reading of Rostow's book, *The United States in the World Arena,* should have been enough to show the Kennedy brothers, who were once admirers and friends of Joe McCarthy, that what the man they had accepted as their mentor represented in the matter of patriotism, national independence, and self-defense against the universal Communist danger was continual withdrawal before the Communist advance, continual advance toward a World Government that could only be Communistic, and, to quote Mr. Walt Rostow himself, "placing the U.S. military power under an effective international control."

For want of space we shall mention only a few of the universally known political events imputable to the Kennedy Presidential tandem — events sufficiently demonstrative of the quality of Kennedy thinking and acting: (1) the Bay of Pigs affair; (2) the formidable hoax of the so-called de-bombing of Communist Cuba; (3) the unilateral dismantling of the U.S. first-strike nuclear power; (4) the General Edwin A. Walker affair; (5) the outrageous treatment of Pérez Jiménez, the former President of Venezuela; and last but not least, (6) the Katanga massacres. The common denominator of the Kennedys' behavior in all the above-mentioned circumstances was accession to Communist desires and Soviet interests.

Have you forgotten the day when, at the Bay of Pigs, two thousand Cuban patriots, encouraged and organized by the Kennedy administration, disembarked from United States craft on Cuban territory, under the solemn promise by the Kennedy administration of air and naval support, and then were abandoned without any support at all, the Navy and the Air Force having received from the same President who had promised their cooperation the personal order to get away as quickly as possible? When later the news came out that the Soviets had transformed Cuba into a nuclear arsenal and a Soviet military stronghold ninety miles off U.S. shores, the Kennedy administration denied the facts as long as denial was possible. When forced to recognize them, the Kennedy brothers did not take the only decision that would have been commensurate to the provocation, the decision required for their country's safety: i.e., total occupation of the island, an operation that could have been completed in forty-eight hours. Instead they set up the greatest hoax perpetrated on a trusting nation since Pearl Harbor. Mock movements of troops and squadrons were paraded before a hoodwinked public, while secret orders to the Navy cancelled out the effectiveness of the so-called quarantine and secret nego- tiations between President Kennedy and Premier Khrushchev – monitored by Robert Kennedy, Secretary of Defense Robert S. McNamara, and Walt Rostow – and an exchange of seventeen letters between Khrushchev and Kennedy brought about the following results:

1. Cuba today is still a Soviet military stronghold in the Caribbean, a third Communist octopus, which has tentacles spreading all over South and Central America; and it has become a submarine base as well.

2. The launching ramps of the Soviet nuclear artillery are still in Cuba, and the missiles are very likely there also.

3. No control over the withdrawal of these missiles was allowed by the Soviets – the assurance that they had been

withdrawn was given by the captain of the Soviet ships that were supposed to transport them.

4. In exchange for the "concession" of Soviet withdrawal, all the U.S. Jupiter nuclear missile bases in the Mediterranean, except those in Libya, were evacuated.*

5. The publicity and the machinery of deception, meanwhile, worked so smoothly under the skillful hands of the Force that has backed the Kennedys throughout their political careers that even now there are people in the United States who believe that this irreversible political and military disaster was a political and military triumph.

It was Walt Rostow, sent to Moscow by John Kennedy to start negotiations with the Soviets when Kennedy was still only President-elect, who came back with the Soviet-inspired idea of dismantling the United States' first-strike nuclear force. Kennedy bought the idea immediately and presented it to the U.S. Senate in a speech that was much admired for the military and technical knowledge demonstrated by a nonprofessional. The truth was that very professional diplomatic and military individuals from the Soviet General Staff and Ministry of Foreign Affairs were responsible for the substance of Kennedy's address. It represented and implemented exactly the desires expressed by Comrade Kuznietzov to Mr. Rostow. "Your policy," the Soviet undersecretary of state had observed, "excludes a surprise attack against us; all your first-strike apparatus is therefore a useless luxury. Give it up and a big step will have been made toward a political understanding between our two countries." Useless to remark that the Soviets did not follow the policy recommended by Mr. Kuznietzov.

We have seen that, faithful to the defeatist policy of his clan, the first manifestation of Edward Kennedy in the Senate after his Chappaquiddick misadventure was a speech against the Anti-Ballistic Missile system. A few days before

---

*Today, those in Libya have also been evacuated.

the misadventure, at a $1000-a-plate political dinner in New York, he had asked for complete and urgent evacuation of U.S. troops from Vietnam. No wonder the Soviet press undertook to defend the Senator strongly in his hour of need.*

The fifty-seven-page book, *Censorship and Survival*, containing the address to the Senate of General Edwin A. Walker, combined with a factual review of the "Walker Case" by New York newsman Ike McAnally, tells of the measure of protection enjoyed by Soviet interests and Communist propaganda under the compact system of control built around the White House during the condominium of the Kennedy brothers.

Briefly, these were the facts: For having launched an educational and training program to "orient military personnel, dependents and friends to the scope of world Communism by studying the philosophies, objectives, and imperialistic expansion of Communism," and for having protested against the revolting fact that the official Army magazine, *The Stars and Stripes,* was sold together with the

---

*Senator Kennedy demands today a new U.S. policy towards Castro Cuba. The pusillanimity of the Kennedy brothers at the moment of the Cuban missile crisis, and what they did afterwards to U.S. defense possibilities, is put in a nutshell in an interview by *U.S. News & World Report* with Secretary of Defense Melvin Laird:

"Mr. LAIRD. However I believe that so much is clear: They [the Soviets] do not want to be in the position they found themselves in when they were confronted with the power of the United States at the time of the Cuban crisis. As you know, at that time President Kennedy had about a 4-to-1 nuclear superiority over the Soviet Union. But I cannot explain why they [the Soviets] are going for such a very large capability of mammoth warheads. Why the Soviets went forward to deploy some 220 of these 99-9s, plus 60 or more under construction, is difficult for me to understand. They have also the SS-11 and the SS-13, of course, both of which are roughly comparable to our Minuteman. They have over 800 of these now and are still deploying them.

Q. Was our policy at that time based on the idea that we should allow the Russians to catch up — that there should be parity between the two countries? Was that one reason we held down our nuclear program?

Mr. LAIRD. That is one reason — but let me emphasize that there was never an estimate that the Russians would develop the kind of momentum they have now. [McNamara computers' estimate, of course.]"

pornographic and pro-Communist *Overseas Weekly,* the General was stripped of his command in Europe and sent to Hawaii.

The Kennedy executioner in this case, in addition to Secretary of Defense Robert S. McNamara, was Adam Yarmolinsky, appointed by the President as special assistant to Mr. McNamara. Like the brothers Rostow, Yarmolinsky belonged to the first American-born generation of a family of foreign extraction, and like them he was fulfilling, in his own key department of government, the office of pro-consul of what is already a virtual anti-national World Government. Also very active in the pro-*Overseas Weekly* campaign were pro-Communist pressure groups such as the ADA (Americans for Democratic Action), which was called by President Kennedy "the minutemen of Democracy"; and, of course, the staff of the *Overseas Weekly.*

To give the reader an idea of the quality of this campaign, we quote here an exchange of words between Senator Strom Thurmond (South Carolina) and Secretary McNamara, who had just declared to the Senate Armed Services Committee that the *Overseas Weekly* was "a repulsive and disgraceful publication":

> Senator THURMOND. Mr. Secretary, the question is not whether you would prohibit free speech. The question is, if you were making the decision today as to whether our servicemen overseas should have this paper, this sexy, malicious, low paper, sent to them with *The Stars and Stripes,* whether or not you would permit it if you were making the decision today.
>
> Secretary McNAMARA. It is an extremely difficult question. I would wish the counsel of my General Counsel [meaning, of course, Yarmolinsky] and the counsel of others in the Department before I made the final answer.

General Walker's affair did not end with his forced retirement from the Armed Services. The statement he submitted to the U.S. Senate left deep scars of rancor in the kidneys of the One-Worlders. His punishment was entrusted to the Robert Kennedy-Katzenbach team. Everybody remembers how General Walker was kidnapped by the Attorney General's stooges at Oxford, Mississippi; how an individual named Dr. Cantor John — who, as head of the Mental Section of the Department of Justice, had the power to impose the same treatment on you — declared the General insane; and how the General was rushed, contrary to state laws and the Constitution, from one state to another, and thrown into a federal prison for the criminally insane, without indictment or trial for any crime, where he was submitted to the most humiliating treatment — an "insane asylum" where he could be rotting still, had he not been General Walker, and had he not had friends powerful enough to cope even with the despotic impulses of the Kennedy brothers. The point of this story is that it was under a Kennedy as Commander-in-Chief of the Armed Forces, and another Kennedy as dispenser of justice, that the career of a gallant, battle-tried, and deserving soldier was destroyed, and that even after his resignation from the Army he was shamefully and wantonly persecuted.

Marcos Pérez Jiménez was president of Venezuela, a fanatical anti-Communist, a great friend of the United States, and an excellent administrator who had brought his country to a state of prosperity, order, and peace it had never known before and has not known since his regime. He was overthrown by a military conspiracy. The new revolutionary government granted him a diplomatic passport and asked the State Department to permit him to reside in United States territory as a political refugee. The permission was granted, and Pérez Jiménez and his family settled in Florida.

Meanwhile, with the help of the U.S. government's dollars and intrigues, the military junta in Venezuela was replaced by the government of Romulus Betancourt, a long-time favorite of the radical State Department clique, a former chief of the Venezuelan Communist party, and of course a sworn enemy of Pérez Jiménez. Betancourt, who knew his Kennedys, asked them to hand over his enemy. The judicial part of the business was entrusted to Robert Kennedy, Nicholas Katzenbach, and the Supreme Court. In an act of perfidy without precedent in the history of international relations, Pérez Jiménez, a friendly former chief of state of a friendly country, who had been officially accepted as a political refugee on U.S. territory, was first seized and thrown into a U.S. prison where, to please radical exigencies, he was treated ignominiously for months, and was then delivered to his enemies.

It is in Katanga, especially during the third and most horrible series of massacres, organized by General Louis Truman, special envoy of President John Kennedy, that we come directly into contact with an essential dimension of the policy of the International Forces whose authority and control the Kennedy clan, after Ambassador Joseph Kennedy's known hesitations, finally adopted for once and for all. It is the dimension where non-Communist and Communist powers, mob and money, anarchy and high finance, chiefs of independent countries and agents of the World Government Camorra, live comfortably together in an obscene symbiosis; where once-powerful empires strive and fight to force regions of the world, in which in earlier days they had brought and spread civilization, back to a tom-tom culture, with the massacre of millions, cannibalism, and chaos.

Hordes of mercenaries gathered from all over the world — some of them, like the Abyssinian contingent, real bandits and cutthroats; all transported and armed at the expense of U.S. taxpayers — were hurled for a third time upon the innocent population of Katanga. When one thinks of the pandemonium that was intentionally created by forcing the hasty and insane withdrawal of the Belgian administration, troops, and police in order to legitimatize the UN invasion, which was sponsored jointly by the United States and the Soviet Union; when one remembers the butchered native and white men, the massacred women and children, the raped women, and all the horrors, bloodshed, and destruction of the three consecutive armed onslaughts on Katanga — especially that last one, prepared with such perfidy by the Kennedy administration, and exceeding everything experienced before then by the Katanga population; when one realizes the stupefaction and indignation that must have shaken this humble, peaceful, industrious people — one almost blushes for the color of his skin.

"Is there in this House a single person who knows what is hidden behind our incredible Congo policy, a policy which has resolved on the destruction of Katanga?" asked Congressman Donald Bruce in the House of Representatives on September 9, 1962. What was hidden behind that act of piracy, brought to the extreme of infamy under a Kennedy administration, was exactly what characterizes the mysterious new amplitude of international policy: (1) sordid financial interests; (2) the tacit understanding between the White House and the Kremlin that was sealed at Yalta, Teheran, and Potsdam and revitalized by the Kennedy-McNamara-Rusk-Stevenson team; and (3) the engineering of an unprecedented victory for the World Government Conspiracy, which for the first time was allowed to make its own laws, to hire an army, to make war, and to conquer a country, in one of the most cynical and brutal colonial undertakings the world has ever known.

It was also under the John-Robert condominium that the major step was taken toward the big merger of the Communist and non-Communist worlds on the spiritual level, when, contrary to the letter and spirit of the United States Constitution, the name of God was banished from American public schools and from American official language.

No "fallen standard of justice, courage, and excellence" was left by the deceased brothers to be picked up by Edward Kennedy. A real chip off the old block, the bequest to which he held stubbornly after the Dyke Bridge tragedy was that of the permanent family drive, by hook or by crook, toward the supreme magistrature of their adopted country. It was for this same purpose that in 1962, under the Kennedy brothers' administration, the laws providing for dictatorship by Presidential Executive Order were established, creating the possibility of a total take-over by a single person of every public and private activity in the United States.

Profaning with characteristic impudence our memories of the enchanting Arthurian saga, the Kennedy publicity machinery has proposed the name of "Camelot" as denotative and symbolic of one of the saddest periods of U.S. post-war history. During that period, the penetration of the Establishment's domination of American life went deeper than in any preceding administration; and during that period also, a President of the United States for the first time officially proclaimed the aims of the International Conspiracy as the new law of the land, when he proudly informed an audience at Columbia University that his was "a proclamation of interdependence and not independence."

The Home Establishment and the One-World Conspiracy are, indeed, inextricably tangled. The social, economic, and financial anarchy, the riots and destructions engineered and provoked by the Establishment (it was under the Kennedys' administration that the system of legiferation under the pressure of black and white government-organized and government-protected mobs was inaugurated), will make it easier to legitimate the growing control of every aspect of American public and private life by the federal government. And it is a paroxysm of this anarchy and carefully supported rebellion that will motivate the total take-over of all liberties, rights, and initiatives of the American people that was anticipated by the Kennedys' Presidential Executive Orders. Without that total take-over it would probably be impossible — despite the long conditioning of the U.S. public by no-win wars, defense dismantling, continuous withdrawals, concessions without compensation, debasing negotiations, and abject begging — to bring this great independent nation definitively, as is required by the Conspiracy, into the universal "Animal Farm" of which the United Nations is only an incomplete prefiguration.

Beware of the Camelot people! They are the framework of the Establishment and the chief operators of the Conspiracy. In the limitlessly competitive electoral game they spur the ambitious, the greedy, and the weak to outdo them in their cuddling of the vociferous minorities, in the wrong choice of their advisers, and in their submission to the Forces of Darkness.

In the White House, in the legislatures, in the courts, on the campuses, or in the streets, they represent all that is necessary to bring about the social, spiritual, and military downfall of the last non-Communist big power. They stand for the identical things for which stood or stand Alger Hiss, Owen Lattimore, Roger Baldwin, Henry Morgenthau, Felix Frankfurter, Walter Lippmann, Arthur Schlesinger, and Drew Pearson. They are diametrically opposed to all that other men — men like Douglas MacArthur, George Patton, Robert Taft, James Forrestal, Pat McCarran, and Joe McCarthy — have dreamed and sought for the greatness and glory of their country.

It was to be expected, therefore, that Establishment and Conspiracy would join their efforts not only in the United States but all over the world, Soviet Russia included, to save from an ignominious end the last in the line of succession of the spurious Arthurian dynasty.

CHAPTER II

A Strictly For Fun Affair

Judging by the first accounts in newspapers and by Senator Kennedy's TV performance, the party on Chappaquiddick Island seemed to have been a devoted gathering of a dedicated group of mourners, where libations were, partly at least, poured on the earth *à l'antique* in memory of some beloved deceased, rather than drunk by participants. "I encouraged and helped to sponsor it," said the Senator; which meant, in less senatorial terms than those employed by Mr. Sorensen, "I ordered it and paid for it."

Less solemnly and more frankly, Miss Esther Newburgh, one of the young revelers who had been "encouraged" by Senator Kennedy to gather that July night at a secluded cottage on a secluded island, called it a "strictly for fun affair," and it was most probably meant to be just that by all of Senator Kennedy's guests.

Who were those guests? Five married young men without their wives; one unmarried chauffeur, aged sixty; and six unmarried young girls, five from Washington, all, we are told, formerly secretaries and aides of Robert Kennedy in his 1968 Presidential campaign. In his TV appearance, Senator Kennedy felt obliged to explain that his wife had been absent "for reasons of health only," letting it be known that Mrs. Kennedy was expecting a baby in February 1970. There was no explanation, either from the Senator or from his four married male guests, concerning

13

the absence of the other four wives, who surely could not all have been pregnant at the same time.*

We want to stress here that in our description of the gathering on Chappaquiddick Island on Friday, July 18, no aspersion whatever on the reputations and characters of the young girls involved is intended. To accept an invitation to a bit of fun is normal and natural at their age. But facts are facts, and in such a somber affair those who seem to be the least important might lead to the much desired elucidation, to the vindication of the innocent and the condemnation of the guilty. If certain circumstances of this affair have the potentiality of leading to unpleasant gossip, the responsibility lies entirely with the sponsor and organizer of the festivities, who must have been aware of the opportunity, detrimental to the reputation of the female guests, offered to rumor-mongers by the seclusion of the place chosen for the cookout and by the absence of all the wives of the married men who were invited.

The males of the Chappaquiddick Island party were, besides Senator Kennedy: (1) *Joseph F. Gargan,* son of a sister of Mrs. Rose Kennedy, and therefore first cousin to the Senator, for whom the Kennedys appear to have secured a post as vice president of the Merchants Bank and Trust Company of Cape Cod. (2) *Paul F. Markham,* for whom Robert Kennedy had obtained appointment as Assistant United States Attorney for Massachusetts; at Robert's re-

---

*In his TV statement, Senator Kennedy gave the impression that if his wife had not been ill she would have participated in the cookout party; to give an appearance of still more respectability, a young nephew of the Senator's was included in this information. Everybody was duly impressed. But if you read the Senator's text more carefully you will discover that that was not at all what he said. It was to the regatta that Mrs. Kennedy and her nephew would have come, not to the cottage party. The conclusion seems to be that if Mrs. Kennedy had been able to come, the "strictly for fun" party in the secluded cottage, at which she would have been the only married woman present, would not have taken place.

Subsequently, in his testimony at the closed-door inquest, Kennedy, answering Judge Boyle's question, declared that he did not know whether his nephew was in Edgartown during the regatta days.

quest he was promoted to United States Attorney by President Johnson in 1967. He has since resigned. (3) *Charles C. Tretter,* a lawyer, who was on Robert Kennedy's staff in Washington. (4) *Raymond S. La Rosa,* a Kennedy politician and friend, known to be a scuba diving expert. (5) *John Crimmins,* an investigator on the staff of the Suffolk County (Massachusetts) Attorney; he had been a driver for President Kennedy and was often used as a chauffeur for Senator Kennedy. All the male members of the party, except the chauffeur, were married and under forty.

There were six girls for the six men of the party, all of them under thirty and all unmarried: (1) *Mary Jo Kopechne,* a member of the staff of Senator Robert Kennedy. She was an ardent liberal, as were, it seems, all the other five girls. (2) *Susan Tannenbaum,* employed on the staff of liberal Congressman Allard E. Lowenstein. (3) *Maryellen Lyons,* assistant to Massachusetts State Senator Beryl Cohen. (4) *Ann Lyons,* Maryellen's sister, an assistant on Senator Edward Kennedy's staff. (5) *Rosemary Keough,* a secretary on the Senator's staff. (6) *Esther Newburgh,* employed in the Urban Institute, Washington, D.C., which allegedly had C.I.A. ties.

Establishing the complete timetable of the "strictly for fun" party prior to the moment of the tragedy is difficult enough because of the silence, reticence, and probably the lies of its members. In the absence of any official investigation, it is impossible to establish it for the hours that followed. To the best of public and journalistic knowledge, however, events ran more or less this way:

It was Joseph F. Gargan, Senator Kennedy's cousin, who about a week in advance of the party made the arrangement to rent the Lawrence cottage for a couple of days at a cost of $200. The cottage is a small two-room affair in an isolated location on Chappaquiddick Island, very likely used by its owner only for summer weekends and holidays. There are two similar cabins nearby, and the cottage has another interesting neighbor: the Chappaquiddick Fire Station, a few yards away on the other side of the road. Here the volunteer firemen, in a region of beautiful but dangerous sand beaches, are always prepared for a life-saving operation. The fire station is always lighted with a red light at night, and an alarm bell is always handy.

Senator Kennedy registered on Friday, July 18, at the Shiretown Inn in Edgartown, on the larger neighboring island of Martha's Vineyard. The young girls were put up at the Dunes Motel, a few miles away, also on Martha's Vineyard. Where the five other gentlemen had left their toothbrushes has never been precisely divulged, but we may surmise that some of them were staying at the Shiretown Inn with Senator Kennedy. At any rate, it is unlikely that the initial intention of ten of the twelve persons in the party had been to spend the whole night in the Lawrence cottage, which held only four beds.

Senator Kennedy took possession of his hotel room in Edgartown on Friday, July 18, at about 6:30 p.m., having been driven in his car to the Lawrence cottage and back at about 1:00 p.m., and having meanwhile taken a swim on the east shore of Chappaquiddick Island and participated in the Martha's Vineyard regatta. After 7:00 p.m., he left Edgartown with the rest of the party, using two cars. Senator Kennedy was again being driven in his four-door black Oldsmobile sedan when the two cars boarded the ferry. On the other side of the 500-foot channel, which is known for its rapid and treacherous currents, Kennedy took — for the third time that day — the two-lane paved road which, with an unmistakable white line separating its two lanes, makes a sharp right turn and leads to the "cottage with the yellow shutters" — the cottage that will haunt the imagination of Edward Kennedy's countrymen for a long time, and that may perhaps keep its secret forever.

So much is precisely known. It is extraordinary that for so long none of the participants in the "fun affair" that ended so tragically were subjected to an open and official interrogation, and that Senator Kennedy was brought to court and his case was settled without a single question having been asked of him by the responsible authorities. But this does not prevent the use of other information that is either complementary or apparently contradictory to the first known facts. For example, according to Miss Esther Newburgh, the only participant in the cookout party who consented to give some stray bits of information, it was at 8:30 p.m. on Friday that Raymond La Rosa picked the girls up at their motel and drove them to the Lawrence cottage, where Kennedy and the other four men were waiting for them. Miss Newburgh also said that four of the girls had already visited the cottage on Thursday evening. From the same source it was reported that, sometime prior to Friday evening, some of the girls had been taken out for a swim by Senator Kennedy and Paul F. Markham, who drove to the beach by the very bridge where the accident occurred.

The party started out of doors, but as cookout parties often do, owing to the number of mosquitoes at large, it moved inside. According to Miss Newburgh, eating ended at 10:30 p.m. According to Senator Kennedy's statement to the police and later on TV, it was at about 11:15 p.m. that he decided to retire, in view of his intention to participate next day in the second part of the yearly Edgartown regatta. He left the cottage with Miss Kopechne, who wanted to start her trip home early in the morning, intending, he said, to catch the scheduled midnight ferry.

This very important time, 11:15 p.m., was not confirmed publicly and under oath by anyone until six months later. When asked about it by newspapermen, the girls generally answered that they had not noticed the absence of the Senator and Miss Kopechne until much later — so "how could they say exactly when they had left?" The men, when asked the same question, remained grimly silent. Some of the girls admit that Markham and Gargan disappeared at a certain time and that both men returned toward 2:15 a.m. They were then in dry clothes, it might be supposed, since they are reported as having bedded down for the night with the rest of the party, whose members, "as there were not enough beds to go around, had to sleep on the floor," we are informed by *Time* magazine.

This raises two important and interlocked problems. Granting that Senator Kennedy did not lie when telling about the efforts of Markham and Gargan to save Mary Jo, and that both young heroes had undressed before their plunge, or had been able somehow and somewhere to change to dry clothes, one might still have expected their long absence to provoke the curiosity of their companions.* If questions were asked, what did they answer? The second problem is: why did those ten persons decide to spend the rest of the night in such uncomfortable conditions? Everybody knew in Edgartown

---

*According to what Markham and Gargan told their female companions that night, they had both jumped instinctively, fully dressed, into the Edgartown Channel. At the top-secret inquest, Maryellen Lyons was interrogated on this point by District Attorney Edmond Dinis:

"Q. – Was there any effort made to go to the ferry and get across, back to Martha's Vineyard?

A. – Well, I believe Mr. Markham and Mr. Gargan said that *they were looking for a boat* and there wasn't any available and there was no ferry.

Q. – You say that they were looking for a boat?

A. – To take us back.

* * *

Q. – And what did they say?

A. – They said that they had been down at the ferry landing and that they had been in the water swimming around, that the Senator had dove in the water because there was no boat available for him and he wanted to get back to the other side and that they dove in after him.

* * *

Q. – And that he had jumped into the water and swum across the channel and they told you that they dove after him?

A. – Yes, they did – no, he dove and they were with him and saw him dive in and I believe they said because of his back, you know, they just sort of instinctively just dove in after him." [Emphasis added.]

and on the Island that even after the last scheduled trip
of the ferry at midnight, a simple phone call would have
brought the ferry across the channel at any time.

The girls, who grudgingly consented to answer some of
the questions asked by newsmen, told them that at about
7:00 a.m. on Saturday Gargan took two of them to their
motel, and came back to fetch the other three *at about
9:30 a.m.; only then did he tell them about the accident.*
But this answer was given days after the tragedy, and might
or might not have been correct. The fact is that, in order
to avoid questions from newsmen, police, or public, all
members of the "strictly for fun" party quickly disappeared from the Island, after clearing away all the debris
and empty glassware from the feast. The girls immediately
checked out of their motel. The men disappeared also
without volunteering any information, except Gargan and
Markham, whose support continued to be essential to the
Senator that morning.

So the most reasonable answer to those two interlocking
problems is that Markham and Gargan did give an explanation for their absence, although it certainly was not everything they knew, and that they swore their companions,
girls and men, to the greatest secrecy – probably until such
time as a decision had been made by Kennedy, with
professional advice, on how the accident should be reported
to the proper authorities. Then they kept the revelers
sequestered in order to prevent any premature and unde-
sired information from reaching the police or the public.

If it is true, as the girls affirm, that Gargan brought the
bad news to them only at 9:30 a.m. – after an absence of
over two hours, during which he certainly got in touch
with the Senator – it is interesting to observe that it was at
about the same time that the Senator finally decided to
break the news to the police.

CHAPTER III

Manslaughter At The Dyke Bridge

"Manslaughter" is the most lenient term that can be used for what happened at the Dyke Bridge on Chappaquiddick Island that night of July 18, even if we take into account only what Senator Kennedy has consented to confess. Knowingly and willingly leaving a human being who might have been rescued to die a slow and tortured death would be considered by many to be, morally if not legally, downright murder.

Although a young woman had lost her life in most mysterious circumstances that night at Dyke Bridge, the Massachusetts police and judiciary authorities during all the following months did not find it necessary to subject the person directly responsible for the tragedy, or those who could have given important information about it, to any form of legal interrogation. The secret proceeding that was initiated after this long delay was of such a nature, and was conducted in such a manner, that the blackout imposed on the Kennedy scandal and on Mary Jo's tragic death was sure to remain in effect until the moment when lifting it would have no practical consequences from a legal point of view, and would hold no interest for the public at large.

Therefore, besides the contradictory and highly suspicious statements of Senator Kennedy and the members of his entourage, some of them implicated in the misdeed, we have only a few, but very valuable, testimonies of independent and courageous individuals, and our own judgment, to help us in attempting to reconstruct — in the interests of Mary Jo, of justice in general, and of the right of the American public to be informed — what could have happened on that fatal summer night. If this public goes along with the official and political set it will never know the truth about a tragedy that, given the status and ambitions of the person implicated, might end by being the tragedy of the American people also.

There is one point of agreement between the statement Senator Kennedy made at the police station and the one he made subsequently over TV. This concerns the time at which he left the Lawrence cottage with Mary Jo Kopechne, which he gave in both statements as 11:15 p.m. This would have placed the pair at the Dyke Bridge a few minutes later. This very important information, on which depends the whole timetable of the events that followed, both on Chappaquiddick Island and in Edgartown, is in flagrant contradiction of the testimony of a most reliable witness, Dukes County Deputy Sheriff Christopher F. Look Jr. Look reported to the Edgartown police, on the morning after the accident, that he had seen Senator Kennedy's black Oldsmobile at the intersection of the paved road going toward the ferry slip and the sand road going toward the Dyke Bridge at 12:45 a.m. — a time when, according to the Senator's statements, that car ought to have been at the bottom of Poucha Pond for an hour and a half. The deputy sheriff reported further that in the car he saw a girl seated beside the driver, who was a man. He suggests the possibility that there may have been another person in the rear seat; this, he says, could only have been another girl or an outstretched garment.

On one point the deputy sheriff is unshakable: the car he saw was Senator Kennedy's black Oldsmobile, with an "L" as the first letter of the license plate and two 7's as the first and last figures.* Look reported to the police that, assuming the driver of the Oldsmobile was having difficulty finding the entrance to the Dyke Bridge road, which was hidden by some bushes, he stepped out of his car and started walking toward the black sedan, which however did not wait for him but immediately took the sand road toward the bridge, despite the fact that the driver probably had recognized his uniform.

Deputy Sheriff Look's version was accepted by the Edgartown Police, who learned that the only other car available to the Lawrence cottage party that night was a *white* 1969 Valiant, rented by Kennedy's cousin Joseph Gargan the very afternoon of the accident. "I know white from black," Deputy Sheriff Look protested when his highly persuasive report was questioned. Like the Edgartown police, we will be brought by the full series of known facts to accept Look's statement as indisputable, and we think that the veracity of the Senator's account of the events that followed must be estimated accordingly.

About the accident itself, described in more or less the same way in both of the Senator's statements, all that we know factually is that at about 8:00 a.m. Saturday two young boys discovered an upturned car submerged in Poucha Pond, and that the body of a young girl, who proved to be Mary Jo Kopechne, was extricated from it the same morning. According to Senator Kennedy, he had been driving the Oldsmobile when it landed upside down in nine feet of water. At the police station Senator Kennedy said that he could not remember how he got out of the car. He did remember, however, that he had made several unsuccessful attempts to rescue his passenger.

---

*The number on Kennedy's license plates was L78-207, and Deputy Sheriff Look recognized the black Oldsmobile without any hesitation the moment it was brought out of the pond. The reader will see how every judicial authority concerned with the case either ignored this essential clue completely, or did his best to call into question the validity of a fact that would have led directly to the solution of what is still the Chappaquiddick mystery. "The dread of knowing more!" — to quote Barry Farrell.

Experiments have been made with submerged cars at a depth of a few feet more than the height of the car itself, with the car not upturned but standing on its four wheels. The conclusion from those experiments was that in those conditions a driver or a passenger who could keep his wits might be able to save himself, especially if the doors and windows were closed. The car being more or less watertight, water enters it slowly, mostly from the bottom part of the car where the water pressure is greatest. This permits the driver or passenger to breathe for a considerable time in the diminishing air pocket that forms at the top of the car. Until the water inside the car reaches a certain height, it is useless to try to open the door, because of the pressure of the water against the outside. The person who can remain calm enough to wait until the water has reached almost to his throat will find the pressure has been equalized, and he will then be able to open the door, and with his mouth tightly shut to make a spurt toward the surface. Extricating himself from the car would obviously be more difficult for the driver, who sits under the steering wheel, than for a passenger.

Senator Kennedy's position at the bottom of Poucha Pond would have been quite different than what we have just described. Imagine him head down and legs up, with the steering wheel in his chest and handicapped by a spinal brace, trying to open the door against the pressure of nine feet of water, or trying, perhaps successfully, to open the window. (The door of the Oldsmobile was found closed by the frogmen who helped to bring the car out of the pond, and the driver's window was open about to the limit.) If the Senator had succeeded in opening the window, then the wider the opening, the stronger would have been the invasion of the water, which would have started to flow in at what was now the lowest part of the car, and at the full pressure of nine feet of water. Water would not have covered his feet first, rising slowly toward his chest, but with all its weight and force would have covered his head and mouth first. We should also note that for a man of Kennedy's corpulence to get through the window, it would have had to be opened to its maximum, so the gush of water opposing his exit would also have been at its maximum.

This writer has been the victim of a similar accident, falling with his car at night from a height of nine feet and landing upside down in a stream only twelve to fifteen inches deep. Judging by this experience, he believes that Senator Kennedy's chances of crawling out of his Oldsmobile in the conditions he describes were *about nil.* Unless he gives a different account of the circumstances, our conclusion is that *HE WAS NOT IN THE OLDSMOBILE SEDAN WHEN IT PLUNGED UPTURNED INTO NINE FEET OF WATER, WHATEVER THE EXACT TIME OF THE ACCIDENT,* and that *MARY JO KOPECHNE WENT ALONE TO THE BOTTOM OF POUCHA POND.*

There is, we think, only one way in which Kennedy could have saved himself: that is by getting out of the car before its immersion. This would have required opening the door of the car in the moment when he felt he was no longer master of it, and instinctively jumping out onto the bridge before the actual plunge. The feat is not impossible, as was proved in a famous police case in Florida a few years ago, and the possibility must not be dismissed simply because Senator Kennedy declared at the police station and in his TV statement that he plunged with the car into the tidal lagoon.

We have again only Kennedy's testimony for what followed the accident and his alleged rescue efforts. Tired and in his water-soaked clothes and shoes, he says that he left the Dyke Bridge and walked a mile and a half back to the cottage, which he would have reached in about half an hour. Counting, let us say, a quarter of an hour for the accident to happen and for the driver to get out of the submerged car and make his rescue efforts, this would put him at the cottage at about 12 midnight, according to the Senator's timetable, or at about 1:25 a.m., according to Deputy Sheriff Look's. This does not take into account the time the Senator says he spent lying exhausted on the grass.

On his way back to the cottage he passed four occupied houses — of these, the Dyke House, the residence of Mrs. Malm, and one other, had lights on, and all of them had telephones that could have brought expert and efficient help from Edgartown in about fifteen minutes. Almost in front of the cottage, on the other side of the road, he passed the lighted Chappaquiddick Fire Station, where help could have been obtained immediately.* According to his report to the police, the Senator did not even enter the Lawrence cottage, but instead climbed into the back seat of the car standing in front of it, which, according to the police, could only have been the white Valiant. Then he asked "someone" to take him back to Edgartown. The "someone" just happened, it seems, to be plural — Paul Markham and Joseph Gargan, Kennedy's cousin.

From that moment until the TV statement Kennedy volunteered after his appearance in court — that is, for a whole week — nothing was said by the Senator or his two companions about where they had been or what they had been doing from that moment until Gargan and Markham, presumably in dry clothes, returned to the cottage Saturday at about 2:15 a.m., and Senator Kennedy appeared, perfectly composed and in perfectly dry clothes, in front of the Shiretown Inn, where he talked with Russell E. Peachey, co-owner of the hotel, complaining about the noise in a neighboring building and asking him insistently for the time.

On Saturday morning we find Kennedy and his two companions again on Chappaquiddick Island, where they were seen between 8:30 and 9:40 a.m. talking calmly with

---

*The testimony before the top-secret inquest proved that the existence of the fire station was well-known to members of the Lawrence cottage party.

various people and giving no indication that they knew anything about an accident. The moment they heard that Edgartown Chief of Police Dominick Arena was already at the Dyke Bridge, they returned quickly to Edgartown. It was not until about 10:00 a.m., when Mary Jo's body had already been taken out of the pond, that Arena was informed that Senator Kennedy was at the police station and wanted to make a report. About ten hours had passed, according to Senator Kennedy's timetable, between the moment of the alleged accident and the moment when Senator Kennedy reported it to the authorities.

Police Chief Arena had been warned at about 8:00 a.m., by a phone call from Mrs. Malm at the Dyke House, that a car was lying wheels up in Poucha Pond. He left immediately for the scene of the accident and himself made an unsuccessful attempt to open the door of the car. He sent then for John Farrar, captain of the Search and Rescue Division of the Edgartown Volunteer Fire Department. Captain Farrar recovered the body of Mary Jo at about 9:00 a.m. At that time, before the arrival of Dr. Donald Mills, associate medical examiner for Suffolk County, Arena already knew that the car belonged to Senator Kennedy, and had tried to reach the Senator by telephone.

Besides Arena's calls, telephone calls had been made during the morning hours from the Island and from Edgartown, by Kennedy or on his account. These had no doubt informed and alarmed Kennedy's family in Hyannis Port and his friends and lawyers in Washington and Boston. It is, however, not necessary to imagine that direct pressure was exercised that very morning on Police Chief Arena and the other legal and medical officials who busied themselves around the submerged car. The Kennedy influence, charm, terror, or whatever you prefer to call it, is in Massachusetts a permanent part of the environment. Everybody harbors the desire to please, or realizes the advantage or the necessity of pleasing, the lords of Hyannis Port Manor.

However that may be, the truth is that the big hush-hush operation, very cleverly and thoroughly carried out by all concerned authorities on behalf of Edward Kennedy in his hour of need, had already begun that Saturday morning. Anybody who has followed the movements of the police and judicial authorities in the Dyke Bridge tragedy from the beginning up to the long-delayed September investigation cannot fail to recognize that the steady purpose of those authorities has been to save Kennedy from the dangerous ordeal of an official questioning, and especially from any public examination and cross-examination under oath, and to allow him to give his promised public statement only under the protection of a final Court decision, with no necessity to do anything but follow freely and without interruption a text composed during seven days of meditation and consultation with lawyers, advisers, and professional speech writers.

That morning of July 19 the all-pervasive influence of the Kennedy clan manifested itself in two ways: in the treatment of Senator Kennedy at the police station, and in the handling of the victim's body on the beach onto which it had been dragged.

Senator Kennedy, after leaving his hotel in Edgartown, had crossed the channel by ferry to the Chappaquiddick side at about 8:30 a.m. Saturday, together with Markham and Gargan, who had joined him at the hotel at about 8 o'clock. For some unexplained but easily conceivable reason, they lingered at the ferry landing for about forty minutes, talking sociably and pleasantly with the people there. When Dick Hewitt, one of the ferry operators, asked whether they had heard about the accident, they answered that they had just heard of it. Then the three night-riders separated immediately. Kennedy and Markham took the ferry back to Edgartown; Gargan headed toward the cottage.

Kennedy and Markham arrived at the Edgartown police station at about 9:30 a.m. Arena joined them there about half an hour later, when he heard that the Senator preferred to meet him there rather than at the scene of the accident. At the police station the Senator, before he handed over his written statement to Arena at about 10:00 a.m., made frantic but unsuccessful efforts to get in touch with his lawyer, Richard McCarran. The statement had been written not by Kennedy but by former U.S. Attorney Markham, and was handed to Arena *unsigned*. Arena was asked not to release it to the Press until it had been controlled — and of course, if necessary, corrected — by Kennedy's lawyer. Here is the text of the document, which, thanks to the precautions taken by a man who had just emerged from a state of shock and partial amnesia, has absolutely no legal or probatory value:

> On July 18, 1969, at approximately 11:15 p.m. on Chappaquiddick, Martha's Vineyard, Mass., I was driving my car on Main Street, Chappaquiddick, on my way to get the ferry back to Edgartown. I was unfamiliar with the road and turned right onto the Dyke Road instead of bearing hard left on Main Street.
>
> After proceeding for approximately one-half mile on Dyke Road, I descended a hill and came upon a narrow bridge. The car went off the side of the bridge. There was one passenger with me, Miss Mary Jo Kopechne, a former secretary of my brother Robert Kennedy.
>
> The car turned over and sank into the water and landed with the roof resting on the bottom. *I attempted to open the door and window of the car* but have no recollection of how I got out of the car. [Emphasis added.]
>
> I came to the surface and then repeatedly dove down to the car in an attempt to see if the passenger was still in the car. I was unsuccessful in the attempt.
>
> I was exhausted and in a state of shock. I recall walking back to where my friends were eating. There was a car parked in front of the cottage, and I climbed into the back seat. I then asked for

someone to bring me back to Edgartown. I remember walking around for a period of time and then going back to my hotel room.

When I fully realized what had happened this morning, I immediately notified the police.*

The simple fact that nine hours had passed between the moment of the accident and Kennedy's reporting it to the police, his failure to ask for expert and professional help in the tragic situation of a human being who might have been rescued, should have made it impossible for a conscientious police officer to be contented with that fragmentary statement, given, moreover, in such a way that any lawyer could have successfully impugned its validity. Nevertheless, despite the fact that Senator Kennedy and Paul Markham spent about four hours at the police station, not one recorded question was asked of them.

When asked by newsmen to explain why he failed to interrogate Kennedy and solicit from him explanations of the obscurities and patent impossibilities in his statement, Chief of Police Dominick Arena replied: "After all, when you have a United States Senator reporting, you have to give him some credibility." Later on, when faced by the same reporters with the accusation of favoritism, in complete contradiction of that former declaration, he protested that Kennedy was treated "the same as anybody else."

The first question Arena ought to have asked, after reminding the Senator of his constitutional rights, is how he and his friend had reached Edgartown after the accident. If Kennedy answered, as he affirmed in his TV statement, that he had swum across the Edgartown channel, Arena should have asked further: (1) Where were his wet

---

*We observe that in the police statement Senator Kennedy does not, as he will do later, cite the darkness of that night as an explanation of his mistake — an explanation which could have been easily challenged at that moment.

garments? (2) Where did he change to dry clothes? (3) *Why did he choose such a dangerous way of reaching his hotel, instead of summoning the ferry, which was on call and could easily have been obtained, even at that time?*

Arena was perfectly familiar with the island and therefore knew all the reasons why Kennedy's explanation that he had taken the wrong turn by mistake was inadmissible. Let us enumerate them to show how wide was the credibility gap Chief Arena was prepared to allow to a United States Senator:

1. The black-top road leading from the cottage to the ferry landing is a two-lane road, its lanes separated by a white line all the way.

2. At the crossroads there is a light signal, a reflecting arrow indicating the direction to the ferry and to Edgartown, which Kennedy could not have missed.

3. Kennedy could not have ridden the 800 yards on the bumpy road to the bridge without knowing that he had left the asphalted road, the Main Street he mentioned in his statement.

4. Kennedy had been driven three times over that high road the very day of the accident, each time in full daylight, and twice, also in full daylight, over the Dyke Bridge. It is incredible therefore that he should have made an error of 180 degrees in direction.

As the explanation given by Senator Kennedy for being on the Dyke Bridge road at that hour was manifestly a lie, it would have been quite natural to ask him for a better one. It would also have been natural to ask him to try to remember the identity of the "someone" (singular or plural) who found him seated in the back seat of the only car remaining in front of the cottage, and how long he stayed there before he was found.*

---

*The top-secret inquest will prove how necessary it was to obtain an early statement on this important point, before La Rosa, Gargan, Markham, and others had time to arrange their testimony.

Senator Kennedy said in his police station statement that he remembered roaming about for a long while in the streets of Edgartown before returning to his hotel. Why was he not asked whether he had met anybody, and whether anyone had inquired about his soaked clothes and his pitiable appearance?

In explaining why he had done absolutely nothing to help the girl who was slowly drowning in his car (except the alleged efforts "to see if his companion was still in the car"), although expert help was readily available, Senator Kennedy says in his statement that he was tired and stunned. It is difficult to understand how Dominick Arena, who had just seen the body of that young and beautiful girl dragged out of the submerged car where she had been abandoned, could have contented himself with such an inadequate explanation.

"When I fully realized what had happened this morning, I immediately notified the police," said Senator Kennedy in the closing sentence of his unsigned statement. Arena did not need any further investigation to know that this was a lie. He knew that the Senator, who left his hotel at 8:00 a.m., had already crossed by ferry to Chappaquiddick Island with his two friends, lingered with them for forty minutes, and used the public telephone booth at the ferry landing to call a lawyer in Washington, before he made up his mind to report at the police station. The police in Edgartown permitted all the members of the Lawrence Cottage party to clear out in haste from the Island and from the town, without asking a single question. Nor were any questions asked of Paul Markham, who stayed in the police station for about four hours and who was allowed to write Kennedy's statement, or of Joseph Gargan, who was also present.

The determination of the police and judiciary authorities *not* to learn officially anything about what had happened during the night of July 18 was so strong that they did not even interview the occupants of the two houses nearest to the scene of the accident, those of Mrs. David Smith and Mrs. Pierre Malm, for instance, as would have been done in the course of any routine investigation.

The scandal of the autopsy confirms still further, and in a more disturbing manner, the intention not only of the Edgartown police but also of the Edgartown prosecutor's office, and higher authorities, to do all they could to hide from the public the exact circumstances that led to the death of Mary Jo Kopechne, and the part played by Senator Kennedy in that tragedy.

CHAPTER IV

Beginning Of The Autopsy Scandal

We are indebted to *Human Events* magazine for gathering the opinions of some of the country's most competent authorities on forensic medicine concerning the failure of the Massachusetts authorities to order an autopsy to be performed on the body of Mary Jo Kopechne. They have all declared that an autopsy should be standard procedure in such an accident as the one in which that young girl met her death, and have expressed the opinion that the real cause of her death could not have been determined without a real post-mortem examination.

Dr. Lester Adelson, professor of forensic pathology at Western Reserve Medical School, observes that "an autopsy could have determined exactly how Miss Kopechne died and put an end to all kinds of ugly rumors and speculations. There is everything to gain and nothing to lose by performing an autopsy in cases of that kind."

Dr. John Edland, Monroe County (N.Y.) medical examiner, a nationally prominent authority in forensic pathology, says: "It is a real farce to bring the body of a dead girl out of a car after nine hours and have someone make a pronouncement that it was a routine drowning . . . . The medical examiner has a responsibility to be an impartial judge of the cause *and circumstances* of the death." (Emphasis added.)

Dr. Sidney Winberg, medical examiner of Suffolk County, New York, and lecturer on forensic pathology at Columbia University, declares that in his bailiwick an autopsy is required as a routine procedure in all cases of death by traffic accident. He adds: "We do not know if the girl died from drowning or from injury, *or if in fact she was not dead before she got into the car.* When you have a young woman of child-bearing age you are doubly suspicious." (Emphasis added.)

In doubtful cases an autopsy can do more than just determine the medical cause of a death; it can change the character of the legal charge. That the Dyke Bridge homicide was such a case was already demonstrated by the more than nine-hour delay in reporting to the police. It was soon to become one of the most mysterious cases an investigator could come across, thanks to the flagrant contradictions between facts and allegations, the lies by commission and omission, and the stubborn silence in which the involved parties wrapped themselves, silence that would be interrupted only by the phony appearance of Edward Kennedy on television.

The responsible Massachusetts authorities knew as well as did Dr. Edland that an autopsy might clear up not only the cause *but also the circumstances* of a violent death; in other words, not only the *medical cause* but also the *legal cause* of that death. They knew as well as Dr. Winberg and Dr. Adelson that an autopsy has also the great advantage of putting an end to all kinds of unjustifiable and ugly rumors. Why then did they not, in their manifest desire to protect Senator Kennedy's interests, order an immediate post-mortem examination in the case of Mary Jo's still unexplained death, as they would have done in any similar case? It is difficult to repress the suspicion that those authorities felt that Kennedy's interests were better protected by suppressing almost irrevocably the possibility of a significant medical examination.

Dr. Donald Mills, Edgartown's assistant medical examiner, stated that Miss Kopechne died from accidental drowning, that the cause of death was obvious, and that therefore no autopsy was necessary. With the consent of Dominick Arena, who declared that he was of the same opinion, Dr. Mills signed the necessary papers and released the body, which was sent to the Martha's Vineyard Funeral Home. There embalming was done, with Dr. Mills' authorization, four hours after the recovery of the body. Within twenty-four hours, without even waiting for a coffin, the body, wrapped simply in a shroud, was flown to Pennsylvania in a Kennedy-chartered airplane, accompanied by Dun Gifford, one of Edward Kennedy's assistants. This created the optimum legal situation for indefinite postponement of any useful medical investigation in the Kennedy-Kopechne case.

At the hour when the body was removed from Massachusetts, Edward Kennedy had already shut himself safely into the Hyannis Port compound, where a high-powered emergency "think factory" had already started to form, for the purpose of drawing the essential lines of the Senator's defense.

Time magazine thought that "neither Arena, Dr. Donald Mills, associate medical adviser, nor Arena's superiors, Prosecutor Steele and District Attorney Edmund Dinis, can brag about the handling of what is probably the most publicized case they will ever be associated with." Many would share that opinion.* The black Oldsmobile sedan was left for hours unguarded, unroped, and unsealed, for anybody to take out of it or to plant in it whatever he wished, or to tamper at will with brakes or engine. A handbag belonging to Miss Rosemary Keough, Edward Kennedy's secretary, was found in the

---

*The situation and responsibility of District Attorney Edmund Dinis are not precisely comparable with those of Prosecutor Steele, Dr. Mills, and Chief Arena. Dinis's office was in New Bedford, not in Edgartown. For him, for the first twenty-four hours, the Dyke Bridge tragedy was just a traffic accident, such as are generally dealt with by local authorities (Steele, Arena, and Mills). Dinis's suspicions were aroused, it seems, when he read Kennedy's police station statement, and grew stronger when he heard the Senator's TV speech.

car and brought to the police station. It was released by a female police official to a man who was not even asked to identify himself. Thus an exhibit that might or might not have been of extreme importance was lost to a possible inquest.

Concerning the particular point of the omitted autopsy, the following extracts from the confidences made by Dr. Mills to Richard J. Connolly of the *Boston Globe* will give an idea of the attitude that prevailed that Saturday morning on the shores of Poucha Pond:

> Of course the word "Kennedy" had been mentioned at the Dyke Bridge, and I don't know who mentioned it. Word went through the group that this girl was a secretary of the Kennedys, and after I did make my examination, on the way back, I remarked to the undertaker, Mr. Frieh, I said, "Good Lord! if there is any Kennedy mixed in it *this is much too big and complicated for me to carry alone.*" . . . I also mentioned to him that this was particularly important because the Kennedy family could be mixed up in it . . . . *I wanted a ruling on an autopsy on this.* [Emphasis added.]

In a decidedly confidential mood, Dr. Mills told Mr. Connolly that the condition of the body (of Miss Kopechne) convinced him that she had drowned. He said, "The body was rigid as a statue, the teeth were gritted, there was froth around the nose, and the hands were in a claw-like position." Dr. Mills did not tell Mr. Connolly what was the color of the froth he observed around Miss Kopechne's nose, and perhaps around her mouth. Dr. Mills, according to his interesting statement, had removed only enough of Mary Jo's clothing to permit him to compress her chest and see some water emerging from her throat. Sea water could not have failed to emerge from her throat after ten hours of immersion. Only an autopsy could have shown, however, whether there was sea water also in her lungs.

According to Dr. Mills, he told the funeral director to

postpone the embalming until he got a ruling from the district attorney's office. He therefore phoned to the Oak Bluffs State Police barracks and asked Trooper Richard P. DeRoche to determine whether or not the district attorney, Edmund Dinis, wanted an autopsy performed. Dr. Mills did not fail to remind the trooper that this was a very important affair because the Kennedy family were mixed up in it. Fifteen minutes later, Dr. Mills said, he received a call from another state trooper, Robert E. Lucas, who quoted a police investigator, Detective Lieutenant George Killen, as saying that if Dr. Mills was satisfied that there had been no foul play, there was no necessity of an autopsy. On the other hand, in the same interview, Dr. Mills explained that he authorized the embalming because, "as Detective Lieutenant Killen did not believe that the autopsy was necessary, he did not believe it either." It seems, really, as if the only persons responsible for the fact that no autopsy was performed on the body of Mary Jo Kopechne were Troopers DeRoche and Lucas.

The only other contact Dr. Mills had with District Attorney Dinis was on July 21, when Mills informed Dinis that, according to blood analysis, Miss Kopechne had consumed about two ounces of alcohol. At this time her body had already been flown away. It was a day earlier, July 20, at 10 o'clock in the morning, that District Attorney Dinis, surprised by certain circumstances in the story of the Poucha Pond accident as related by Senator Kennedy at the Edgartown police station, called Detective Lieutenant Killen on the telephone and said that he wanted an autopsy. Lieutenant Killen then informed him that the body had already left Massachusetts. Dinis learned later that this was not true, and that Mary Jo's body, which had been delivered first to a mortician and then to one of Senator Kennedy's secretaries, did not in fact leave Martha's Vineyard airport for another two hours — that is, not until noon on July 20.

So Chief of Police Dominick Arena, declaring that "the accident was strictly accidental," and that "there was no sign of negligence," charged the Senator simply with "leaving the scene of an accident." Kennedy was not present at the Dukes County Courthouse on July 22, when Arena filed the complaint. Attorney Richard McCarran, representing Kennedy, petitioned for a hearing on July 25, and got it.

Did the charge chosen by Arena and accepted by Prosecutor Steele and later by Judge Boyle correspond with the facts of the case? Even an accident can lead to a charge of manslaughter, depending on the circumstances under which it occurs. District Attorney Dinis was given the opportunity to remember this only after almost insuperable procedural difficulties had already been placed in the way of such a charge against the Senator.

One cannot compare the case of a driver who dents another car and hurries away, or that of one who forces another car into the ditch and whizzes past, but stops at the first telephone booth to call police, so that help comes soon, with that of a brute who runs down a pedestrian at top speed and leaves him bleeding to death on the pavement in the middle of the night. Yet all these have "left the scene of an accident." Let anybody decide which of these three cases is most similar to the Kennedy-Kopechne tragedy.

There were other investigators at Poucha Pond that morning: the members of the Edgartown Volunteer Fire Department. It was John W. Farrar, captain of the Search and Rescue Division, who removed the dead body of Mary Jo Kopechne from the submerged Oldsmobile. Captain Farrar declared to reporters that the girl could have stayed alive for as long as several hours in the air pocket which had formed in the submerged car, judging by the position of the car and the position in which the girl was holding herself, with her head in the foot well of the back seats — which had become the topmost part of the vehicle, so that the air pocket had formed there. "Her hands," says Farrar, "were still holding the back seat in what I should say was an attempt to keep her head in this pocket. I must say that there remained a chance that the girl's life could have been saved if rescuers had got into the car earlier."

Captain Farrar's statements are not contradicted by those of Dr. Mills, who said that Mary Jo probably died from five to eight hours before 9:30 a.m., when he had the opportunity of examining the body. This would mean that she lived until some time between 1:30 and 4:30 a.m. Time enough in any case for rescue to have reached her if Kennedy or his confederates had seen fit to summon it.

It has been rumored that Kennedy's lawyers entrusted to some specialized agency a series of experiments designed to prove that Mary Jo's death was instantaneous. It is much to be regretted that those Kennedy-chosen investigators did not have at their disposal the results of a regular autopsy, which by an examination of the digestive organs and other tests could have determined more precisely than did Dr. Mills the time of Mary Jo's death. Lacking such data, the only information upon which a conclusion about the possibility of Mary Jo's survival can be based is furnished by the records of other similar accidents in the past. This is what such records show:

1. An air pocket may form in a totally submerged car, with either open or closed windows, whether overturned or not.

2. In a totally submerged car that remains upright, a person or persons who have been able to avail themselves of the air in the air pocket *might* be able to save themselves without outside help.

3. In a totally submerged car that is overturned, so

that the air pocket forms in the foot well, the trapped persons can be saved only by outside help.

Only a thorough inquest could have decided whether these data were sufficient to prove that the Senator was ever in fact submerged in Poucha Pond in his black Oldsmobile sedan, with Mary Jo Kopechne.

CHAPTER V

Between Police Station And Court

The moment Kennedy and Markham left the police station, the Senator hastened to the family stronghold at Hyannis Port, where until his appearance in court only his lawyers, his intimate associates, and his professional speech writers would be admitted. Besides his unsigned statement at the police station he refused to give any other explanation, letting it be known that some sort of detailed account would be released "at the proper moment." The members of the cottage party, instructed by lawyers and other advisers, also clammed up hermetically, the girls resisting even generous financial offers from newspapermen.

The seven-day delay between the accident and the appearance in court seems to have been very usefully employed. There was a dangerous crisis to be faced and it could not be done without expert and friendly advice. Sixteen members of the old New-Frontier brain trust hurried to the rescue of the last of the Kennedy brothers, "crowding" — as *Time* magazine put it — "the famous Hyannis Port compound, taking every spare bed." Only the house of Jacqueline Onassis escaped service as a dormitory. Present at this dramatic conclave were:

Robert McNamara, notorious former Secretary of Defense.

Theodore Sorensen, President Kennedy's speech writer and admirer, author of *Kennedy* and of *Decision Making In The White House,* both works of great historical inaccuracy.

Richard Goodwin, special counsel to President Kennedy

on Latin-American policy; author of the text of the Alliance for Progress; constant advocate of a pro-Castro policy.

Burke Marshall, former Assistant Attorney General under Robert Kennedy.

David Burke, Senator Edward Kennedy's administrative assistant.

Milton Gwirtzman, a Washington lawyer and Edward Kennedy's friend.

Stephen Smith, Kennedy's brother-in-law.

Sargent Shriver, another Kennedy brother-in-law.

Frank O'Connor, one of Kennedy's assistants.

Richard McCarran, town attorney for Edgartown and Senator Kennedy's lawyer.

John Driscoll, another of Kennedy's lawyers.

Robert J. Clark, another of Kennedy's lawyers, former District Court Judge for Massachusetts.

Robert J. Clark III, son of the foregoing and another of Kennedy's lawyers.

Paul Markham, Kennedy's friend, former U.S. Attorney for Massachusetts.

Joseph Gargan, Kennedy's cousin.

Kenneth O'Donnel, a friend of the family.

Additional advice was also sought by phone from:

Arthur Schlesinger Jr., a founder of Americans for Democratic Action, special assistant to President Kennedy, a writer of history whose heroes are Franklin D. Roosevelt, Harry S. Truman, John F. Kennedy, Robert Kennedy, Adlai Stevenson, Juan Bosch, and Fidel Castro.

John Kenneth Galbraith, appointed by President Kennedy as Ambassador to India; a socialist politician and writer; advocate of admission of Red China to the United Nations.

Abraham Ribicoff, Senator from Connecticut.

It was necessary to determine the broad lines of Kennedy's defense before the legal authorities and before the U.S.

public. The unfolding of subsequent events permits us to reconstruct, without inside information, what decisions were taken on this crucial subject by the nineteen advisers involved. They appear to have been as follows:

1. To avoid for the moment any contact with newsmen, and, if this proved impossible, to refuse to answer any of their questions; and to persuade all the members of the Lawrence cottage party to follow the same line of conduct.

2. To negotiate an arrangement with the court and the prosecuting authorities to spare Senator Kennedy the dangerous ordeal of an official and public interrogation, and especially a public examination under oath.

3. To prepare in advance a public explanation to be given immediately after the expected court decision, anticipating and trying to attenuate the amazement sure to be provoked by its unaccountable mildness.

4. Once the public statement was given, to refuse grimly to be drawn into any discussion about it, and flatly to deny the truth of any conflicting information.

Protecting Senator Kennedy from the inquisitiveness and the rigors of the law was only a part of the task his lawyers and friends, feverishly at work at Hyannis Port, had taken upon themselves. There was also Kennedy's political future to salvage from what seemed to be irremediable wreckage. The "confession" which it was decided that Kennedy would deliver on TV following his plea of guilty would inevitably bring, it was realized, the question of the advisability of his resignation as Senator from Massachusetts. It was evident, however, that his Senate seat had to be saved at any price. The possibility of again bringing the Presidency of the United States into the Kennedy family was not the concern of the moment.

According to columnists Robert S. Allen and John A.

Goldsmith, it was Richard Goodwin who had the bright idea of asking the people of Massachusetts to help the penitent and wavering Senator to reach a decision about his resignation. "It would take them. That has sex appeal," Goodwin is reported to have said. The same columnists further report that already, before the TV speech, "the word was being spread by telephone and other means to Kennedy's liegemen and devotees throughout the country to make every effort to ensure a deluge of favorable responses. A boiler-room team was set up to solicit supporting messages from all parts of the country." The whole Kennedy electoral apparatus seems to have been set in motion. There was evidence, said *Human Events*, that many of the letters and telegrams received after the TV appearance were generated by the Kennedy organization. Columnist Ted Lewis wrote in the *New York Daily News* that "loyal precinct workers in Rockwell, Lexington, Concord, and Chicopee Falls were responsible for getting out the favorable missives." Labor's policy makers joined in the effort, said the *Wisconsin State Journal,* and gave orders to their people in Massachusetts to express confidence in the Senator. So did the Soviet press. The *Komsolskaia Pravda,* among others, came openly to the defense of Edward Kennedy, "the young chief of American Liberalism," and affirmed that he was a victim of the U.S. rightist clique.*

We may suppose that the Hyannis Port special brain trust had to decide also whether or not Senator Kennedy should appear at Mary Jo's funeral. "Senator Kennedy gravely wounded in an auto accident," had been the way in which the international press first broadcasted news of the Dyke Bridge tragedy. Dr. Robert Watt of Hyannis Port, Edward Kennedy's physician, told reporters, while the Senator was in strict seclusion with his advisers and lawyers, that Kennedy "was suffering from a slight concussion and was bruised and

---

*For a long while *Pravda* mentioned and discussed the accident without mentioning Mary Jo.

shaken up." However, Kennedy's appearance, alert, dapper, and talkative, in Edgartown and on Chappaquiddick Island during the night of the accident and the next morning belied such information. Therefore a public demonstration seemed advisable to substantiate the theory of shock and amnesia *basic to Kennedy's defense*. So it was decided that he would appear at the funeral in Larksville, Pennsylvania, between his wife and his sister-in-law, with a dashing neck-brace under his open shirt. Unfortunately, this attire was dismally reminiscent of Dr. Sam Shepherd, presenting himself in court in similar garb while he attempted to convince the jury that two black men, with black masks, riding in a black car, had beaten him almost to death.

The Senator's appearance in Larksville put him in direct contact with newsmen for the first time since the accident, and gave him the opportunity to teach them manners: "I have just attended the burial of a very lovely girl. It is not the moment to make commentaries. I will release a declaration when it is necessary." It was announced the same day that this declaration would be made on television — far from the insistent inquisitiveness of the press and the dangers of cross-examination in court. At Larksville, Kennedy tactlessly enough offered to pay the expenses of the funeral, an offer that was, said the Press, curtly declined by Mary Jo's parents.

This brings us to an interesting question: What were the results of the investigation by the company with which Kennedy's car was insured? An insurance agent appears as a matter of course, as promptly as possible, at the scene of any accident. He makes his proper inquiries and fixes the responsibility of the company according to what he learns. Presumably the records of this separate and independent investigation could be subpoenaed by the proper authorities. In the case of the Kennedy accident, what was paid? To whom? By whom? For what?

"Some members of the press," said Arena on July 21, "get

irritable because they believe all I have to do is to wave a magic wand and everyone concerned with the incident will talk. But those close to it are extremely reluctant to talk." We do not know in whose hands was the magic wand of the law — in Chief Arena's, Prosecutor Steele's, or District Attorney Dinis's. What we do know is that none of them used it at the proper time to break the guilty reluctance of eleven first-class witnesses (the star witness, Senator Kennedy, included) and to force them to assist the Law in its "due process" with whatever they knew about the violent death of Mary Jo Kopechne, who had been a companion and friend of all of them. And we know that it was Prosecutor Steele who had the initial responsibility and the authority to prosecute in the Kennedy-Kopechne case, as in any other similar case in his jurisdiction. We also know that it was Prosecutor Steele who ruled out the more serious charge of negligence, and thus took the case out of the hands of District Attorney Dinis.

Prosecutor Walter Steele is known to be a close friend of Senator Edward Kennedy, with whom he served as Assistant District Attorney of Suffolk County under District Attorney Garrett Byrne. We understand very well the irritation of the prosecutor when reporter Dan Tommasson alluded to this friendship, and we are even willing to believe that it played no part in determining the prosecutor's behavior in the Dyke Bridge tragedy. But we cannot fail to observe that it was this behavior that blocked any official interrogation of Senator Kennedy or his ten companions, male and female, before the appearance of the Senator in court.

CHAPTER VI

Justice After A Fashion

The laws of the Commonwealth of Massachusetts provide for two months to two years of internment in a house of correction for unlawfully leaving the scene of an accident. Two months with suspended sentence is the lightest possible penalty, reserved for the least culpable offenders; two years with no suspension of sentence is the heaviest, given to offenders who have shown the greatest disregard for the rules of traffic safety *or for the well-being of persons injured through their fault.* Between these two extremes the judge had at his disposal a whole range of possible penalties.

The dictionary definition of manslaughter is "culpable homicide without malice aforethought." For a charge of manslaughter to be brought, the laws of the Commonwealth of Massachusetts require "willful and wanton conduct," which does not imply the intention to kill, still less premeditation.

In filing his charge of "leaving the scene of an accident *without negligence involved,"* Police Chief Dominick Arena explained to the press that he had asked Lieutenant George Killen, as a personal favor, to question those who were at the cottage the night of July 18 and July 19. Before the same reporters, Dukes County Prosecutor Walter Steele confirmed Killen's mission and informed the newsmen that one of the purposes of the investigation was to determine whether any additional charge should be brought against Senator Kennedy, besides that chosen by Police Chief Arena.*

It would have been logical and in agreement with normal procedure to let the announced investigation – which could have started on July 19, before all the important witnesses were scattered over the Eastern States – determine, before the Senator's appearance in court, whether there were aggravating circumstances that might, as suggested by Prosecutor Steele, have led to a more serious charge than "leaving the scene" – to a charge of manslaughter, for instance.

The promised public investigation never took place. The witnesses were allowed to disperse; none was subpoenaed. Mary Jo's body, an autopsy on which might have substantiated even graver charges than manslaughter, was sent safely out of the jurisdiction of Police Chief Arena, District Attorney Dinis, and Prosecutor Steele. Thus, Senator Kennedy would be brought before Judge Boyle in the Edgartown court house on July 25 without having been subjected to any form of interrogation.

Even on the basis of the little Senator Kennedy cared to disclose in the written statement he left at the police station the day after the accident, with no supplementary interrogation; even with the charge limited to that of "leaving the scene," the prosecution could not normally have presented the case as one of the less culpable in its category. The accident had had a fatal issue. Almost ten hours had passed before the defendant reported it to the police, and he had meanwhile neglected all the possibilities of professional help that were immediately at his disposal: police, fire station,

---

*To newsmen Lieutenant Killen declared: "It is not true that I have been assigned to this case. I have no intention of interrogating any witnesses. All I know is that to all intents and purposes the investigation is over." As for Prosecutor Steele, far from trying to find out whether any additional charge should be brought, he suppressed even the possibility of adding "negligence" to "leaving the scene of an accident," by stating in his report – nobody knows on what basis – that Kennedy was driving "with extreme caution."

Coast Guard. More than that, he had asked his companions not to summon help.

If the Senator and his ten companions had been subjected immediately to a normal legal interrogation, it could very likely have been proved that Kennedy had not taken the sand road by mistake, and he would have been obliged to give another explanation for leaving the Lawrence cottage with Mary Jo than the desire to catch the last scheduled ferry. This would have changed the whole aspect of the case and might have brought to the consideration of the prosecutor and of the court the advisability of a more serious charge than leaving the scene of an accident. Even if the autopsy had not brought up other probatory elements, this more serious charge could not have been less than manslaughter, since it was wantonly and willfully that, by Kennedy's conduct, Mary Jo Kopechne was denied the assistance that, in all reasonable probability, might have saved her life.

There must have been reasons why the prosecuting authorities failed so conspicuously to fulfill their routine obligation in a case of death by external means. To a majority of public opinion in the United States and abroad those reasons appeared to be:

1 The concern of the responsible authorities was not so much with the tragic death of a girl as with how to spare a Senator and a potential candidate for the Presidency of the United States the prison penalty he deserved, and to save his political future.

2. During this week of hard reflection and discussion among members of the Hyannis Port special brain trust, and of negotiations between Kennedy's lawyers and the prosecution, an agreement had been reached by which, in exchange for a plea of guilty to the minimum charge possible under the circumstances, Kennedy was promised that he would be spared any question, put publicly and under oath, that might

have helped to uncover what really happened the night Mary Jo met her death.

Kennedy's friends affirm that the Senator had desired a "show-cause" hearing at which some legal defense could be offered. We do not know whether this is true or not. In any case his lawyers and advisers must have realized quickly that such a hearing would lead to just what the Senator and his defense were desperately trying to avoid: public examination and counter-examination of the defendant and the known witnesses; public surprise testimony; and medical consultations and counter-consultations that could have completely demolished Kennedy's statements concerning shock and selective amnesia. It was quickly realized also that there was only one way of avoiding any dangerous questioning: that was to plead guilty to a charge in response to which the defense had been previously assured that the prosecution would not ask for any penalty that could result in the Senator's imprisonment for even twenty-four hours.

The hearing, originally fixed for Monday, July 28, was held on Friday, July 25. It was a hearing for trial, not to show cause, and the stage was set in the nicest way possible under the circumstances. Senator Kennedy appeared at the Edgartown Court House at 8:15 a.m., 25 minutes before the scheduled opening of the trial, this time without neck-brace, and between his wife and brother-in-law, Stephen Smith. They were accompanied by three of the Senator's lawyers and one bodyguard, and followed by a caravan of cars, and they were received by a waiting and not altogether friendly crowd of local people and newsmen.* There were some preparatory consultations between lawyers, prosecution, and defendant. When asked for his plea, Senator Kennedy answered twice: "Guilty. Guilty!" — the first time in a low

---

*The following Sunday Kennedy was met at the entrance of his Hyannis Port church by a crowd of youths bearing placards with comminatory inscriptions such as "Teddy, tell the truth!"

voice; and he did not utter another word during the *nine-minute* session.

Attorney Richard McCarran asked for a suspended sentence, explaining that "the Senator's character is well-known in the United States and in the world." Dukes County Special Prosecutor Wilbur Steele could not resist such an argument, and joined in asking that the defendant be spared imprisonment. The Court concurred, and Judge Boyle pronounced the lightest possible sentence, the sentence provided by the law for the least culpable cases of leaving the scene of an accident: two months in a house of correction, suspended for one year. Senator Kennedy was not put on probation, as another delinquent probably would have been, but under one year's special court supervision. This permitted him not only to leave the state of Massachusetts but even, as was later shown, to travel abroad on important official missions as a representative of the United States Senate.

In an intervention that was the only surprise in those few minutes in court, Judge Boyle asked whether there had been "a deliberate effort to conceal the identity of the defendant." This happened before the appearance of the Drew Pearson column that accused the Senator of having tried to duplicate the youthful performance that once got him expelled from Harvard, by asking his cousin, Joseph Gargan, to "take the rap" for him.* Had Judge Boyle received a tip from some mysterious informer? The fact is that both lawyers and prosecution seemed suddenly apprehensive — and with good reason, since the more than nine hours' delay in reporting the accident, and all the mysterious comings and goings of that tragic night, amply legitimated the Judge's suspicions. Here is the exchange of words that ensued:

---

*Possibly for the first time in the history of cheating in examinations, young Edward Kennedy had had the bright idea of paying a comrade who looked more or less like him to take an examination in his place. Discovered, both young men were expelled from the University.

Judge BOYLE. — I would be most interested in determining, from the defendant or from the Commonwealth, if there was a deliberate effort to conceal the identity of the defendant.

Chief ARENA. — Identity of the defendant . . . . Not to my knowledge, your Honor.

Prosecutor STEELE. — *Thank you, Chief.* [Emphasis added.]

The thanks were well deserved. The efforts of Prosecutor Steele and Chief Arena to help the Senior Senator from Massachusetts as much as possible had been and were obvious. When giving what he called a summary of the evidence, Chief Arena told Judge Boyle:

I returned to the station and was advised by Mr. Kennedy that he had been the operator of the vehicle involved. Mr. Kennedy advised me that *he believed that the accident happened sometime after 11:15 p.m. on July 18, 1969.* [Emphasis added.]

Kennedy never expressed himself in that way about the time of the accident, either in his police station statement or in his TV script. He did not use the phrase, "I believe"; he did not say "sometime after 11:15 p.m.," which would cover the whole night. On both occasions he said very precisely: "I left the cottage with Miss Kopechne at about 11:15 p.m." — which put him at the Dyke Bridge some minutes later than 11:15.

Arena and Steele knew, no doubt, at that time that Kennedy had lied about the time of the accident, and that the unshakable testimony of Deputy Sheriff Look, firstly adopted by the police, had proved that Kennedy's car was still far from the bottom of Poucha Pond at 12:45. By editing Kennedy's answer, and not revealing Look's testimony, Arena was concealing this fact from Judge Boyle and preventing him from forming a just appreciation of the veracity of the rest of Kennedy's statement. *Two days earlier, Prosecutor Steele had described to newsmen as "un-*

fortunate" Arena's disclosure of Look's testimony. Arena corrected his unfortunate error in Judge Boyle's court.

When Judge Boyle expressed concern "with the question of disposition, mitigating and aggravating circumstances," the Commonwealth, in the words of Chief Arena, had already given its answer:

> Investigation of the accident and of the accident scene produced no evidence of negligence on the part of the defendant; however, it appears that there were opportunities for the defendant to have made himself known to the proper authorities immediately after the accident. Therefore a complaint was sought against him for leaving the scene of an accident without immediately making himself known.

Contrary to Arena's statement, there had been absolutely no investigation of the accident, no interrogation of witnesses, no verification of even the little information Kennedy gave Arena. And if willfully neglecting for more than nine hours to summon the assistance that was within immediate reach for the rescue of the slowly drowning girl, and forbidding his two companions, Gargan and Markham, to do so (a fact which investigation would have promptly brought to light) — if this was not a sufficiently aggravating circumstance, then there is something wrong either with the Massachusetts laws or with those who interpret them when Senators are involved.

It would have been rather difficult for the defense to find any mitigating circumstances for Kennedy's behavior, but Counselor McCarran — who, by the way, is also the chief attorney of Edgartown municipality, which employs Dominick Arena as police chief — did not miss the opportunity offered by the Judge's question, and responded quickly, giving an answer which, though it sidestepped the question, presented his client from a favorable angle of repentance and courage, saying: "The defendant is adamant in this matter, that he wishes to plead guilty."

McCarran tried, however, to convince the court that some legal defense would have been possible on behalf of Kennedy. Judge Boyle, rightly irritated at that bit of professional cheek, interrupted him abruptly. Everybody had to help, and Prosecutor Steele did his best, bringing this family scene to a happy conclusion in the following exchange:

> Mr. STEELE. – May it please your Honor, the Commonwealth suggests for your Honor's consideration that this defendant be incarcerated in the house of correction for a period of two months and that the execution of this sentence be suspended.
>
> It would seem that, having in mind the character of the defendant, his age, his reputation prior to this occurrence, the ends of justice would best be served were he given a suspended sentence.
>
> Judge BOYLE. – There is no record, Mrs. Tyra?
>
> Mrs. HELEN TYRA (in charge of the local probation office). – None, your Honor.*
>
> Judge BOYLE. – Considering the unblemished record of the defendant – and the Commonwealth represents that this is not a case where he was trying to conceal his identity . . . .
>
> Mr. STEELE. – No, sir.
>
> Judge BOYLE. – Where it is my understanding, he has already been and will continue to be punished far beyond anything this court can impose – the ends of justice would be satisfied by the imposition of the minimum jail sentence and the suspension of that sentence, assuming the defendant accepts the suspension.
>
> Mr. McCARRAN. – The defendant will accept the suspension, your Honor.

So even Mrs. Helen Tyra did her bit. There was actually a long record of traffic violations against the Senator, a record so amply reported by the press during the preceding week that it would have appeared impossible for anyone to ignore the fact that, at least in the matter of

---

*When it was discovered that Kennedy's driving license showed absolutely no sign of immersion, it was explained that the Senator drove without his license that night. Mrs. Tyra, to whom the license had lately been delivered, might have added this item to the Senator's already rich record.

traffic offenses, the Senator's record was not unblemished.

Judge Boyle was completely wrong when he implied that the penalty he had just pronounced was the strongest the court had at its disposal. It would need an effort of the imagination to describe a case more deserving of the maximum penalty — two years in a house of correction — that the Massachusetts law provides for "unlawfully leaving the scene of an accident." Judge Boyle's excuse for his fatherly indulgence was that it was not until the next day, after Senator Kennedy's performance on TV, that he had reason to suspect how little the Senator deserved it.

There is one important point that should not be forgotten when assessing the legality and the morality of the treatment with which Senator Kennedy was favored through all the judicial proceedings in the case of Mary Jo Kopechne's tragic death. *Everybody knew that the defendant had decided to plead guilty to a minor charge because that was the only way of avoiding public examination under oath about the circumstances of the girl's death. Everybody knew, therefore, that there was something the defendant wanted to hide, obviously something more incriminating than the charge to which he had consented to plead guilty.*

It was only after he was brought to believe that no official investigation would ever force him to disclose more than he wanted to about the part he played on that fatal night, that Senator Edward Kennedy announced briskly, to the newsmen and the onlookers who crowded around him on his departure from the court house, that he would finally make his long-promised public statement: "I have made my plea, and I want time on the network tonight to speak to the people of Massachusetts."*

---

*Later, when his lawyers realized that some sort of inquest would finally be unavoidable, Kennedy asked the Massachusetts Supreme Court to rule that it be top-secret.

Time was already secured on all channels, unpaid and with priority, and the speech that was to be delivered that night had been carefully and painfully put together during seven days of gestation by a troupe of devoted scribes at work in Hyannis Port.

CHAPTER VII

On T.V. – Facts And Anti-Facts

The result of the labors of the speech-writers in the Hyannis Port compound, offered to the U.S. public at 7:00 p.m. on July 25 via all TV channels, consisted of two interlaced plots: a contrived structure of events, actions, and attitudes and a sensitivity-training performance specially designed for the benefit of the Massachusetts electorate.

It has been said by one of Senator Kennedy's colleagues, and was felt by millions of listeners, that his TV broadcast on the evening following his appearance in court was "a perfect piece of propaganda and public relations literature." Millions of others, it seems, recognized in it "the sincerity and the courage characteristic of the great Kennedy style," feeling at certain moments that they heard "not the Senator, but his brother, the murdered President."

We do not think that there is any fundamental contradiction between these two impressions. "A man does what he must, in spite of personal consequences, in spite of obstacles and dangers and pressures," wrote President Kennedy in *Profiles of Courage*; and these identical words were used by his brother the Senator in his self-exculpatory speech. The big style is there in both cases, and in both cases there is the abysmal discrepancy between the lofty words and the actions to which they seem to refer – the Dyke Bridge affair in the one case, and the Bay of Pigs in the other.

The intention, or the necessity, to deceive appears with the very first words of the Senator's speech:

Prior to my appearance in court it would have been improper
for me to comment on this matter. *But tonight, I am free to
tell what happened* and to say what it meant for me. [Emphasis
added.]

The Senator had spent four hours on the morning of the
accident in the Edgartown police station, where he was not
only free but bound to give a complete and truthful
account of the fatal mishap in which a young girl had
perished, while he himself had emerged unscathed. Instead
of doing so, he left in the hands of Chief Dominick Arena,
after long hesitation and several attempts to reach a lawyer,
a short statement that was at variance with the TV address
on almost all essential points, both in what was said and in
what was omitted. If he had believed that truth would
serve his interest, nothing in law or in propriety would
have prevented him from making it public immediately, at
the police station. Therefore, telling his listeners that he
had not been free until the night of July 25 to explain
what happened the night of July 18 was an absurdity,
and an obvious first attempt to bamboozle them. Others
followed:

When I left the party around 11:15 p.m., I was accompanied
by one of the girls, Miss Mary Jo Kopechne . . . . A little over
one mile away, the car that I was driving on an unlit road went
off a narrow bridge which had no guard rails and was built on a
left angle to the road.

In his police statement Senator Kennedy had presented
quite a different version of that part of the Dyke Bridge
mishap:

On July 18, 1969, at approximately 11:15 p.m., on Chappaquiddick, Martha's Vineyard, Massachusetts, I was driving
my car on Main Street, Chappaquiddick, *on my way to get
the ferry back to Edgartown. I was unfamiliar with the road*

and turned right into the Dyke Road instead of bearing hard left on Main Street. [Emphasis added.]

In the TV statement the crucial parts of this information are missing. His rash and hasty statement about being unfamiliar with the road and taking a 180 degree wrong turn by mistake had meanwhile been exploded by a public roar of protest, and by all the observable circumstances that made such a mistake impossible. It is true, as the Senator mentioned on TV, that it was an "unlit road"; what he did not mention was the reflective arrow, at the fork of the road, which pointed the way to the ferry landing, and the fact that the two lanes of the asphalt road from the cottage to the ferry landing were separated by a visible white line.

In the police statement Kennedy states that he was driving his car on Main Street on his way to get the ferry back to Edgartown. On TV he leaves his millions of listeners in absolute ignorance of the reason why he and Miss Kopechne were on the Dyke Bridge dirt road at that hour. An explanation was all the more necessary because *the time (11:15 p.m.) mentioned in both statements has been proved to be untrue.* The black Oldsmobile could not have been submerged, wheels up, in Poucha Pond before 12:45 a.m., the time at which it was seen and identified by Deputy Sheriff Look, deliberately taking the Dyke Bridge direction. The car Mrs. Malm heard passing a short time before midnight, without being able to identify its direction, could have been any vehicle; if it was Kennedy's Oldsmobile, it would have proved only that the car had passed over the Dyke Bridge several times safely earlier that same night.*

About the accident itself, Kennedy said in his TV statement:

---

*Mrs. Malm told the press: "A short time before midnight I heard a car passing. I thought it was going pretty fast."

The car overturned in a deep pond and immediately filled with
water. I remember thinking as the cold water rushed in around
my head that I was for certain drowning. Then water entered my
lungs and I actually felt the sensation of drowning. *But somehow
I struggled to the surface alive.* I made immediate and repeated
efforts to save Mary Jo, by diving into the strong and murky
current, but succeeded only in increasing my state of utter
exhaustion and alarm. [Emphasis added.]

The police statement was somewhat different:

The car turned over and sank into the water and landed with
the roof resting on the bottom. *I attempted to open the door and
window of the car* but have no recollection of how I got out of
the car. I came to the surface and then repeatedly dove down in
an attempt *to see if the passenger was still in the car.* I was
unsuccessful in the attempt. [Emphasis added.]

On TV Kennedy said that "the car immediately filled
with water." He did not mention this in his original
statement. Water could indeed have rushed immediately
through broken windows, but in the upturned position of
the car an air pocket would have formed in any case in the
foot well of the rear seat, which was higher in the water
than the front part of the car. It was in this air pocket that
Captain Farrar believed that Mary Jo had tried to keep her
head.

Senator Kennedy's grim silence and strict seclusion between the tragedy and his TV broadcast, the strange torpor
of the investigating and prosecuting authorities, the universal knowledge that the TV statement had been prepared by a
high-powered group of lawyers and speech-writers, together
with the mysterious circumstances that surrounded the
tragedy, justified any suspicion, even the wildest. That the
suspicion increased rather than diminished following the
Senator's public statement is entirely his own fault and that
of his advisers. None of them can complain if Kennedy's

factual description of the accident from which he escaped
alive is not believed by so many.

How did the Senator get out of the sunken and overturned
car? Its doors were found closed; according to his own statement it seems that the windows were closed also when the car
made its plunge. How did the Senator open one of them with
the water rushing in around his head? With batteries and engine
submerged, electrical devices, if any, were of course out of action. Did the Senator wind up the window crank until the
window was opened sufficiently for him to pass through it?
How long did this operation take, *with the Senator's head already in the rushing water?* If it was through a broken window
that the Senator crawled out, did he tear his clothes, or lacerate
his hands or face or other parts of his body? *Why did nobody
see him in soaked clothes?* What kind of injury permitted him
to appear normal and alert on the morning of July 19, forced
him to wear a rigid neckbrace on July 23 when he appeared for
the first time in public, and then permitted him to discard the
brace before appearing in court on July 25 – when its presence
could have suggested the necessity of a medical examination?

In fact, an increasing number of persons asked themselves,
after reading and hearing the two statements, whether the
Senator was really in his car when it overturned and submerged in Poucha Pond; asked themselves further, *"How did
Mary Jo Kopechne really come to her tragic death?"*

To everybody's bewilderment, Senator Kennedy introduced two new and sensational pieces of information in his
public statement about which not one word had been said or
written by him or his companions either at the police station
or at any other time between the accident and the TV appearance a week later.

In his initial statement Kennedy had told the police that,
after giving up his efforts "to see if the passenger was still in
the submerged car," he walked back, soaked and exhausted,
to the cottage, and there climbed into a car that was parked

in front of it and asked for "someone" *to take him to Edgartown.* He told quite another story on TV, where he said:

> Instead of looking directly for a telephone *after lying exhausted in the grass for an undetermined time,* I walked back to the cottage where the party was being held, and requested the help of two friends — my cousin Joseph Gargan and Paul Markham — and directed them to return immediately to the scene of the accident with me — this was sometime after midnight — in order to undertake *with me* a new effort to dive down and locate Miss Kopechne. Their strenuous efforts, undertaken at some risk to their own lives, proved futile. [Emphasis added.]

Why did not Kennedy, Gargan, or Markham tell Arena the next morning about these last heroic efforts to rescue the drowning girl? Nobody could have blamed them for that. Was it perhaps because they could not have produced their soaked clothes or explained how they got into dry ones?

If it was true that the Senator and his two friends visited the place of the accident again that terrible night, it could not have been to make a last effort to save the trapped girl, because the Senator (who allegedly was in a state of shock) and also Gargan and Markham (who presumably were in possession of all their wits) all refrained carefully from utilizing any of the surprisingly numerous means of summoning assistance that were at their disposal, not only in Edgartown and farther afield, but on Chappaquiddick Island itself. Let us listen on this basic subject to Hall Bruno, news editor of *Newsweek* magazine, one of the journalists who courageously took upon themselves the investigating duties the responsible local and state authorities had not cared — or dared — to fulfill:

> Another thing that a walk on Chappaquiddick reveals is just how much help was immediately at hand for anyone willing and able to call for it . . . .
>
> There are at least four houses on the route back from the Dyke Bridge to the cottage, and the occupants of at least two of them have said that they had lights burning at the time of the accident. A

phone call from any of them would have brought immediate response from the police and the fire department . . . . I discovered some 500 feet before I got to the cottage *a large red light glowing from a cinder block building just a few yards from the road.* This is the Chappaquiddick Volunteer Fire Station. You have to pass it every time you go to or from the party cottage. *The red light is left on all night.*

I talked with Foster Silva, whose house is just across the road from the fire house and *practically next door to the party cottage.* Silva is proud of his volunteer fire company. He is its captain. If he had been called from near the bridge, or *if someone had pulled the alarm inside the unlocked fire house,* Silva would have been on the bridge immediately. *"I would have been there in three minutes,"* Silva said, "and my volunteers and half the people on the island could have showed up within fifteen minutes." [Emphasis added.]

The millions of listeners to the TV broadcast have the right to ask themselves, as did the inhabitants of the island interviewed by Hall Bruno: "What were those three trying to hide out there?"

In Kennedy's initial statement, when he had not yet decided how to explain his appearance in Edgartown the night of the tragedy — an explanation everybody expected, which finally had to be given — the Senator said, in writing:

I was exhausted and in a state of shock. I recall walking back to where my friends were eating. There was a car parked in front of the cottage and I climbed into the back seat. I then asked for someone to bring me back to Edgartown. *I remember walking around for a period of time* and then going back to my hotel room. [Emphasis added.]

The TV version was remarkably different:

Instructing Gargan and Markham not to alarm Mary Jo's friends that night, I had them take me to the ferry-crossing. The ferry having shut down for the night, I suddenly jumped into the water and impulsively swam across, nearly drowning once again in the effort, and returned to my hotel about 2 a.m., and collapsed in my room . . . . I remember going out at one time and saying something to the room clerk. [Emphasis added.]

Why did Kennedy, in a state of shock and utter exhaustion, take this highly dangerous way of reaching Edgartown, and why did his two companions let him do it, when a simple telephone call was all that would have been required to bring a ferry to the Chappaquiddick side of the channel for anyone giving a sensible reason for the request — especially a Kennedy in Kennedy country? Captain Farrar, the professional diver, and two young sportsmen tried the same feat by daylight the next day, clad in swimming trunks, and as a result of the experiment they concluded that it was very doubtful that the Senator could have done it at night, in a state of shock and encumbered by a back brace, a concussion, and already-soaked clothing and water-logged shoes, unless he had either started much farther upstream or landed much farther downstream on the opposite shore.

Kennedy and his two companions — who in a space of less than two hours had been plunging and swimming all around Chappaquiddick Island, extricating themselves miraculously from submerged cars, attempting heroic rescues, crossing dangerous channels — were never seen by anybody during that fatal night otherwise than in dry and pressed clothes. The Senator did not mention in his initial report having met and chatted *at about 2:25 a.m.* with Mr. Russell E. Peachey, the co-owner of his hotel, the Shiretown Inn, and he mentioned it in only a few words in his TV report. His listeners would have liked to know whether it was before or after he collapsed in his room that he changed his drenched clothing for the unremarkable garb in which Mr. Peachey saw him at 2:25 a.m., looking calm and composed, asking Mr. Peachey for the time and complaining about the noise coming from a nearby building. Was it after this conversation that he collapsed in his room — so that only at about ten o'clock the next morning, "with [his] mind somewhat more lucid," could he report to the police?

The truth is that nobody knows what Senator Kennedy and his two companions were doing during the two hours or so which, according to the Senator's TV statement, passed between his return to the cottage from the scene of the accident and his appearance in front of the Shiretown Inn.* Nobody knows, either, the real reason why it was essential to Kennedy's interests that this portion of the tragic night's events remain unknown to law authorities and the public.

In our last quote from Senator Kennedy's TV statement there is one sentence that should not be overlooked. It is perhaps the most credible and at the same time the most self-incriminatory sentence in the long "confession," if the words reported are, as seems likely, the actual words that were used when he was "instructing Gargan and Markham not to alarm Mary Jo's friends that night." If at that moment of shock, cerebral concussion, and utter exhaustion the Senator still had enough presence of mind and considerateness to recommend that Markham and Gargan spare Mary Jo's friends the emotion of the tragic news for "that night," surely the same presence of mind and feeling of responsibility should have prompted him to ask his two friends to cross the road − if he was too exhausted to do it himself − and to ring the alarm bell of the Chappaquiddick Fire Station, whose door was open and whose red light was burning the whole night. That bell would have summoned the good will, competence, and equipment that would have permitted immediate rescue of the young girl, whose life could perhaps, at that time, still have been saved.†

---

*According to Deputy Sheriff Christopher Look, the elapsed time could not have been longer than an hour and a quarter.

†During a "white-washing" panel discussion of Kennedy's two statements on NBC television, John Chancellor, the commentator, had the effrontery to compare Kennedy's TV performance with President Nixon's "Checquers" speech of 1952, answering a smear attack on him by the press. Mr. Chancellor commented that the only major difference between the two was "that Mr. Nixon was running for office at the time." The same kept press provided large repercussions to Mr. Chancellor's brain wave, confirming the opinion of many that Vice President Agnew was very moderate in his criticism of the activities of the news industry. He could have used a much bigger stick.

Nobody can doubt today that Kennedy's injunction to his confederates was not to alarm anybody until something had been decided about the least incriminating way of reporting Mary Jo's death. If some doubts persist as to this, the inexcusable conduct of Gargan and Markham should quickly clear them away. This conduct, by the way, makes them not only guilty of withholding information and obstructing justice — a charge that could be brought, probably, against a number of the Lawrence cottage revelers — but also of being accessories after the fact, whatever this fact may have been.

CHAPTER VIII

On T.V. – Sensitivity Training

In the first tirade of his TV appearance, Senator Kennedy objected vigorously to the accusation that he had driven under the influence of liquor, and to ugly speculations about his relationship with Miss Kopechne or about the characters of any of the girls present at the Lawrence cottage party.

One can easily believe Senator Kennedy's denial of having drunk too much the night of the tragedy. His behavior between the first moment of what he called "the incredible incident" and his appearance at Edgartown police station demonstrated a singleness of purpose and a consistency in execution incompatible with a state of real drunkenness. As for the reputations of the six girls in whose defense the Senator felt obliged to break a knightly lance, nobody would have had any reason or even any opportunity to speculate about that subject before the tragic conclusion of the party to which they had been invited, perhaps without knowing that they were to meet there six men, five of whom were married but unaccompanied by their wives. And it was immediately after the impetuous volley in which the Senator was supposed to be defending Mary Jo's character that he provided an opening for some "widely circulated assumptions" by ostentatiously suppressing from this public statement, to the great astonishment of millions of listeners, the more or less acceptable motive he had given in his police statement for his presence with Miss Kopechne in the black Oldsmobile sedan — at 11:15 p.m. according to his version; at 12:45 a.m. according to the police version — on the sand road to the Dyke Bridge, going in a direction diametrically opposite to that leading to the ferry landing.

After the benevolent verdict of the Edgartown court, there were, it seems, two attitudes that Senator Kennedy might have adopted: (1) he might have wrapped himself in the armor of *res adjudicata,* and avoided making any other explanation "then or ever," letting time do its healing and sometimes dirty work; and (2) he might have resigned his Senate seat, and in a short address to the Massachusetts electorate explained that he believed it his duty to let them decide in the next election whether, after that verdict, he was still qualified to represent in the United States Senate the state which had sent to that respected body men like John Quincy Adams, Daniel Webster, Charles Sumner, and the elder Henry Cabot Lodge.

The old Kennedy hands and the members of the Kennedy clan assembled at that moment at Hyannis Port very likely found both of these two solutions to the alarming crisis too risky for the Senator's political future, upon which so much had been staked. So a third course was decided upon, which involved, besides the enumeration of a carefully measured number of facts and anti-facts, a public confession of guilt. Should that confession shoulder without restriction the responsibility of the mentioned facts and anti-facts, or should it try to find an excuse for what had happened and to offer it together with a plea for forgiveness? Senator Kennedy tried to have it both ways, combining a manly attitude of unqualified contrition with a specimen of the sensitivity-training type of confession as abject as could be desired by a modern educator, aiming much less at self-castigation than at the awakening of a whole arpeggio of favorable emotions in his listeners:

My conduct and conversation during the next several hours, *to the extent that I can remember them,* make no sense to me at all.

Although my doctors informed me that I suffered a cerebral concussion as well as a shock, I do not seek to escape responsibility for my action by placing the blame either on the physical and emotional trauma brought on by the accident, *or on anyone else.*

I regard as indefensible the fact that I did not report the accident to the police immediately . . . .

All kind of scrambled thoughts, all of them confused, some of them irrational, *many of which I cannot recall* and some of which I would not have seriously entertained under normal circumstances, went through my mind during this period. They were reflected in the various inexplicable, inconsistent, and inconclusive things I said and did, including such questions as *whether the girl might still be alive somewhere out of the immediate area ,* . . . whether there was some justifiable reason for me to doubt what had happened *and to delay my report,* whether somehow the terrible weight of *this incredible incident* might in some way pass from my shoulders.

I was overcome, I am frank to say, by a jumble of emotions: grief, fear, doubt, exhaustion, panic, confusion, and shock. [Emphasis added.]

It is no wonder that the Senator insists on the "scrambled thoughts" that he cannot recall, and on "the extent [to which] I can remember them," in talking of his conduct and conversation following the accident. Selective amnesia is an important part of his self-exculpatory thesis. One can also easily understand his introduction of the question of "whether the girl might still be alive somewhere out of the immediate area." Skipping the romantic evocation of the "Kennedy curse," this led directly to "some justifiable reason for me to doubt what had happened *and to delay my report.*" But who was the enigmatic "anyone else" upon whom the blame might be placed, and in what way did the Senator imagine that the "terrible weight" of the Poucha Pond tragedy "might . . . pass from my shoulders"? Was there in those suggestions anything more than a diverting touch of suspense and mystery, introduced into the text by some inventive co-writer? An honest inquest might have elucidated these points.

Senator Kennedy was frank in saying at the beginning of his TV speech that it was to his Massachusetts constituents, the custodians of his political future, that it was addressed. Its fundamental inspiration must, therefore, be looked for in that obsessive concern, characteristic of the third generation of American Kennedys, with the winning and upholding of political power as a prerequisite to the supreme magistrature of the nation.

It was this overwhelming concern — shared by all the Kennedy henchmen who had repaired to Hyannis Port from all over the United States to help the Senator decide what to remember and what to forget — which directed all the decisions and activities of the Senator from the first moment of the tragedy, whatever its exact circumstances may have been, until the opening of the inquest on January 5, 1970, when his seven lawyers were still using all their skill and resorting to every legal possibility to avoid for their client the obligation to either confirm under oath all the statements included in his address to the Massachusetts electorate, retract them, or invoke the Fifth Amendment.

It must indeed have been this obsession that made the Senator resolve to abandon to her fate the girl in the submerged car, and prompted him to maintain this inhuman resolve for nine hours, in the hope that some subterfuge could be found that would remove from his shoulders the responsibility for the fatal mishap and avert its political consequences.

This subterfuge was found, a little later, by the resourceful conclave at Hyannis Port: a quick plea of guilty before a court guaranteed to be overindulgent and a speech in the comfortable surroundings generously donated for the use of the millionaire orator by the ABC, CBS, and NBC networks, under conditions that would not subject the Senator to the possibility of a perjury charge or to the pointed interruptions of a press audience.

Everyone knows the emotion-creating possibilities of this newest medium of communication; but many still succumb to its blandishments. The normal ability of the speaker to affect, to touch, or to persuade by his oratory are multiplied when the hearer can also see him as he speaks — his looks, his sincere demeanor, his expression, strained, sorrowful, or repentant, as the case demands. The visual spell often prevails over the actual words, preventing the listener-viewer from detecting even the most obvious distortion or evasion of the truth (as, for instance, in the first half of Kennedy's remarks), or the most brazen double-talk (as in its peroration, specially designed for the Massachusetts voters).

Almost in the same breath with which the Senator humbly implored the advice, the expression of opinion, and the prayers of his fellow citizens to help him reach a decision on whether or not to resign his seat in the U.S. Senate, he proclaimed virtuously:

> And that is the basis of all human morality. Whatever may be the sacrifice he faces if he follows his conscience — the loss of his friends, his fortune, his contentment, even the esteem of his fellow men — each man must decide for himself the course he will follow.

While Senator Kennedy was bracing himself for a decision, all the Kennedy machinery had been put in movement to orient in the right direction the advice, the opinion, and the prayers of those who were asked to help him "to put this most recent tragedy behind me and make some further contributions to our State and mankind" — to quote the Senator himself.

The Senator's speech was a hit, we are told, with his

constituents. Ten to one according to one version; two to one according to another, of the telegrams and telephone calls received at the Kennedy Boston office asked the Senator to keep his seat in the Senate. Even Mrs. Kopechne, the mother of the drowned girl, under the spell of the TV magic, wired him her sympathy. But this magic did not last long outside the doctored, Kennedy-tied segment of the Massachusetts electorate and the callous hard core of New Frontier politicians and henchmen who had already decided to support further the man of their choice.

What the other, the hostile telegrams and telephone calls received in reply to Kennedy's appeal, may have told him we will probably never know, but we can easily figure it out from the curt remarks gathered by reporters in Kennedy territory from the man in the street, and from articles and editorials in publications, the majority of which are generally favorable to the Kennedy clan. For example, from the man in the street:

> How gullible does he think people are?
> He's got to come up with something better than that!
> If he couldn't save her, why didn't he go to the nearest house to call for emergency help?
> If he was strong enough to walk to where his friends were, why didn't he ask them to phone to the police immediately?
> They behaved like three men that were more concerned with a reputation than with the girl trapped in the car.
> I think the man proved himself a coward. I just cannot imagine him leaving the scene.

From the *Manchester Union Leader,* one of the most honest publications on this continent:

> Of course it is quite obvious that the Kennedys did not want any inquiry into what really happened in connection with the death of the poor secretary, Mary Jo Kopechne, but the public is entitled to know the full details of the situation — not simply the Senator's version. It should not be brushed under the table as is now being done . . . .

There are entirely too many mysteries in this case, and they ought to be cleared up.

For once in his life Teddy Kennedy should be made to stand up like a man, take his medicine, and face the reality of the world as it is. He should not be permitted to give only his own version of the tragic accident.

From the *New York Times*:

His emotion-charged address leaves us less than satisfied with his partial explanation for a gross failure of responsibility, and more than ever convinced that the concerned town, county, and state officials of Massachusetts have also failed in their duty thoroughly to investigate the case because of the political personality involved.

From *Time* magazine:

The appearance did in fact answer a few questions, but left the most serious one unanswered, and raised a few that had not been asked before.

From *Newsweek*:

For the hard fact was that Teddy's TV account of the tragedy of Chappaquiddick Island — and in particular of his indefensible ten-hour delay in reporting to the police — has not been enough to remove the suspicions, the doubts, the contradictions, and the unanswered questions that hang about the case.

From an editorial in *Life* magazine, which has never been accused of anti-Kennedyism:

There was also some decidedly awkward talk of morality and courage, including an eloquent passage from his brother's book, which Teddy recited as though oblivious to the way the meaning rebuked him. He was simply hustling heartstrings, using words, cashing in on the family credibility . . . .

It was like a parody of the Cuban missile crisis, all surviving New Frontiersmen scheming to extricate their man from the scandal of the accident.

Mr. and Mrs. Joseph Kopechne, a hard-working, respect-able, retiring couple, who ask only that as little tumult as possible be raised around them and their daughter's death, have nevertheless, according to *Time* magazine and the *New York Post,* demanded some answers, even after Judge Boyle's verdict and Kennedy's speech — answers to which they are entitled by every consideration of humanity and legality. Mrs. Kopechne said:

> Reading all the versions of what has happened, it really gets you confused. Why was not help called for my daughter by Markham and Gargan? I can understand shock, but I do not see when Markham and Gargan went into shock. They are my puzzle, I mean they are human. I don't think anyone can have that control over you. [Mrs. Kopechne refers to Kennedy's control over his two friends.]
>
> I would like to hear the whole story, just a continuation from when I was informed that Mary Jo said she wanted to go back to the motel that evening. She was tired, sunburned, and Senator Kennedy offered her a lift. I never understood what time that was. There are so many questions about that time. I would like to hear everything about what happened, good and bad. I would like to hear all of them, Senator Kennedy and the others, all of it pieced together. The girls know they could lessen the heartache we have by giving some answers. Those girls are not going to talk.
>
> We have reached the breaking point many times, but I am controlling myself for my husband and he is controlling himself for me. We are holding up together. My husband does not sleep. We try to find ways to avoid going to bed. We walk around and keep the light on. When we finally go to bed and the lights are out, we can't help thinking . . . .

The Kopechnes seem to have been too honest to under-stand what was really going on at that time in the Kennedy clan, or to imagine what really happened on Chappaquiddick Island. Mrs. Kopechne was somewhat unjust in saying to *Time* magazine that everybody seemed to be on the Kennedy side. Any honest man's sympathy is with their daughter and them. But what cannot be understood is why, knowing that only through an inquest would they ever know the truth, they endeavored to prevent it, or to postpone it indefinitely, by opposing an autopsy. In fact, they had nothing to worry about; the Kennedy influence is so ubiquitous that the responsible authorities in Pennsylvania would never have ordered the exhumation asked by District Attorney Dinis until it was too late for an exhumation to have served any useful purpose. The parents' opposition served only to confuse those who otherwise would have been massively and entirely on the Kopechne side and would have helped them to find the truth, not for political reasons but for reasons of justice and humanity.

Mrs. Rose Kennedy, also a *mater dolorosa,* expressed deep sympathy for the parents of Mary Jo. We think she could have manifested it more concretely by persuading her son to tell the whole truth about the circumstances of their daughter's death; or, if his special brand of amnesia did not permit him to do that, then to liberate Markham, Gargan, and all the rest of the surviving revelers from the pledge of silence which was apparently exacted from them.

It is still up to her son, Markham, Gargan, their three other male companions, and the five surviving girls, all of them friends and comrades of the victim, to alleviate the anguish of Mary Jo's parents by satisfying their legitimate desire to know: *What are all of them helping to hide?*

CHAPTER IX

The Senator's State Of Shock

There are two distinct questions here: (1) Was Senator Kennedy in a state of shock after his immersion in Poucha Pond? (2) Does this explain the ten-hour delay in reporting the accident to the police?

The answer to the second question is immediately evident: Kennedy's state of shock cannot explain a misdeed for which the responsibility was shared by two other men, Markham and Gargan, who had no excuse for having lost their wits. Their behavior is an important first clue to the Senator's physical and mental state. There can be no possible doubt that it was the Senator who influenced his two companions to refrain from summoning professional assistance for the rescue of the girl in the car; not the other way around. The first impulse of the two men, seeing their friend soaked and exhausted and hearing from him the shocking story of the accident, must surely have been that of any normal human being: to rush to the nearest telephone, or to the Chappaquiddick Fire Station, almost directly across the road from the cottage, to get help for the victim, and to take, or ask others to take, appropriate measures for the physical comfort of their friend. The force of persuasion the Senator must have used to induce his companions not to do the normal thing is not symptomatic of a blurred and vacillating mind; and such a mind at such a moment would surely not have prevailed over the will and the objections of two experienced lawyers.

The essential characteristic of shock consequent on physical or psychological trauma is a state of prostration. It is quite possible that one of its effects may be an impairment of memory involving more or less extensive areas of experience. But it would be a strange case of prostration that would have permitted the Senator, encumbered by a back-brace and soaked clothes and shoes after his near-drowning at the bottom of Poucha Pond, to walk a mile and a half back to the cottage; to seek out two of his companions *without alarming the others;* to explain what had happened; to take them back to the accident scene; to direct their efforts to save the trapped girl; and a few minutes later to jump into the strong current of the Martha's Vineyard channel, which is 500 feet wide, swim across it, and reach the harbor, without being carried farther downstream, and reappear composed and dry at 2:25 a.m. that same night, standing in front of his hotel neatly clothed and talking and acting in a way that betrayed no strain or emotional disturbance.

The Senator's intermittent and selective amnesia presents some interesting problems.* Medical science knows of cases of

---

*The Senator himself described with a remarkable lucidity the periods of oblivion and recollection through which he passed after the accident. We read in the certificate delivered after a neurological examination by Dr. Milton F. Brougham on July 22, 1969:

"In describing his recollections of the events occurring at the time, he states that he can recall driving down a road and onto a bridge, and has some recollection of the car starting off the bridge which he thinks was a realization that the car had struck a beam along the side of the bridge; however, he remembers nothing immediately following this; has no recollection of the car turning over or of any impact of the car against the water or any solid object. There is a gap in his memory of indeterminable length, but presumably brief, and his next recollection is of being in the front seat of his car which was filling with water. He somehow escaped from the car, *but does not know how he did this.* He states further that he can recall making repeated efforts to get back to the car by diving. Subsequent events are recalled in somewhat fragmentary fashion with an impaired recall of their exact time relationship . . . . At the time of this examination the patient is alert and fully oriented. Examination of the scalp reveals *a zone of tenderness approximately 3 cm. in diameter.*" [Emphasis added.]

This certificate was neither asked for nor presented at the trial in which the Senator received a two-month suspended sentence, despite the fact that it is easy to believe that with his lawyers' assistance it could have exonerated him completely.

unconsciously directed nepenthe which helped the patient through a period of physical or mental trouble or distress; but the rapidity with which the Senator repeatedly fell into oblivion and snapped out of it can, we think, seldom have been paralleled in the clinical history of shock. Consider the following points:

The Senator remembered attempting to open the door and window of the submerged car, but had no recollection of how he got out of it.

At the police station at 10:00 a.m. the next day, he forgot all about that last attempt at rescue, and about swimming the channel to get back to Edgartown. He remembered it, though, before his TV appearance a week later. The same morning at 8:30, he had remembered to keep his appointment at his hotel with his two friends, and the necessity of calling a lawyer in Washington and making other calls from the phone at the ferry landing; but he remembered to inform the police only after those calls were made.

On his walk back to the cottage from the accident scene, he forgot to report the accident and call for help, but he remembered the details of the accident perfectly when he told the story to his friends.

At the police station he remembered walking around for a period of time in Edgartown before going to bed, but he had forgotten this when he reported on TV.

Also at the police station, he remembered that his purpose in leaving the cottage with Miss Kopechne had been to catch the last scheduled ferry, but he had forgotten this important detail before his TV appearance, only to remember it again later.

Of all his "scrambled thoughts," he remembered only those that provided justification for his delay in reporting the accident to the police.

Back at the cottage, he forgot the existence of the fire station, almost directly across the road, but remembered, as he brought his two friends back to the site of the accident, that there was a submerged car there.

At the ferry landing with Markham and Gargan, he apparently forgot the existence of both the telephone booth and the ferry, but he did not forget the necessity, whatever it was, to leave the island as quickly as possible and without outside help. Once on the other side of the channel, he forgot again to inform the police, as he had allegedly promised his two companions to do.

Far from being in a state of shock, it seems, the Senator in these critical hours had retained all his wits and even the aptitude for scheming of his Harvard days. This aptitude was demonstrated, according to the Senator's own statements, by the precautions he took not to be observed directly, upon his return to the cottage, by any other than his close friends, Gargan and Markham; and, if the story of his new plunge into waters in which he had already almost lost his life that night was not a fabrication, by the hidden but firm purpose that made him choose that strange way of locomotion.

And if this story was not true, it must still be considered as a part of the whole fabric of concealment and obfuscation, which cannot have been the product of blurred memory and impaired reasoning.

Nobody is obliged to believe the story of the Senator's plunge, or that of the belated and useless attempts at rescue made by Markham and Gargan. They were not mentioned in the more or less spontaneous report written by Markham at Kennedy's dictation the morning after the accident at the police station, and might have been contrived during the week of collaboration between lawyers, speech writers, and assorted supporters that followed in the Hyannis Port refuge.

A routine, honest inquest, held at the moment and on the spot, might have shown that the testimony of Remington Ballou contained the explanation of the Senator's mysterious appearance outside his hotel at Edgartown at 2:25 a.m. on

July 19. At about 2:00 a.m., Mr. Ballou and his family saw a fifteen- to seventeen-foot motor boat in the Edgartown harbor approaching a small sailboat moored nearby. Its lights were then immediately doused and its engine switched off. Mr. Ballou and his passengers saw three persons in the motor boat.

When Markham and Gargan told Maryellen Lyons that they had been looking for a boat at the ferry landing (without explaining why they had not simply phoned for the ferry), they might have spoken the truth. Perhaps they found the boat they sought; this would explain why all of them were in dry clothes when seen by other people later that night.

CHAPTER X

The "Thing"

Senator Kennedy declared publicly that those who expected to find "a 'thing' in the Chappaquiddick tragedy will be very soon disappointed." We think the deception will take longer to come out because of the decision to push the inquiry into the circumstances of this tragedy from the lower courts to the Massachusetts Superior Court, then to the Massachusetts Supreme Court, and from there to the secret inquest.

Nevertheless, the United States public — and the public at large — has the right to try to discover the nature of the "thing" in which one of the most conspicuous political personalities of the day, a potential candidate for election to the Presidency of the United States, was involved that fatal night on a remote coastal island. Their desire for information is all the more justifiable because Senator Kennedy, after an eclipse of only a few days, during which he was covered by the protection of a very exceptional maze of jurisdictions and procedures, imperturbably re-entered the political arena in both the national and international fields. He did it on what might certainly be called a false pretense if the "thing" that happened at Poucha Pond was such as to disqualify him morally and rationally as a would-be leader of men and generator of opinion.

Let us observe immediately that it is highly improbable that the "thing" which so many people are so assiduously helping to hide is the fact that the Senator drove his car, that fatal night, under the influence of rather more liquor than people are expected to imbibe at a cook-out party. The Senator and the two gentlemen who were with him share the responsibility for the ten-hour delay in reporting the accident and for wilfully denying the girl trapped in the submerged car the assistance that might have saved her life. They were all trained lawyers and sufficiently well-informed concerning the laws of their state and their country to know that the position of the Senator was bound to become more critical, legally and morally, through his acting as he did than through reporting the accident immediately, and immediately summoning professional help. This would still have been true even if the amenable Arena had thereby been given opportunity to detect a suspicious whiff of alcohol on the breath of the Senator and his friends — a possibility that would not have posed any real inconvenience, thanks to the leniency of Massachusetts regulations respecting such accidents. The "thing" that had and still has to be hidden must have been something much more damnable than that.

Similar considerations must be borne in mind when trying to find out the reason for Kennedy's initial lie, which may hide the reason for all the other fabrications and concealments in the TV statement. Why did Senator Kennedy say at the police station that he had left the cottage with Miss Kopechne in order to catch the last ferry at midnight, and that he had taken the Dyke Bridge road by mistake? Could he have said it to protect Miss Kopechne's or his own good reputation? With regard to Miss Kopechne, this idea must surely be dismissed, since the Senator did not do very much to protect even her *life*. Did he? As for the Senator's own reputation, there would have been nothing very improper in the return of two or several members of the cottage party at night to the beach where they had bathed and sunbathed during the day. All the other guests at the Lawrence cottage took short or long walks by twos or threes that evening.

There was no reason there to risk the inconvenience of a lie that was bound to be exploded the next day by the protests of the local population. The "thing" behind this falsehood was something more than that Kennedy, "jovial, relaxed, and perhaps high," said to the girl, "Come on, Mary Jo, let's have a look at the ocean" — as *Time* magazine suggested.

What is more striking in Kennedy's statements than their contradictions, their evasions, and the improbability of the facts related, is the incredibility of the alleged behavior and reactions of the actors. One never feels it more strongly than on the spot where the tragedy occurred, trying to imagine oneself in some of the situations described by the Senator.

From the bridge near the Dyke House, let us look down at the deep waters and the swift current into which the car plunged and overturned. Imagine yourself, after you have miraculously succeeded in scrambling out of it, you can't remember how — probably through an open or broken window — plunging into the black waters again, several times, in an effort to save your passenger's life; then dragging yourself up the bank exhausted, and finding yourself a few feet from a house, the Dyke House, with windows ablaze with lights. Here, you know that just by knocking at the door or even by raising your voice you will find sympathy and comfort, and you know that a telephone call from here will bring immediate assistance to the person you tried to rescue, a few minutes ago, at the risk of your own life, and will bring your friends to your side. Could *you* ignore these immediate possibilities? Would *you*, exhausted and in water-heavy clothes and shoes, undertake the 1.6-mile trek to the cottage, passing by not only other lighted houses close to the road, but also the lighted fire station, almost opposite the cottage, without seeking help somewhere?

Again, stand on the ferry wharf on the Chappaquiddick side of the Martha's Vineyard channel; look again at that powerfully running expanse of cold, dark water, and see the efforts the oncoming ferry has to put forth to cross it in a straight line. Imagine yourself standing there at night, exhausted, in a state of shock, with two devoted friends beside you and the emergency telephone, which could bring the ferry to your side of the channel in just a few minutes, at arm's length — would *you* choose instead to dive headlong into that channel and swim across it? Would your friends let you do it?

Your answer would be that of the inhabitants of Chappaquiddick Island, who have seen the Dyke Bridge so often and who cross the Martha's Vineyard channel every day: no such situations and reactions can ever have occurred, nor can so many of the others that Kennedy's statements try to make us accept. *They are no truer than the false Kennedy who presented himself at that Harvard examination, or than the heroics of the Cuban missile crisis, or those of the P.T. boat back in World War II.*

Failing a regular, open inquest, which now will never take place, the only help in finding out what did and what did not happen the night of Mary Jo's death is to remember that it surely was not to help him tell the truth, but to help him hide it more effectually, that Senator Kennedy summoned advisers, speech writers, and defense attorneys to Hyannis Port. We must probe carefully, therefore, all that his statement contains, and base our reasoning on known facts and reliable testimony.

Those facts and that testimony are, in more or less chronological order, as follows:

Fact 1. The Lawrence cottage cook-out-cook-in party begins at 6 p.m. July 18. Present are six unmarried girls, Mary Jo Kopechne among them; one unmarried man, the chauffeur; and five married men without their wives, among them Senator Edward M. Kennedy.

Fact 2. There is a telephone booth at the ferry slip on either side of the channel. A ferry can be summoned to Chappaquiddick Island at any time, day or night.

Fact 3. At 12:45 a.m. on the night of the tragedy, a black Oldsmobile sedan with Massachusetts plates L7 — 7 is seen on dry ground by Deputy Sheriff Christopher Look. The driver is a man; a girl is sitting beside him. Look also sees on the rear seat something that might be either a garment or another person. The car is Senator Kennedy's.

Fact 4. A few minutes later, on the main road, Look talks with two girls and a man who are walking toward the Lawrence cottage.

Fact 5. The Silva family, neighbors of the Lawrence cottage, observe that the noise coming from the cottage ceases suddenly at about 1 a.m.

Fact 6. Sometime after 2 a.m., Remington Ballou sees a boat with three persons aboard passing his boat in Edgartown harbor and mooring near a sailboat there.

Fact 7. Russell E. Peachey, co-owner of the Shiretown Inn, finds Senator Kennedy, calm, composed, and in dry clothes, standing in front of the hotel at about 2:25 a.m. Kennedy says he has mislaid his watch and asks Mr. Peachey for the time.

Fact 8. At about 8:20 a.m., two young boys discover a submerged and overturned car in the waters beside Dyke Bridge. Chief of Police Arena comes immediately to the scene. At about 8:40 the body of a girl — later identified as Mary Jo Kopechne — is recovered from the car.

Fact 9. Meanwhile, between 8 and 8:30 a.m., Kennedy chats with friends in front of his hotel.

Fact 10. At 8:30 he is joined by Paul Markham and Joseph Gargan and talks with them in his room for about half an hour.

Fact 11. At about 9 a.m. the three friends are seen at the ferry slip on the Chappaquiddick side of the channel. Asked if they have heard about the accident, they answer that they have just heard about it. Kennedy and Markham then leave immediately for Edgartown.

Fact 12. At about 9:30 Police Chief Arena is informed at the scene of the accident that Senator Kennedy wants to talk to him at the police station.

Fact 13. At about 10 a.m., an unsigned report of the accident is handed to Chief Arena by Kennedy. This report has been written by Markham at Kennedy's dictation. Kennedy insists that the report be communicated to the press *only after it has been controlled by his lawyers.*

Fact 14. Arena complies with Kennedy's request by not releasing the report until 4 p.m., when it has become clear that the lawyers cannot get there that day.

Fact 15. At 9:45 a.m., Dr. Donald E. Mills releases the body of Mary Jo Kopechne to the Martha's Vineyard Funeral Home, after a ten-minute on-the-spot examination; at 12:30 he gives permission for embalming to be done.

Fact 16. At 2:30 the same day, Dun Gifford, Senator Kennedy's legislative assistant, enters Dr. Mills' office and hands the doctor a death certificate already filled out, stating that Mary Jo Kopechne died by drowning. Dr. Mills signs it and Mr. Gifford takes it away with him.

Fact 17. On July 20 at 10 a.m., District Attorney Dinis is erroneously informed by phone that the body of Mary Jo Kopechne has left Martha's Vineyard for Pennsylvania.

Fact 18. The body of Mary Jo actually leaves the Martha's Vineyard airport at 12:30 p.m., in custody of a Kennedy secretary, the man who had presented to Dr. Mills the already filled out death certificate, and to whom the body was delivered during the morning.

No official investigation ever really tried to fill the gaping holes between these landmark facts.

PART TWO

THE COMEDY
July 31, 1969 - February 18, 1970

CHAPTER XI

The District Attorney's Initiative

"Come here, Ted, you're right back where you belong!" called Senator Mansfield, the Senate majority leader, to his colleague, Senator Edward M. Kennedy, as he hesitated on the threshold of the Senate chamber.

The group of politicians to which Senator Kennedy belonged is that which, with the help of the prostitute news media industry, has for twenty-five years used the false dilemma of capitulation or nuclear annihilation to legitimate all the withdrawals and renunciations that will soon leave the Soviet Union as the only Big Power in the world.

Members of this group, again with the help of the controlled press, have brought the people who have put their trust in them to forget that the real issue in the Vietnam war is not the rapidity with which "the boys are brought home." Rather it is the question, why two million young Americans have been sent to Southeast Asia and more than a quarter million of them slaughtered or maimed, though from the beginning it had been determined, and the enemy duly informed of the decision, that this war, which could have been won in two months, must end, after years of tremendous efforts and sacrifices, in a self-inflicted American defeat.

It is to this group of politicians that the United States owes the permanent protection of the enemy's friends and agents, who are dug into the most sensitive offices of the government, and the political and moral assassination of those who, like Senator Joe McCarthy and Otto Otepka, have tried to smoke the "un-Americans" out of their lairs.

It is this same group that by malfeasance or nonfeasance has encouraged and still encourages the endemic rebellion of the hairy, integrated troglodytes, draft dodgers, vandals, snipers, and arsonists who plague the cities and universities of the U.S., in unmistakable rehearsal for the all-annihilating revolution needed by the Communist Conspiracy. It is thanks to the complacency and complicity of the same political set that Presidential administrations, one after another, have unconstitutionally surrendered the legislative and even the executive authority of the nation to federal courts packed with notorious abettors of treason, rebellion, crime, and pornography — and that those same administrations have unopposedly prepared the surrender of their country's sovereignty to a monstrous fiction of which the United Nations is only an ominous prefiguration.

It is among them, the comrades-at-arms of the Kennedy clan, that we find the baiters of the police, the detractors of the armed forces, those who ask that the standards for admission to the Federal Bureau of Investigation and other security offices be lowered to such an extent that their ranks could be filled with the very rabble-rousers and rabble they are supposed to protect the nation against. Among them also are those who want control of military operations withdrawn from the military and entrusted to civilian authorities in case of war.

And above all, it is to their indifference and complicity, and that of corrupt educators, that a mysterious and satanic power whose identity they are afraid even to investigate has been able to create, in the last forty years, a new type of young Americans, a growing rabble of drugged robots, of pernicious zombies, owning neither God, law, nor country.

It so happened that the man whom Senator Mansfield greeted with such sincere warmth was himself, since the suspended sentence handed down by the Edgartown court, an evaded issue. Indeed, the question that was in every mind when he stepped out of the blue car driven by a friend and hurriedly climbed the steps of the Capitol building was no longer, as until then it had very naturally been, "Will the Senior Senator from Massachusetts go to prison or not?" — but, "How much has his political standing been damaged? Will he be able to run for the Presidency of the United States in 1972 or 1976?"

In the Senate chamber, after having thanked Senator Mansfield "a million," Kennedy was warmly welcomed by his Republican opposite number and patted on the back by colleagues of both parties. He declared to the news-papermen that he was glad to be back but that he would not have any other comment to make *"then or ever"* about the Chappaquiddick affair, other than those he had already made in his two statements. This position was soon to be taken also by his friend Markham, who told reporters that he saw "no necessity of talking about it ever," and by his press secretary, Richard C. Drayn, who said even more conclusively: "The Senator made it clear in his statement, and if it was not clear, I am not going to elaborate."

Later, Mr. Drayn informed reporters that the Senator had received more than 10,000 telegrams in answer to his appeal to the Massachusetts electorate, and that they were ten to one in favor of his remaining in office. In the Senator's mail was one most special message expressing support and sympathy, which outweighed hundreds that may have been adverse or insulting. This was the message in which the parents of the victim ex-pressed confidence in the Senator and asked him to keep his seat. The Senator could not, evidently, do less than accede to such a significant exhortation, added to those of the people of Massachusetts "who rushed to support him."

There were, however, some dissenting voices, and these came from newspapers and publications generally favorable to the Senator. For example, from the *New York Times*:

The police chief in Edgartown and county officials might understandably be awed at having to deal with their U.S. Senator, a political power in their state and a potential candidate for the Presidency, but it was no favor either to Senator Kennedy or to the public for them to have allowed that awe to inhibit their official conduct as it seems it has done. *Too many questions remain unanswered and as yet unasked.* [Emphasis added.]

And from the *Washington Post*:

But even if there are no further legal proceedings the matter will not rest, of course, because it will not be allowed to rest by those with genuine reservations about it, as well as those who see one purpose or another in bringing Senator Kennedy down. And it won't rest because the Senator put his conduct last weekend as a political issue before the people of his state.

The *Washington Post* was right. The Senator learned the very day of his appearance at the Capitol that a fortnight after the accident, Dukes County District Attorney Dinis had, by a letter directed to Chief Justice G. Joseph Tauro of the Massachusetts Superior Court, requested the assignment of a Superior Court judge to conduct, in the matter of Mary Jo Kopechne's death, the inquest about which nobody had bothered until then.

The Dinis letter opened a new phase of the Chappaquiddick affair just at the moment when it might have been thought that the case was closed by the suspended sentence and the provisional withdrawal of the Senator's driving license. But with the controversies and frictions; with the play between the various Massachusetts authorities, and between all of them and their counterparts in Pennsylvania; and with the duration and complexity of the procedures and the insignificance of their results, this phase looked more like the first act of a long comedy than the last act of a tragedy.

It was evident that Prosecutor Steele — the former colleague and intimate friend of Senator Kennedy — who, by reporting that the Senator had driven his car over Dyke Bridge with *extreme caution,* had saved him from a charge of negligent or wanton behavior, was not pleased with the District Attorney's sudden initiative. He expressed to reporters his regret that he had not been consulted before the step was taken: "Both Chief Arena and I are surprised. We have had no discussions at all since Kennedy pleaded guilty, with Mr. Dinis, as to the evidence in the case."

It seems that Dinis had good reason to be on his guard with Prosecutor Steele, whose only step toward the solution of the Dyke Bridge mystery had been to request by mail from every member of the Lawrence cottage party a written statement, *controlled in each case by the individual's lawyer.* This request is reminiscent of Chief Justice Warren's advice to Jack Ruby to say nothing if he thought talking would be dangerous to him.

Dinis's move to the Superior Court, passing, not quite according to regulations, over Judge Boyle's head, was a snub to the latter also. Superior Court Judge Tauro, perhaps correctly enough, declined jurisdiction and sent Dinis back to Judge Boyle, who had already rescued the Senator and his companions once from the perils of an inquest by accepting Kennedy's plea of guilty without prior investigation and without any interrogation of witnesses.

Judge Boyle neither accepted nor rejected Dinis's petition, but asked him on August 6 for a new request, on the ground that the first one was "unclear." Judge Boyle also asked whether District Attorney Dinis was calling on the court to "exercise its discretionary power" or acting under his own "mandatory power." And he wanted to know whether or not Dinis had "an intent to submit evidence that an unlawful act of negligence caused or contributed to the death [of Mary Jo Kopechne] or that the cause of death is contrary to the published report of the medical examiner's findings." Dinis answered that he was exercising his mandatory power. He rewrote his petition, and this time made it clear enough, it seems, since Judge Boyle granted his request and fixed a preliminary hearing for August 28.

It was obvious that what Dinis was looking for was evidence of an unlawful act that would constitute another charge in addition to the one already disposed of by Judge Boyle on July 25, and that he had, or believed he had, reason to think that the cause of death might be other than that hastily determined by Dr. Mills. According to Massachusetts law, however, the *medical* cause of a death caused by external means can be determined only by an autopsy. In the case of Mary Jo, because of the negligence of the Dukes County authorities, including District Attorney Dinis, no testimony whatever had been taken from possible witnesses, and without the help of an autopsy, determining the *legal* cause of death also presented a difficult problem. Dinis therefore belatedly initiated his painful and macabre litigation with the Pennsylvania authorities to get the necessary authorization for an autopsy on Mary Jo's body, which was now protected by a double legal obstacle: the change in jurisdiction, and the necessity of exhumation.

We have already had the opportunity to observe that the reluctance to become involved and to find out the truth in the case of Mary Jo's death reached its climax in the matter of the autopsy. So we should not wonder that District Attorney Dinis met with much less than an enthusiastic response when concomitantly with his petition for an inquest he addressed himself to District Attorney Blyth Evans, his opposite number in Lucerne County, Pennsylvania, to ask his assistance in the matter of exhumation. District Attorney Evans wanted the world to know of his disapproval; therefore he told it to the press: "I really don't know what he [Dinis] is asking . . . . First of all I consider it a Massachusetts case. The burden of proof is on Mr. Dinis, to prove to the courts of his own state that an autopsy is necessary. I view this as a major burden for Dinis. After all, there has been a medical finding in this case which was unchallenged and was accepted until now. *I definitely will not do anything of my own volition.* If the Massachusetts court hands down an order, then we are ready to collaborate. But everything will be done according to the book." (Emphasis added.)

What the book would say when the time came was easy enough to guess in view of the no doubt impartial but severe attitude of Judge Bernard C. Brominski of the Lucerne County Court of Common Pleas, who seems to be as formidable as his name. It is only fair to point out that Judge Brominski was caught in cross-fire from three directions: from the "book"; from District Attorney Dinis, who wanted an exhumation; and from Mr. and Mrs. Kopechne, who did not want their daughter's grave disturbed. "She is dead, nothing will give her back to us," said Mr. Kopechne. District Attorney Dinis had to fight on two fronts also: first, in the Pennsylvania court, against the "book" as interpreted by inflexible Judge Brominski and District Attorney Evans; and second, against the Kopechnes, who seemed no more eager to unravel the riddles that surrounded their daughter's death than was the Kennedy family to expose the falsehoods of the Warren report and learn the truth about the murder of the President of the United States, John F. Kennedy.

His first and second petitions for exhumation were declared insufficient by Judge Brominski, despite Dinis's presence at the second hearing, finally a third petition was accepted for consideration. On this occasion Dinis sent his assistant, Armand Fernandes, to face Attorney Flannagan, acting for Mr. and Mrs. Kopechne. Flannagan wanted any hearing in the case to be postponed until after September 3, when a decision was to be taken by the Edgartown court concerning the inquest requested by Dinis. Fernandes argued that, on the contrary, the autopsy should be performed first, in order to determine the necessity for the inquest and to help in carrying it out. This turtle race between inquest and autopsy seemed likely to last until neither proceeding would hold much interest for a forgetful public. On September 3, when the preliminary hearing alluded to by Attorney Flannagan resulted in a suspension and an appeal to the Massachusetts Supreme Court, Judge Brominski finally ruled on both the Dinis and the Kopechne petitions. He dismissed Attorney Flannagan's allegation that the Lucerne County Criminal Court had no jurisdiction and therefore no authority to order an autopsy. But he called again for an amended petition from Dinis – who decidedly had no luck with his scripts – on the ground that the original petition had not set forth sufficient facts to warrant an autopsy under Pennsylvania law.

Before District Attorney Dinis could come back with the amended petition, a strange fact, still unexplained but fitting perfectly into the general pattern of the Chappaquiddick affair, turned up in Dukes County – a fact that would gravely diminish the effectiveness and authority of this new Dinis intervention. Robert W. Nevin, M.D., the medical examiner for Dukes County, who had been off duty the day the body of Miss Kopechne was recovered and whose function had been performed by Dr. Mills, had signed District Attorney Dinis's petition for exhumation. Dr. Nevin now withdrew his support of the last Dinis petition without informing Dinis that he was doing so. Asked for his reason for not having warned the District Attorney before his about-face, Dr. Nevin said he had not done so "because Dinis had not contacted him." The question is: Who *had* contacted Dr. Nevin?

CHAPTER XII

Judge Boyle Wants
To Rout Out The Truth

We must not be too severe either with District Attorney Dinis for not having started his case while witnesses were still on the spot, the trail hot, and Mary Jo's body still in his jurisdiction, or with Judge Boyle for having muffed his first opportunity to rout the truth out of Senator Kennedy. District Attorney Dinis resides not in Edgartown but in New Bedford. The Poucha Pond accident was for him, that morning of July 19, nothing more than a fatal traffic accident, which could normally have been left in the hands of local Police Chief Arena and Assistant Medical Examiner Mills. As for Judge Boyle, imagine Counselor Perry Mason and Prosecutor Hamilton Burger both invoking the reputation and the excellent conduct of the defendant and together asking the Court not to send him to prison. In such a situation, what could Judge Boyle do? Only next morning, after he had heard Senator Kennedy's statement on TV, could he have realized that Prosecutor Steele and Chief Arena had not told him all they knew about the case.

Quite different are the cases of Prosecutor Steele, Chief Arena, and Dr. Mills. They were on the spot. Dr. Mills had no direct contact with Dinis before he released the girl's body to the funeral home and to the Kennedy people. When Dinis, alerted by certain mystifying circumstances, asked for an autopsy at 10:00 a.m. on July 20, the day after the recovery of the body, he was told that the body had already left Massachusetts. This was not true. Until

12:30 p.m. that day, the body was on Martha's Vineyard in the safekeeping of Kennedy's men.

Prosecutor Steele and Chief Arena already knew very well at the time of the trial, on July 25, that even the Senator's plea of guilty was based on two capital lies, and that its purpose was to avoid the subpoenaing of witnesses whose examination and cross-examination might have laid bare what those lies were designed to hide.

Arena at least showed some nostalgia for the vanished truth when he said wistfully to assembled reporters: "If I had been out there at the Dyke Bridge *at one in the morning,* who knows what I might have found." No similar nostalgia was evident in Prosecutor Steele, "who had been on a first-name basis with Kennedy since they served together in 1961 as assistant district attorneys in Boston." At the beginning of this new and, for Kennedy, extremely perilous chapter of the Dyke Bridge affair, opened by Dinis' petition for an inquest, Prosecutor Steele proved once again his faithfulness to old friendship by going out of his way — during the impassioned efforts of Kennedy's nine lawyers to block any attempt at questioning of witnesses — to declare to newsmen: "It is my educated guess that the Senator wants to get it over with as quickly as possible. My guess is the lawyers do not want it." From Boston, Kennedy's friends had already let it be known that the Senator, far from opposing an autopsy, had wanted one from the beginning. Once more Senator Kennedy tried to have it both ways: to appear as the man who wanted as much light as possible thrown on the Chappaquiddick tragedy, while nine lawyers, including some of the best, fought like hell in court to prevent entirely, or to obstruct as long as possible, the inquest that could have thrown the desired light on the tragedy and perhaps led to a new indictment.

We talk about nine lawyers and not about five, because we count the four who were hired to represent the other ten members of the Lawrence cottage party and to prevent their questioning — or at any rate their public and unhindered questioning. These four worked as hard for Senator Kennedy as his own quintet of high-powered attorneys, and perhaps even more usefully. It was this fact that Judge Boyle had perhaps in view when, in a preliminary hearing, he established the rules under which an inquest would begin on September 3, according to laws that have applied in Massachusetts for more than a century. Nevertheless, as a consequence of a blitz intervention by the nine lawyers of the defendant and his friends, a judge of the Massachusetts Supreme Court amazed millions in the United States and abroad by ordering the postponement of the inquest on the ground that the rules laid down by Judge Boyle imperilled Senator Kennedy's constitutional rights.

Judge Boyle apparently knew what he was doing when he held fast to all the power the Massachusetts laws granted him in setting the ground rules for an investigative — not accusatory — proceeding. Edward Kennedy had already, on July 25, been sentenced in connection with the charge of leaving the scene of an accident and failing to report it for ten hours. Any question which, in an accusatory proceeding, might have been put to him in connection with that charge could have been objected to immediately by his lawyers on the ground of *res adjudicata*. Even in an investigative rather than an accusatory proceeding, some difficulties might have been made on this same ground by Kennedy's lawyers, or by those representing his associates, despite the fact that there was no closed case against any of them.

It was for these reasons, we suppose, that Judge Boyle, at the end of a two-day pre-inquest hearing, fixed for the proceedings of the inquest that was to begin September 3, the following rules:

Only one witness at a time will appear in the courtroom. The witness may be represented by counsel.

Counsel may advise the witness only on his constitutional rights.

When the witness leaves the courtroom, counsel must leave with him.

Counsel can make private arrangements to obtain stenographic reports of the proceedings.

Sequestering of witnesses will be decided by the judge at the appropriate time.

No microphones, listening devices, or cameras will be allowed in the courtroom.

The seats in the courtroom are reserved exclusively for representatives of the news media.*

Judge Boyle added that the presence of Kennedy was essential to the inquest and that, if necessary, he would be subpoenaed.

A session at the Boston law office of Ropes & Gray, the law firm of Edward E. Hanify, the man who would from now on be Kennedy's chief attorney, had decided upon the particulars of a common strategy. This could not have been difficult. A battery of the cleverest defense lawyers money could buy had been assembled to face Judge Boyle, and they had been assembled on the same initiative and had the same purposes in mind: to avoid any inquest if possible; to postpone it indefinitely if avoiding it proved impossible; and to keep it hushed behind closed doors when it could no longer be postponed. The three motions these lawyers presented to Judge Boyle asked that he conduct the inquest as he would a criminal trial, contending that the proceedings were in fact accusatory; and that *all witnesses* be given the same constitutional protection they would have as defendants in a trial, i.e., the right to cross-examine witnesses, to produce their own witnesses, and even to decline to

---

*This was certainly an exceptional measure, and one that gave Kennedy's lawyers a solid peg on which to hang their appeal to the Massachusetts Supreme Court. It is difficult to understand why Judge Boyle went to this extreme.

answer, and to refuse to take the stand. "Take for instance the young ladies," said Clark, who was Kennedy's lawyer and not the young ladies', "are they to be pilloried?"

Judge Boyle certainly had no intention of permitting anybody to be pilloried with irrelevant questions; all he and the prosecution wanted to know was how, when, and where Mary Jo Kopechne met her death. The situation was comical enough — a judge ruling that nobody was under accusation, that nobody was indicted, and nine lawyers insisting that their clients be granted the status and the constitutional protection of indicted persons, and that the proceedings be criminal proceedings.

Such demands, from Kennedy's own lawyers might perhaps have been understandable. There was something in Hanify's contention that Kennedy, as the driver of the car in which Miss Kopechne lost her life, had been and was the object of "more pre-trial publicity than in any other fatal accident in Massachusetts or in the United States." But what about the lawyers of the five eligible girls, the four non-eligible married males, and the eligible sixty-year-old chauffeur, Crimmins? What right had their clients to special treatment? The five surviving young ladies decidedly seemed to cause a not very flattering concern on the part of their lawyers, who were afraid of the legendary feminine volubility. "Are they going," exclaimed Attorney Redmond, "to be asked not only their name, age, and address but every friend they had in high school? What school they went to, and the like? Is it going to be in the nature of a slander case, where someone's whole life is laid open?"

Judge Boyle, who had no interest in the young ladies' whole lives, but only in that part of them that had been spent on Chappaquiddick Island, rejected on August 28 all three motions of the nine associate lawyers, and fixed September 3 for the beginning of the inquest. On September

2, as we have already noted, Justice Reardon of the Massachusetts Supreme Court declared that Judge Boyle's rules imperilled the constitutional rights of the summoned witnesses, especially those of Senator Kennedy, who had been the object and victim of so much publicity; and he ordered the inquest suspended until the full Supreme Court of Massachusetts could rule on the matter. This, as was to be expected, produced consternation and disappointment among the 370 newsmen from all over the world who had assembled in Edgartown to follow the inquest proceedings, and who now rushed angrily home prepared to unload much more publicity than Justice Reardon could have anticipated as a result of his ruling. Here are some quotes from the hundreds that could be assembled.

From the *New York Times*:

> Throughout the country there is a feeling that Senator Kennedy was getting special treatment — that he was getting off without an autopsy on Mary Jo Kopechne and without an official inquest.

From the column of Max Lerner, certainly no Kennedy-hater:

> The trouble with the postponement of the Kopechne-Kennedy inquest is clear enough. Judge Reardon understandably wanted to protect Senator Kennedy from too much publicity, yet it is the people themselves who are troubled about the Kopechne case. Somehow, somewhere, sometime a way has to be found to resolve their trouble and answer their legitimate questions. . . . If the law and the courts cannot get an honest exploration of the Kopechne death, with all its questions and doubts, then something is seriously wrong with the law and the courts. And if the normal function of the courts is being twisted because Senator Kennedy is a somebody and not a run-of-the-mill nobody, then we had better know and face it.

From the (Martha's) *Vineyard Gazette*:

The kind of talk you hear up and down the street is that the Kennedys have money and power and that they will be able to stall this thing off.

From the sedate, scrupulously objective, and respected *U.S. News & World Report*:

Why did Senator Kennedy, who is reported to want an inquest into Mary Jo Kopechne's death as soon as possible, permit his lawyers to bid for delay? *The answer appeared to be* that the Senator's lawyers convinced him that delay — even with the risk of heightening speculation as to his motive — was preferable to going through with the inquest as prescribed by Judge Boyle. [Emphasis added.]

But this is no answer to the other question: *why did the nine lawyers of the Kennedy party fear, on behalf of their star client, a public inquest into the death of Mary Jo?* They were to have their field day and to burst out with their full blast in the fall sitting of the Massachusetts Supreme Court — where we will follow them. The amplitude and the vehemence of their efforts to suppress any testimony that could publicly contradict Senator Kennedy's already contradictory statements will be the best, and probably the only, valid indication we will ever have of the gravity and the significance of the thing these efforts were meant to conceal.

CHAPTER XIII

Titicut Follies

Justice Paul C. Reardon's ruling of September 2 brought the Kennedy team of lawyers, strongly reinforced, before the Massachusetts Supreme Court on October 8. Not one but two or more months' delay was thereby won in that turtle race between the Massachusetts and the Pennsylvania courts toward the much feared goal. Nobody could have expected the Massachusetts Supreme Court to give a ruling on this case more speedily than was its general custom.

About the substance of that ruling there was no reason to entertain more illusions than did Judge Boyle, who foresaw that it would give the Kennedy lawyers the opportunity to appeal even to the Supreme Court of the United States, an appeal that could take months and even years. The outcome of the two hours' pleading by the Kennedy lawyers was a motion to "liberalize" the 1867 Massachusetts law on inquests, enforced without a hitch for a century, by an "infusion of constitutionality." The recommended "infusion" included the provision that the inquest proceedings be conducted in secret.

Legal briefs were presented by Attorneys Edward R. Hanify for Kennedy, Joseph P. Donahue Jr. for Gargan, and Paul J. Redmond for the other members of the Lawrence cottage party. The briefs contended that by opening the inquest to the press, Judge Boyle sanctioned "publicity so widespread as to taint with irremediable prejudice any subsequent judicial procedure." Chief Justice Raymond C.

Wilkins ruled immediately that, in any case, the press would not be barred from the Massachusetts Supreme Court chamber.

As there was much discussion of publicity in the argument presented by the Kennedy team, a short description of the setting in which that two-hour hearing before the Massachusetts Supreme Court took place will be in order. Five justices were sitting: Chief Justice Raymond C. Wilkins and Justices John V. Spalding, R. Ammi Cutter, Jacob J. Spiegel, and Paul C. Reardon. Justice Paul C. Kirk had disqualified himself because of his son's political connections with Senator Edward Kennedy. The courtroom seated about 100 persons, in addition to seventeen seats reserved for lawyers and others occupied by special arrangement. To accommodate the overflow of spectators and newspaper, radio, and television reporters, two other rooms, provided with loud speakers carrying the proceedings to the listeners, had been assigned. The seats, together with silver identification buttons, were distributed on a first-come-first-served basis.

The oral arguments were presented in the following order:

1. For the Kennedy party: Representing Kennedy, Attorney Edward R. Hanify, assisted by Attorneys Robert C. Clark Jr., Thomas G. Dignan Jr., John M. Harrington, Robert A. Hayes, and John S. Hopkins. Representing Kennedy's chauffeur, Jack Crimmins, and the other Kennedy companions, male and female: Attorney Paul J. Redmond, assisted by Attorney Daniel Daly. Representing Joseph Gargan: Attorney Joseph P. Donahue Jr. No motion was presented at this time by former U.S. Attorney Paul Markham.

2. For Judge James Boyle, respondent in the case: Assistant Attorney General Joseph J. Hurley. Also present were Attorney General Robert M. Quinn, Assistant Attorney General Walter M. Mayo, Assistant Attorney General James P. Kiernan, Ruth Abrams, and William Searson. In court also were legal assistants Peter Wylie and Robert Conlin.

Seven lawyers for Kennedy, *two* for his companions, eight for the state, and five sitting justices were to discuss before more than 300 reporters and millions of newspaper readers how to call a United States Senator as a witness without provoking too much publicity.

The tasks of the two groups of Kennedy lawyers seemed to be at least equally difficult, if not quite impossible. Those representing the chauffeur Crimmins and Kennedy's nine other companions had to demonstrate that what they were trying to avoid for their clients was only a public intrusion into the most secret arcana of their intimate lives, and not the necessity of answering publicly and under oath pertinent questions regarding the circumstances of Mary Jo's death — which was the sole purpose of the inquest they had tried to postpone indefinitely.

Kennedy's freshly completed string of lawyers had to show that the public prominence of their client created an exceptional situation which called not for still more clarity, candor, and openness toward the people who had put their confidence in him and brought him into that prominence, but on the contrary for special measures of dissimulation and protection against publicity. They had further to prove that those exceptional measures should include rulings that the inquest be secret, and also that the Senator be allowed to appear protected by all the rights of a defendant in a criminal case — rights that would give his lawyers countless excuses to obstruct the proceedings and appeal to higher courts. Hanify and his assistants had to perform this difficult task without betraying — and here lay the impossibility — that what they feared for their client was not too much publicity, stimulated by the continuous cover-up, but rather the consequences of a thorough inquest that could demonstrate publicly that the Senator's two statements were two bundles of lies.

Hanify and his assistants asked that the right provided by

the Sixth and Fourteenth Amendments to an indicted person in a criminal proceeding be secured to their client — although he had not been indicted and the proceeding was not a criminal one — and claimed for him a range of privileges not provided in the 1867 Massachusetts law governing inquests. They argued for the following rights:

1. To call witnesses.
2. To cross-examine witnesses.
3. To present evidence.
4. To seek rulings from the court.
5. *To have the proceedings conducted in secret.*
6. To have the results withheld from the public until a "proper" length of time should have elapsed.
7. To have the court review the constitutionality of the inquest procedure established by the 1867 Massachusetts law.
8. To order that Judge James A. Boyle disqualify himself because he had made it clear in advance that Senator Kennedy would be requested to be present at the inquest.

Hanify asked the court to quash Judge Boyle's rule concerning the admission of news media representatives to the inquest, which was of such a nature, Hanify said, that it would deprive his client "of the right of fair trial by jury in the event, however unlikely, that *any subsequent criminal charge may be brought against him."* (Emphasis added.)

In regard to the question of constitutionality, the following exchange of words occurred between Hanify and the Court:

> Mr. HANIFY. I am asking this court respectfully to view the statute [the 1867 law] and to determine whether or not the statute must be constructed so as to permit a mechanism like this prospective inquest to operate, to determine that the statute is unconstitutional.
> Chief Justice WILKINS. Before you make your point, I was going to ask: Do you claim that the inquest is unconstitutional anyway, no matter how it is conducted?

Mr. HANIFY. No, your Honor. I claim it is possible for the honorable Court to infuse the inquest with constitutional vitality and relieve it from the present infirmity. And those basic infirmities, I believe, are curable by appropriate directives.

Chief Justice WILKINS. Do you mean it is always accusatory, no matter how it is conducted?

Mr. HANIFY. I think, your Honor, that it has always the potentiality of being an accusatory proceeding. In other words, it may start to be accusatory because the district attorney, who required it, intends it to be such. It may commence to be investigatory, and after five minutes of evidence it may be accusatory.

Attorney Redmond, who appeared for Kennedy's chauffeur and companions, argued that his clients, "as private citizens who live in an era of political assassination, should be protected by the court from invasion of their rights so they would not be the victims of verbal assassination." The theme of Attorney Donahue, appearing for Gargan, was substantially the same. In their arguments, as in that before the Edgartown court, the exhortation not to let their clients be "pilloried" and have their privacy invaded before the press of the world resounded loudly and continuously as a battle cry. The pathetic thing about these exhortations is that no reasonable person could believe in their sincerity. Nobody, least of all those five experienced justices, could for one instant suppose that Judge Boyle or any other judge designated by the New Bedford Superior Court would permit chauffeur Crimmins, or the five young girls, or Gargan, to be "verbally assassinated" by questions having no bearing on the case at issue.

But such was the intensity and the vehemence, not of what was said by the alarmed counselors but of what could not be put into words — their fear of the eleventh-hour evidence that could put an end not only to the political future but to the liberty of their star client — and such was the eloquence and cleverness of that devoted team of defenders, that they succeeded in transmitting their anxiety to their learned audience, and it was from the court itself that the suggestion of a satisfactory compromise came.

> Justice REARDON. Mr. Hanify, would you have any constitutional complaint, *assuming the hearing was private,* if a record of this proceeding was kept and published and could no longer do the damage that you describe under those particular rules? [Emphasis added.]
>
> Mr. HANIFY. Well, on the assumption that the publication of the record would take place at a period when there was no danger of damage under the ground rules . . . .
>
> Justice REARDON. Let us assume that the judge at the conclusion of the inquest makes a finding that there is no responsibility in any direction, would you have any objection to an immediate release of the transcript?
>
> Mr. HANIFY. I would not, your Honor.
>
> Justice REARDON. Assuming the judge finds there is some difficulty or possible criminal problem, would it then be your thought that such a release might be delayed until such time as the proceedings against the individual in question would have been concluded?
>
> Mr. HANIFY. That is correct.

The language of the two learned jurists was not very clear about the moment at which this release would no longer be harmful to Senator Kennedy. Should a possible trial also be kept behind closed doors? If not, how could the findings of the inquest be kept secret?

Assistant Attorney General Joseph J. Hurley talked very reasonably for the state, but his argument did not seem to go so far and so deep with the Court as those of the Kennedy lawyers.

> Justice SPIEGEL. Do you know of any inquest in Massachusetts that was conducted publicly similar to the rules laid down in this case?*
>
> Assistant Attorney General HURLEY. I do not, your

---

*The part of Judge Boyle's ruling to which Justice Spiegel alluded was that all seats in the courtroom be reserved exclusively for the press, national and international. An exceptional stipulation indeed, and one that was manna for Kennedy's lawyers.

Honor . . . . I have tried to put myself in the position of Judge Boyle when he made this ruling, and I think there are two good reasons why this inquest, which is an unusual inquest — and I suggest it does not matter whether inquests are generally private or not — I suggest there are two great reasons why this inquest should be public and not private. The first is perhaps a practical reason. We all know that extreme public interest is directed upon this affair. I suggest that Judge Boyle concluded that because of this extreme public interest, manifested through the press, it would not be possible to keep the inquest secret. You might close the doors, make it private, but you could not keep it secret. Now, which is better, as a practical matter: for the press to have access, to be able to report directly and accurately what is going on in that inquest room, or to be reporting what they are able to find out second, third, or tenth hand? I think there is only one answer. It is better to have the press there and reporting what they hear themselves, directly.

Assistant Attorney General Hurley observed that the constitutional requirement had been amply met when Judge Boyle ruled that each witness be attended by his lawyer to advise him, or her, about his constitutional rights. He argued also that there were neither federal nor state constitutional dispositions guaranteeing any general right to privacy, and that there was no reason to suppose that the inquest under Judge Boyle's rulings would violate the rights that are guaranteed by constitutional amendments and Supreme Court rulings.

According to Attorney Donahue it was not only Crimmins's privacy that was about to be illegally invaded, but also that of Joseph Gargan, a "private person caught in the vortex of massive coverage and forever branded by the single incident in which the glare of attention is focused on him." Attorney Redmond, asked by Justice Spiegel whether, as far as his clients were concerned, he was taking the same position as Attorney Hanify, answered that his clients "were in the same position, under the control of the state, as the inmates of the Bridgewater State Hospital who were protected by the Supreme Court in a recent ruling from being shown publicly in the motion picture called 'Titicut Follies.' "

We will follow those other macabre follies, with their never-present star performer, their sonorous chorus of defense lawyers, their silent troop of ingenues and extras, whether they lead to some medieval closed-door proceeding or to the Supreme Court in Washington, with the blood-stained garments of Mary Jo in a plastic bag as the only and reproachful props.

CHAPTER XIV

Asparagus Juice And
The Chief's Bleeding Toe

The comedy was acted out on two interdependent stages: in Massachusetts when it concerned the inquest, in Pennsylvania when the exhumation and the autopsy were concerned. In a turtle race, where the winner is the contender who reaches the goal last, the best technique is, obviously, short or false sprints with longer rest periods. But certain rules have to be observed. With the hearing of October 8, Massachusetts had done its bit. It was Pennsylvania's turn to act, and Judge Brominski played up.

On October 9, Mary Jo being three months dead, Judge Brominski — after nine weeks of mature reflection, after three postponed decisions, and in possession of District Attorney Dinis's last amended petition — issued a decision of approximately 2000 words, from which the following is a quotation:

> . . . at the moment the issue before the court is not whether an exhumation and autopsy should be allowed, but whether, based on the allegations of fact in the amended petition, a hearing for the petition should be conducted.
>
> This leads the court to the conclusion that, while we are not judging at this time that an exhumation and autopsy should be allowed, a hearing should be held in order to allow the petitioner the opportunity to prove the allegations for the amended petition and for the Kopechnes to exercise their prerogatives in the ultimate question: whether or not an exhumation and autopsy should be allowed.

Accordingly, Judge Brominski set the hearing for Monday, October 20, at 10:00 a.m. On October 20 the faithful crowd of newsmen from all over the United States and from various foreign countries showed up again at the courthouse at Wilkes-Barre, Pennsylvania. They were all the' more eager because, after the questions they had heard addressed to the Kennedy lawyers by five Justices of the Massachusetts Supreme Court, they were convinced that the secrecy asked by those lawyers was as good as granted, and that these hearings were probably their last opportunity to witness some judicial action in the case. They were not altogether disappointed. It was the first time witnesses in the Kennedy scandal had been interrogated publicly and under oath, and very likely it would be the last.

Before we come to the highlights of the three Wilkes-Barre hearings, it is not irrelevant to signalize certain moments in the proceedings relating to the reliability of Dr. Donald Mills' memory. A fact that was confirmed several times by Dr. Mills himself, and made very clear once again in the Wilkes-Barre proceedings, was the deep impression made upon him by the circumstance of Kennedy's involvement in the case. One detail brought out during Dr. Mills' interrogation by Assistant District Attorney Fernandes seemed to indicate that some persons even suspected that in his partiality for a member of this prominent family Dr. Mills might have gone so far as to try to help the Senator in the alleged attempt at alibi construction, by letting it be believed that Mary Jo was driving, herself and alone, the car that plunged into Poucha Pond:

> Mr. FERNANDES. Do you know, or did you assume, what part of the automobile she [Miss Kopechne] was found in?
> Dr. MILLS: I remember Mr. Farrar said she was in an inverted — that is, the car was upside down, and she was this way up, but everything else was just —
> Mr. FERNANDES. Let's see if I can refresh your memory,

doctor. Do you remember making a statement that indicated you were of the opinion that the young lady was in the driver's seat? Does that refresh your memory?

Dr. MILLS. That was probably a statement I had made with the blood samples going to the police. That would have been based on something I had been told — that she may have driven the car. *These things are very garbled because the situation was garbled.* [Emphasis added.]

Dr. Mills' memory lapses have a special importance where they concern the question of releasing Mary Jo's body without performing an autopsy. One thing is absolutely indisputable: Dr. Mills, as official local medical examiner, had the legal power to refuse to release the body of any person killed by external means for as long as he thought it necessary. By the same token, it was up to him to advise District Attorney Dinis on the medical aspects of the case, and not the other way around. Nevertheless, he repeated in court at Wilkes-Barre what he had said a month earlier to Richard J. Connally of the *Boston Globe*: "For reasons of personality, I felt it was more than I wanted to handle on my own."

He asserted in court that, before releasing the body at 9:45 a.m. to Mr. Eugene Frieh, the Edgartown funeral director, he told him not to embalm it until he received further word; in fact, to wait until Dr. Mills got a clearance from District Attorney Dinis. The following exchange of questions and answers ensued between him and Assistant District Attorney Fernandes:

Mr. FERNANDES. Now, doctor, you have testified that you made inquiries to determine whether there should be an autopsy?

Dr. MILLS. Yes, I did.

Mr. FERNANDES. And you did that by placing a telephone call to whom?

Dr. MILLS. To the state police, the district attorney's office.

Mr. FERNANDES. Who did you call, and who did you talk to?

Dr. MILLS. Well, the state police barracks is located in Oak

Bluffs. That is on Martha's Vineyard Island, and it has been customary with me, and as per an earlier directive from the Department of Public Safety, that these calls are routed through the state police.

Mr. FERNANDES. And was that the call that you referred to that you made about 10 o'clock in the morning?

Dr. MILLS. That's right.

Mr. FERNANDES. Who did you talk to, doctor, if you know?

Dr. MILLS. I talked with Officer . . . I don't know what officer.

Mr. FERNANDES. Was that Officer DeRoche?

Dr. MILLS. DeRoche?

Mr. FERNANDES. And what did you say to him, doctor?

Dr. MILLS. I told him, "Would you please contact the district attorney's office, tell them that I have the case of a girl who has been drowned in a submerged vehicle, that I am quite certain I am fully satisfied with the diagnosis of drowning by immersion, that I don't know who she is but she was reputed to be connected with the Kennedy family as an employee, that if it was the judgment of the district attorney or his assistant that an autopsy was indicated, then I was asking for one."

Mr. FERNANDES. Did you hear anything more from the district attorney's office that day?

Dr. MILLS. I did.

Mr. FERNANDES. At what time and from whom?

Dr. MILLS. The office of — This message went out from my own office right after I got back from my examination on Chappaquiddick Island, and the lieutenant called back and said the district attorney's line was busy but he would call me as soon as he could get an answer on it.*

Mr. FERNANDES. Do you know who the lieutenant was who called you?

Dr. Mills did not remember that name either, in Wilkes-Barre, although he remembered both State Troopers De Roche and Lucas very well in his interview with Mr. Connally, adding then that "as Detective Lieutenant Killen did not believe that the autopsy was necessary I did not

---

*With little effort Dr. Mills could have talked directly with Dinis in New Bedford.

believe it either." According to Dr. Mills himself, he never came into direct contact with District Attorney Dinis while Mary Jo's body was in Dukes County. And it was at second and third hand, from persons whose names he had already forgotten, that he got what he called "clearance from the District Attorney's office." His testimony concerning his responsibility in releasing the body to the morticians prematurely was so hazy that it could not be taken as a contradiction of District Attorney Dinis's, which was of impressive precision.

Answering Fernandes' question, Dinis made it known that there was no obligation in the statutes for him to make personal and immediate investigation in every fatal accident occurring in his district; that it was customary for district attorneys to take charge only in cases of "suspicious or unattended death," or when the investigations by local authority were "unsatisfactory or incomplete." Asked by Fernandes when the medical findings were made available to him, Dinis answered: "Not within the first twenty-four hours, and not before the body left the island."

Mr. FERNANDES. What did you do when you received the report?

Mr. DINIS. I ordered an autopsy.

Mr. FERNANDES. And could you tell this court when you ordered an autopsy?

Mr. DINIS. Ten a.m. on July 20.

Mr. FERNANDES. Would this be Sunday, the day after the body was discovered?

Mr. DINIS. That is correct.

Mr. FERNANDES. To whom did you make this request?

Mr. DINIS. I made this request to Lieutenant George K. Killen of the state police.

Mr. FERNANDES. What, if any, information was given to you with reference to an autopsy at that time?

Mr. DINIS. I was informed by Lieutenant Killen that the body had already been flown off the island by the Kennedy people.

Killen's information was erroneous, and Dinis was fooled, as shown by another very special witness, K. Dun Gifford, Senator Kennedy's secretary. Mr. Gifford informed the court that the departure of the plane chartered by Senator Kennedy to carry Mary Jo's body out of Massachusetts and out of the district attorney's territory, which was scheduled for 9:30 a.m. July 20, had been held up until 12:30 p.m. because of bad flying weather and mechanical difficulties. It was Mr. Gifford who had custody of the body until it was safely delivered to Pennsylvania authorities.

The Kopechnes were represented in court by three lawyers of ambivalent loyalties: they did their best for their clients, but they did not forget Senator Kennedy's interests either. They very naturally tried to prove that an autopsy was unnecessary. Attorney Flannagan, the Kopechnes' chief counsel, wanted to know why Dinis had not taken legal action earlier. Dinis answered that he was not obliged to do so before he had satisfactory information on which to base a determining judgment, and that he had such information only after Senator Kennedy made his national TV appearance on July 25, explaining his part in the accident.

Concerning the necessity of the autopsy at the time of the accident, and its usefulness four months afterwards, the experts brought by both parties could not agree. Dr. Joseph W. Spelman, former state medical examiner of Vermont, and Dr. George T. Katzas, another expert on forensic medicine summoned by District Attorney Dinis, agreed that factors contributing to death or producing it could not be determined solely by a ten-minute external examination such as that conducted by Dr. Mills. Asked by Assistant District Attorney Fernandes whether he "felt with reasonable certainty that other causes of death besides drowning were excluded," Dr. Spelman answered with a categorical "No!" An external examination alone, said Dr. Spelman, "even if it is conducted carefully and completely, frequently fails to disclose internal injuries, fractured skull, bruises in the brain, broken ribs or ruptured internal organs, or natural disease processes."

Asked by Fernandes what effect the fact of the body's having been buried for four months or more would have on the usefulness of an autopsy, Dr. Spelman observed that in fifteen, twenty, or more cases he had performed autopsies on bodies that had been buried for varying periods of time, some for as long as five years, and said: "The interpretation of the results would be somewhat more difficult. Still it would be entirely possible to make many observations and draw many conclusions therefrom."

Dr. Mills and the experts on his side stated firmly their opinion that the ten-minute external examination had been sufficient to determine the cause of the girl's death. Dr. Spitz's opinion was that an autopsy should not be performed, because "even if it were to show internal injuries, it could not be determined if they had occurred before or after drowning."

Two Massachusetts state chemists testified that bloodstains were found on Miss Kopechne's clothes. Dr. John McHugh, supervisor of the laboratory at the Massachusetts Department of Public Safety, testified to the presence of blood, determined by benzidine tests, on the back, left sleeve, and collar of the girl's white blouse, with a maximum of positive results on the collar. The first chemist of the same laboratory confirmed Dr. McHugh's findings and added that the other articles of clothing gave a negative reaction to the test. About the pink froth noted by Dr. Mills in the nose and around the mouth of the victim, every expert agreed that this was usually, but not exclusively, found in cases of death by drowning. The following dialogue on the subject took place between District Attorney Dinis and Dr. Spitz, another medical expert:

Dr. SPITZ. That foam is the combination of water and protein that is being shaken, and the shaking action is the breathing action.

Mr. DINIS. So she breathed?

Dr. SPITZ. That girl, she breathed.

Mr. DINIS. She was not dead instantaneously?

Dr. SPITZ. That can be eliminated. You won't find a case of instantaneous death, whether you exhume or you don't.

The question of the blood on the collar, the sleeves, and all over the back raised a more disquieting question for the Kopechnes' lawyers, who seemed to double as Kennedy's lawyers too. Thus chief counsel Flannagan, cross-examining Chief Arena, asked him in the best Perry Mason manner whether he had hurt his toe during his maneuvers around the submerged car before taking the body of Mary Jo on his lap. When Chief Arena answered affirmatively, Flannagan asked him whether that toe could have bled. The chief answered that it could have done so. Everybody in court got the message, but doubly sure is better, so Flannagan, who had done his homework thoroughly, asked the two chemists if it was not true that asparagus or potato juice stains could react the same as bloodstains to the benzidine test. They could, said the experts.

Another painful moment occurred when Assistant District Attorney Fernandes was examining Dr. Mills:

Mr. FERNANDES. Are you of the opinion, doctor, that your external examination, keeping in mind reasonable medical certainty, excluded other causes of death?

Dr. MILLS. To all practical purposes, yes.

Mr. FERNANDES. What of a fractured skull, doctor? Would an external examination establish that a person died of a fractured skull?

Dr. MILLS. A skull fracture?

Mr. FERNANDES. Would you answer that yes or no, please.

Dr. MILLS. I am sorry, would you mind rephrasing it?

THE COURT. Read the question back, please.

Dr. MILLS. I would have to answer that as yes.

Mr. FERNANDES. It is your opinion, therefore, that it would establish it. What of manual strangulation?

THE COURT. I don't know how he would answer that question, counselor, the way you phrase it.

Mr. FERNANDES. Doctor, as I understand your position, you are satisfied that your external examination conclusively established the cause of death?

Dr. MILLS. Yes.

Mr. FERNANDES. And I ask whether or not you had considered at that time a fractured skull, in terms of whether or not that would be established by an external examination; and secondly, I ask you whether or not manual strangulation . . . .

Here Attorney Flannagan interrupted to object to the question, and his objection was sustained by Judge Brominski. The question had nevertheless to be taken care of. A man like Judge Brominski could, after all, allow the exhumation; with a former quarterback you never can tell. Attorney Flannagan found his opportunity while cross-examining Chief Arena:

Attorney FLANNAGAN. When was it that you first learned there was a body in the car?

Chief ARENA. When Mr. Farrar went under and came up with it.

Mr. FLANNAGAN. When he went under, how did he go about getting the body out?

Chief ARENA. I believe he put a rope around her neck and then probably worked her out. Once again I am only assuming.

Mr. FLANNAGAN. He was under the water and you were on top of the car?

Chief ARENA. Yes, sir.

Mr. FLANNAGAN. Now, how did you know he was coming up with the body?

Chief ARENA. I felt a pull on the rope.

Mr. FLANNAGAN. Then what did you do?

Chief ARENA. I started to pull up the rope.
Mr. FLANNAGAN. What happened after that?
Chief ARENA. Miss Kopechne came up simultaneously with
Mr. Farrar.

Chief Arena's last answer was nicely worded. You could
see him pulling on the rope, with enough force to bring up
both the girl and the scuba diver, and this rope knotted
around the girl's neck. Under examination Farrar had
already said that, to make certain that the strong current
didn't separate him from the girl's body, he had passed a
rope around the portion of the body that came to his
hand at that moment. But he insisted that he had never
left the body, and that the rope and the knot had never
been taut.

Chief Arena, Dr. Mills, and all witnesses who had had the
opportunity of seeing Miss Kopechne's body were asked by
the Kopechne lawyers whether they had seen open wounds,
blood, or other signs of violence. The answer had always been
negative.*

One can understand Flannagan's objections to any questions that might turn up a good reason for authorizing the
exhumation; there the Kopechnes' interests and those of
Senator Kennedy were, by chance, parallel. But objections to
the admission as evidence of the statements made by Senator
Kennedy at the Edgartown police station and on TV because
they were hearsay did not seem to belong to Mr. and Mrs.
Kopechne's case. Then why did their lawyer object?

Of all the statements heard by Judge Brominski's court,
the most important was probably that in which Deputy
Sheriff Christopher F. Look Jr., questioned by Dinis,
confirmed under oath the time at which he had seen, still on

---

*From Funeral Director Frieh's testimony: "Very little water was expelled from
the lungs. I raised my eyebrows because I expected much more water." This was
in direct contradiction of Dr. Mills' statement at the secret inquest that "this
girl was completely filled with water."

dry ground and on its four wheels, the car that, according to Senator Kennedy's statements, had at that time been under nine feet of water for an hour and a half. The following reproduces the incomplete transcript as it appeared in the press.

District Attorney DINIS. Now at some time on your way back to your home, was your attention diverted?

Deputy Sheriff LOOK. Yes, sir.

Mr. DINIS. Will you tell the court what you saw?

Deputy Sheriff LOOK. I saw the headlights of an automobile approaching me on Chappaquiddick Road, and knowing the road, I slowed down, because there is a sharp corner back to the ferry and usually people will turn and cut the corner too close. I wanted to make sure this didn't happen to me. So I came almost to a complete stop, and the car passed right in front of me, about 25 or 30 feet away — *a black car.*

Mr. DINIS. Did you observe how many persons were in that automobile?

Deputy Sheriff LOOK. There was a man driving, a woman in the front seat, and either *another person or some clothing, a sweater or a pocketbook or something, in the back seat; what appeared to be a shadow of some kind.*

Mr. DINIS. Did you see anything further when this car approached?

Deputy Sheriff LOOK. Yes, sir.

Mr. DINIS. What?

Deputy Sheriff LOOK. It passed in front of me and went into what we call Cemetery Road, maybe 10 or 15 feet. By this time I had proceeded around the corner a little bit and was approximately 30 feet away. I saw through my rear window that the car was backing up. I thought they wanted information, or were lost or something. I got out of my automobile and started to walk towards them. As I got to approximately 25 or 30 feet away, the car backing up towards me and the tail lights showing all over my uniform, I started to ask, but the car took off towards Dyke Bridge.

Mr. DINIS. Will you tell the court what time this happened to you?

Deputy Sheriff LOOK. It was approximately 12:40 to 12:45 a.m.

Mr. DINIS. Did you make any observations as to the registration of that car?

Deputy Sheriff LOOK. Well, I did make a sort of photographic thing in my mind that it had a seven.*

Mr. DINIS. What did you do then, after the car drove down Dyke Road?

Deputy Sheriff LOOK. I walked back and got into my car and proceeded towards my home. I met three people, two women and a man. One woman was tall and there was another shorter woman and the man was short, with curly hair. I stopped and asked if they would like to have a little lift. The tall girl said, "Shove off, buddy. We aren't pick-ups." [Emphasis added.]

From John N. Farrar, captain of the rescue division of the Edgartown fire department, Judge Brominski's court heard the following testimony when Farrar was under interrogation by District Attorney Dinis:

Mr. DINIS. Was the rope used at all?

Mr. FARRAR. No, sir — well, it was not drawn taut at all.

Mr. DINIS. Did you bring the body to the surface?

Mr. FARRAR. I came to the surface with the body, holding the body all the time.

Farrar's description of the position of the body in the car did not correspond at all with Dr. Mills' volunteered suggestion that Mary Jo might have been in the driver's seat.

Mr. FARRAR. I went into the water and checked the car from the left-hand — that is, the driver's side.† I looked through the

---

*At another point during his examination, Deputy Sheriff Look declared: "The moment I saw the registration of the Oldsmobile I went to the police officer and told him that it was the same car I had seen previously, the night before, at approximately 12:45 a.m., on Chappaquiddick Road." According to the complete official transcript of the Edgartown Court Inquiry, Deputy Sheriff Look declared under oath that the registration number of the car he saw at the crossroad began with L7 and ended with another 7 (L7 – – – 7).

†About the state in which he found the car, Farrar said: "The car windshield was shattered but not knocked out. The two right windows were knocked out completely and shattered. The driver's door was locked, its window was rolled down to within three quarters of an inch of being completely withdrawn."

open window and saw nothing immediately just inside that front window. Then I swam around to the back of the car and saw two feet together on the top side of the right rear window. I then proceeded around to the right side of the car and went in, protruding myself into the broken window, and observed the victim inside the car. Her head was taut. Her face was pressed into the footwell, hands holding onto the front edge of the back seat.

District Attorney Dinis, very understandably, did not ask Farrar in court for his opinion concerning Miss Kopechne's chances for survival. Such questions would have been immediately challenged as irrelevant or hearsay by the doubly watchful lawyers on the Kopechne-Kennedy side. But Farrar had on this subject very pertinent and interesting information to give. He did it in the interview granted to *U.S. News & World Report,* from which we quote the following:

Q. — You are quoted as saying that Miss Kopechne might have lived if a diver had been called in time. What were the odds that she might have been saved?

A. — I think the odds were rather good, for these reasons:

First, the way the car entered the water, which would have caused it initially to trap a large amount of air.

Second, the position of the car on the bottom. It was resting on the hood ornament and the brow of the windshield, with the rear end slightly below the surface of the water.

Third, the consciously assumed position of the victim, as previously described.

Fourth, the fact that air bubbles emanated from the car as it was removed from the water 10 or 11 hours after the accident was said to have happened.

And fifth, the fact that there was a large area void and a lack of water in the trunk of the car when it was removed.

Only recently there have been two incidents in New England in which people lived for some time by finding an air bubble in a submerged car. In one a woman lived for two hours, and in the other a woman lived for six hours . . . .

Q. — How long would it have taken you to get to Dyke Bridge?

A. — No longer than it did that next morning.

The newspapers presented the same day, one of them on the same page, the picture of Farrar, the man who has made rescuing other men's lives one of the reasons of his existence, and one of Senator Edward Kennedy, the man who left Mary Jo under tidal waters for ten hours, who had been surreptitiously shunted off to Europe as a part of Operation Rehabilitation. He was shown addressing the Belgian senate.

The Kopechnes' appearance in court was extremely moving; but the arguments of their lawyers gave the uncanny feeling that there were not two parties, as Mrs. Kopechne had said — one that of the Kennedys, and the other that of the Kopechnes — but rather that the Kennedys and the Kopechnes were on one side and the dead girl alone on the other.

CHAPTER XV

The Senator Is Gratified

Having listened patiently to what was probably the only public testimony that would ever be heard in the matter of the Kennedy scandal, Judge Brominski withheld his decision and declared again that he needed more time to think. He promised that the press would be warned twenty-four hours in advance of publication of the decision. In this slow-motion, alternating play of hearings and rulings between Massachusetts and Pennsylvania courts, it was now the turn of the Massachusetts Supreme Court to speak.

It spoke, and its ruling gave Chief Arena and Prosecutor Steele new occasion to express their feelings. "I thought that a new inquest law might result," said the former. "The decision is just about what I figured it would be," said the latter. Senator Kennedy was caught by the newsmen just out of an official dinner offered by the Massachusetts Historical Society, where he had been solemnly introduced by the society's president, Thomas Boylston Adams, and had had the opportunity, as guest of honor, to recommend that historians "tell facts as they are." About the Massachusetts Supreme Court's decision he told the press that he was "deeply gratified that the Court acted so expeditiously, and that he hoped any additional proceedings would be held soon." This was, of course, all humbug. If the Senator had really desired an expeditious liquidation of his case, he would not have hired a whole commando troop of the most aggressive lawyers in the United States to delay as long as possible any public hearing, and if possible any hearing, any obligation on his part to confirm publicly and under oath, or to repudiate, his statements at the Edgartown police station and in his TV appearance. Everybody could understand, however, the Senator's gratification. *His lawyers had won their major point: the Supreme Court had decided that the inquest in the case of Mary Jo Kopechne's death would be "closed to the public and to all news media."*

The Massachusetts Supreme Court completed its decision with the following orders:

1. Upon completion of the inquest, Judge Boyle's report and the transcript of the proceedings shall remain impounded.

2. Access both to the Judge's report and to the transcript shall be afforded only to the attorney general, the appropriate district attorney, and counsel to any person reported to be actually or possibly responsible for Mary Jo Kopechne's death. Any witness at the inquest shall be permitted to check the accuracy of the transcript of his own testimony.

3. The transcript of the inquest and Judge Boyle's report shall be made available to the public only upon order of a judge of the Superior Court and only if one of the following conditions is met:

   a. The district attorney has filed with the Superior Court a written certificate that there will be no prosecution.

   b. An indictment shall have been sought and not returned.

   c. The trial against the person named in the record as responsible shall have been completed.

   d. A judge of that Superior Court shall determine that no criminal trial is likely. [Emphasis added.]

The Massachusetts Supreme Court did not forget to insist upon the fact that the new rules established for the Kopechne inquest would apply from then on to any future inquest held in the state of Massachusetts, and that what it had taken into consideration was that opening any inquest to the public and to the news media could in general jeopardize the right to a fair trial for the defendant if a criminal proceeding should result.

Hundreds of inquests have been held in Massachusetts and all over the United States with open doors; open coroner's inquests by the thousands have been held for hundreds of years in Great Britain; and the fact that there were no secrets has always been regarded as a guarantee of impartiality and as homage paid to democratic principles. The sudden decision that all inquests must be held *in camera* was undoubtedly a legal rarity, all the more surprising because the Massachusetts laws already provided for the right of the presiding judge in exceptional cases to close the doors "to all persons not required by law to attend."

What made the Supreme Court's order most remarkable was that, according to Massachusetts law, a petition for a writ of certiorari (a petition to review a ruling of a lower court) *cannot be brought in the Supreme Court until the case is finished in the lower court.* The Massachusetts Supreme Court, however, considered that the Kennedy petition for a writ of certiorari was "only technically improper," whatever that meant, and acted on it positively and, beyond all question, in a manner contrary to the existing law. The fact is that, following the illustrious example of the United States Supreme Court, the Massachusetts court had legislated, *it had made new law,* as was remarked by the guileless Chief Arena and discreetly admitted by Massachusetts Attorney General Robert H. Quinn when, in commenting upon the court's decision, he spoke of "the twilight area between legislation and judicial interpretation."

The Court took the trouble to say that, although the Kennedy case presented an unusual problem, it would not make a ruling on it but would prescribe general rules for the future. Nobody believed it. This new "law" was made for the benefit of Senator Kennedy — no matter that all future inquests will have to submit to it, no matter what assurances to the contrary are given. It was only one feature, though a major one, in the constant attitude of protection (against what?) that has been adopted toward the Senator by the responsible authorities in the case of Mary Jo's death.

When would the transcript of the proceedings and the report of the judge to the Supreme Court be made available to the public? The language of the court was very ambiguous on that point. It said they would be made available *"only upon order of a judge of the Superior Court and only if one of the four prescribed conditions is met."* According to this text, the order from the Superior Court is essential and paramount to the fulfillment of the four conditions enumerated. This order is necessary in any case, which makes any final decision on the matter entirely dependent on a Superior Court judge.*

The Supreme Court ruling might hold some further surprises for those who believe that they have a right to know the precise circumstances under which a fellow-citizen and a fellow-human, a young working girl with a whole life of hope before her, met her death in Senator Kennedy's car. An inquest is not legally a part of a subsequent trial, but its results may be used in any accusatory proceeding. How could that be done under the Supreme Court ruling? — logically, only in a closed-door trial, and perhaps not even then. Would the Supreme Court use the "right of superintendency," which it had discovered in a law passed in 1790 to help Kennedy in such an eventuality also?†

Public opinion, bored into lethargy by a year or two of

---

*In fact, Judge Paquet of the Suffolk County Superior Court was to be the one to throw, with the pious assistance of a Catholic priest, the last judicial spadeful of earth upon Mary Jo's grave.

†In fact, this is exactly what happened.

legal quibbling and casuistry, might after all permit it, and permit even the total evaporation of the Kennedy-Kopechne case, as it permitted, among others, the cases of Owen Lattimore and Judith Coplon to evaporate. For the moment, however, the so-called silent majority was, no doubt, of the same opinion as the Sigma Delta Chi Society of Professional Journalists, expressed as follows by its president:

> We find it extremely ironic that the Court cites "great public interest" as a reason for closing the hearing to the public .... There is further irony in the Court's own statement that it will not make "any special rule for a particular case."

CHAPTER XVI

The End Of The Autopsy Scandal

Almost five months after the still unexplained death of Mary Jo Kopechne, and three months after being asked by the Dukes County authorities in New Bedford, Massachusetts, to allow the exhumation of her body, which had been surreptitiously removed from Massachusetts jurisdiction — the Lucerne County (Pennsylvania) Court of Common Pleas finally rejected Massachusetts' request. Mary Jo's body will never be submitted to serious medical examination.

Among the arguments with which Judge Brominski justified his decision, one will certainly stand as a landmark in the history of forensic medicine in the United States, for it refuted one of the most firmly established tenets of the profession. It has always been admitted by forensic medical specialists that an autopsy has at least, and in any case, the great advantage that it puts an end to all the unjustified assumptions and wild rumors provoked by death caused by external means. For many of the most experienced specialists, therefore, an autopsy is routine even in the most normal and everyday cases of death in traffic accidents.

Nobody who heard or read Senator Kennedy's two contradictory and evidently untruthful reports would put the Dyke Bridge tragedy in the category of normal and everyday highway accidents. Even the *New York Times*, the *Washington Post, Newsweek,* and *Time* magazine, always favorably disposed toward the Senator and his political

137

activities, warned him about the justifiable suspicions aroused by his deportment after the accident, his dodging of any public investigation, and his obviously phony TV explanations. With courageous contempt of old and hackneyed formulas, Judge Brominski, however, opening absolutely new grounds in forensic medicine, ruled that permitting an autopsy in the Kennedy-Kopechne case would "give rein to speculations unsupported by medical facts." Many might have believed, before this bold piece of medical jurisprudence, that an autopsy would, on the contrary, put an end to "speculations unsupported by medical facts." How wild these speculations were in the aftermath of the Dyke Bridge tragedy, Judge Brominski, who mentioned manual strangulation in his commentary, knew as well as anybody else.

Judge Brominski decided that the hearing he presided over brought out only minor discrepancies between the two Kennedy reports, and that these did not "alter the original determination of the cause of death." Not even the fact that Kennedy's car was seen by Deputy Sheriff Look *on dry ground* an hour and a half after the time the Senator affirmed that it had plunged with him and Mary Jo into Poucha Pond, seems to have interested Mary Jo Kopechne's parents and Judge Brominski. The judge did not in any way take into account in his ruling the impossibility of fitting the events described by the Senator in between the time he was seen in his car by Christopher Look and the time he was seen by Mr. Peachey in dry clothes and perfectly composed, in front of his hotel in Edgartown. This fact alone, however, belied the Senator's account in its totality.

In a rather surprising part of his fourteen-page ruling, Judge Brominski asserted that the Massachusetts authorities had "voluntarily" passed up their right to perform an autopsy before burial. Judge Brominski disregarded thereby the fact, stated under oath by District Attorney for the

Southern District of Massachusetts Edmund Dinis and not refuted by the defense, that it was against his will and by a stratagem that Mary Jo Kopechne's body was flown out of his jurisdiction in a Kennedy-chartered plane, two and a half hours after he was falsely informed that it had already left Massachusetts.

Attorneys for the Kopechne family and the experts they produced were of the opinion that after such a long time an autopsy could hardly disclose anything of real importance. Experts produced by District Attorney Dinis were of quite a different opinion. Judge Brominski chose to decide that "even if the autopsy showed injuries, they could have been caused in the accident, and would not necessarily change the findings of death by drowning." It is quite true that the long delay and the embalming would have prevented the detection of certain facts, such as the quantity of alcohol consumed before death or the presence of certain other toxic or hypnotic substances. But the facts that *could* have been detected, despite the lapse of time and the embalming, were exactly those that could have substantiated or disproved some of the most incriminating but justifiable assumptions provoked by the Senator's contradictions, falsehoods, and dissimulations, which had been brought to the status of a real international scandal by his plea for a closed inquest.*

The presence of blood detected by the benzidine test, not only on the sleeves and the collar but also on the back of the victim's blouse, does not seem to have aroused the curiosity either of Judge Brominski or of Mr. and Mrs. Kopechne. They were all contented with the explanation that the origin of the bloodstains could have been "the slight froth from the nose, common to drowning, that could have run down Miss Kopechne's face to the back of

*We refer the reader to the absolutely unbiased opinions of some of the top authorities in legal medicine mentioned in Chapter Four.

the neck and shoulders," not wondering how such a slight froth could have become "set" in the fabric during immersion without being first washed out by the strong current passing through the overturned car, whose windows were all either open or broken.

Both the Kopechnes and Senator Kennedy declared themselves satisfied with Judge Brominski's ruling. Mrs. Kopechne told reporters that she "could never have gone to that cemetary again if the grave . . . had been disturbed." And Senator Kennedy said he felt happy because of what the ruling meant for Mr. and Mrs. Kopechne.

Senator Kennedy added that he hoped the Massachusetts authorities would "move forward so that the entire matter could be concluded as soon as possible." There was no contradiction between this laudable request of the Senior Senator from Massachusetts and the five-month-long effort of nine Kennedy lawyers to delay or even impede an inquest in the Dyke Bridge tragedy, since the situation had completely changed in the meantime. According to Massachusetts law, only an autopsy, ruled out by Judge Brominski, could have found another *medical* cause for Mary Jo's death than the one proclaimed by Dr. Mills without an autopsy and after a cursory, strictly visual examination. The possibility of uncovering another *legal* cause, learning the true circumstances in which the drowning took place, could, however, still have been investigated by interrogation of witnesses. But meanwhile, the case had been so hermetically sealed against such interrogations by the ad hoc decisions of the Massachusetts Supreme Court that not even the parents of Mary Jo were allowed to be present at the inquest and to take direct cognizance of the questions put to the witnesses, of their answers, and of how many of them — including perhaps even Senator Kennedy — might have chosen to hide behind the cloak of their constitutional rights.

It is true that the facts revealed by the inquest, according to the Supreme Court decision, would eventually be revealed to the U.S. public (and not just the facts, it was to be hoped, but also Senator Kennedy's explanations of his fanciful assertions and contradictions) — but only when such a revelation would be "fair to all parties." Nobody knew what this formula meant and what span of time it would cover.

Meanwhile so many things could happen to draw public attention away from the last tortured moments of Mary Jo! Senator Kennedy himself provided one of them, of ghastly impact, with the statement that not 110 or 526 South Vietnamese civilians were murdered during the Vietnam war, as reported by the well-paid army slanderers tracked down by Mr. Seymour Hersh, but 300,000 — *the great majority of whom were slain by United States forces,* so the Senator contended.

Since Senator Kennedy's sensational declarations were made, the My Lai frame-up has, indeed, developed into "an indictment of the whole United States Armed Forces," to the great relish of the *New York Times* and other anti-American sources of information.

CHAPTER XVII

From The Tarpeian Rock
To The Capitol

There is a charming story concerning a duel between Édouard Drumont, the fiery French publicist, and Arthur Meyer, the placid director of *Le Gaulois* and recorder of Parisian social events. It was *"l'affaire Dreyfus"* and an objectionable article in Arthur Meyer's paper that brought these two gentlemen to face one another, swords in hand, at Longchamps, where such jousts used to be fought. Poor Meyer, who had no aggression in him, started the combat by seizing his opponent's sword with his left hand. He was forgiven the first time, but when he repeated the performance he was "disqualified" by the four seconds and sent home. On his way back to Paris, shamed and contrite, he spoke to his friends these memorable words: *"Il faudrait une guerre pour que le monde oublie cela."* ("Only a war could make the world forget that.")

It is more likely that Kennedy and his friends would content themselves with a revolution.

William F. Buckley Jr. has very rightly observed that when a politician gets into serious trouble, the instinctive thing for him to do is "to take a hard tack to the left, where he is sure to find adherents and protection." He might have added that the more serious the trouble, the harder must be the tack.

It would be difficult to figure more trouble for a politician than that which Edward Kennedy found himself in after the body of Mary Jo Kopechne was discovered in his submerged car. This trouble was, moreover, of the permanently irritant nature of a Damoclean sword; and Senator Kennedy, like his brothers, had learned long since all the advantages offered, without danger to the fortune and privileges to which he was born, to an ambitious young man who adopts radicalism as a profession. It could have been foreseen, therefore, that the moment the Senator felt himself able "to put behind [him] this most recent tragedy" he would try, as he so nicely put it, "to make further contributions to [his] state and to mankind." In both the domestic and the foreign political fields, this contribution could only have been of the kind that has brought to the Kennedy clan the support and admiration of the new breed of young humans, hairy and vociferous, of both sexes and all colors, and the approbation of Moscow, Peking, and Hanoi.

Immediately after the Chappaquiddick affair, the Senator had an opportunity to discover the protective quality of the political environment he had chosen. To everybody's surprise, certain news organs belonging to the liberal establishment, laboring under the irresistible effect of the ugliness of what was known of the Dyke Bridge tragedy, and afraid of what might still be discovered, seemed to have turned their backs on the Senior Senator from Massachusetts. But these brief and virtuous manifestations of independence — to be attributed, for the most part, to the professional honesty of the reporter on the spot of the accident — were soon smothered under the adulation of the faithful and the favorable headlines of the national and foreign press.

Here are some examples of the latter, collected from both domestic and foreign newspapers: *Telegrams Flood The Senator. — Public Backing Ted. — Why Kennedy Can Fight It Out. — Massachusetts Backs Kennedy. — Kennedy Still Eligible. — Faith In Ted Unshaken. — Humphrey Backs*

Kennedy. — Public Stands By Kennedy. — Thousands Support Kennedy. — Thousands Write "Ted Don't Resign." — For Ted Time Is Great Healer. — Senators Admire Kennedy, But Many Question His Judgment. — Senator's Statement, First Step Toward Recovery. — Top Hill Democrats Support Kennedy. — A Tragic Accident Imperils A Great Career. — and so on, and so on.

That was long ago. Today you cannot open a U.S. newspaper any day of the week without being struck by Senator Kennedy's name in the headlines again. But since the magic wand has come down with a bang on the tables of the newspaper staffs, defending and denouncing the Senator are both, and equally, bad manners. It is his uninterrupted patriotic and philanthropic activities that must appear in the news. The second phase of Operation Rescue is well under way.

Those activities are multiple and of every possible character. It is not business-as-usual that the salvaging brain-trust has prescribed, but business-much-more-than-usual. Here are some pertinent headlines: *Senator Kennedy Is Informed About Drug Problems In Greater Boston Schools. — Senator Kennedy Tours Boston Hospitals To Prepare Key Speech. — Kennedy To Hold Hearings On Draft Law. — Senator Kennedy Seeks Draft Law Credit. Hopes To Beat President To The Punch. — Kennedy Calls Draft Laws Unfair To Youth, Negroes And Poor. — Kennedy Declares Serious Question Exists About Confirmation Of Judge Haynsworth. — Ted Rejects Everett Mayor. — Kennedy Sees War Causing Violence Here. — Senator Says War Is Impossible To Win. — Senator Wants Gaps To Be Filled. —* and so on, and so on. And crowning the whole was a surprise picture of Senator Kennedy addressing the NATO Assembly in the Belgian Senate Chamber, and announcing to his hearers that there was "a great likelihood that the U.S. Senate would soon adopt a resolution calling for withdrawal of some of the U.S. troops from Western Europe."

The most remarkable public activities of Senator Kennedy after his reappearance at the Capitol, safely rescued from what at first seemed to have been a political Tarpeian plunge, were his two speeches on the war in Vietnam, and his violent intervention in the Senate on behalf of the Gun Control Act. The two issues are not quite so far apart as one might believe.

It was on September 14, 1969, at a dinner of the American Cancer Society, that the Senator delivered his first post-Chappaquiddick speech. Its subject was not cancer at all, or any related matter. To everybody's bewilderment, he asked for an immediate and total withdrawal of United States troops from Vietnam and for a new government in Saigon that would include Communists, replacing the present "corrupt and oppressive administration." If the Thieu government did not comply, he said, it ought to be told: "This is your war; you must fight it alone."

This speech was only a preliminary to the October "Moratorium" activities of Senator Kennedy.* On October 15 the Senator spoke to the World Affairs Committee in Boston. In the street, he had answered greetings with the modified "V" sign, which, whatever it may mean, does not mean "Victory in Vietnam." In the meeting room, he was received, according to the press, with an eighty-second ovation. His speech was repetitive, but included an interesting warning: "We can expect more division, *even violence,* among our people as the war works its corrupting effect on every aspect of the national life."

Senator Kennedy knew whereof he spoke. He has never

---

*It is of interest that one of the principal organizers of the Moratorium Movement, the man who gave it its name, was Sam Brown of Harvard, who had officiated for a time, under Adam Yarmolinsky, in that part of the University bought and controlled by the Kennedy family.

been afraid of the most subversive and seditious company, so long as the subversion and sedition is leftist in character.* As companions in the steering of the Moratorium Movement he had Arnold Johnson of the New Mobilization Committee, the public relations director of the Communist Party, USA; two members of the so-called "Chicago Eight," then still on trial for rioting; two members of the American Civil Liberties Union (whose founder, Roger Baldwin, gave his full approval to the right of all, citizens and aliens alike, to advocate political assassination†); and also Donald Kalish and Franz Schurmann, Richard Falk and Martin Peretz, all of them extreme leftist agitators. Among the top speakers with Kennedy in the Boston Moratorium campaign were William Sloane Coffin Jr. and Mitchell Goodman — co-defendants with the notorious Dr. Benjamin Spock in an anti-draft conspiracy trial.

The Gun Control Act provides for the registration of every weapon in the country in possession of private persons. It is, of course, a necessary first step toward confiscation of all weapons at the proper moment. It would be almost an insult to the intelligence of our readers to remind them that such

---

*Neither were his brothers. An article appearing in the July 1968 issue of the Spanish magazine *Historia y Vida* seems to substantiate, with text and photographs, the fact that John F. Kennedy, the future President of the United States, spent some time in 1938 in Spain, on the Communist side of the Civil War, where no doubt his sympathies were also engaged. (See Appendix C.)

†From the transcript of an investigation by a U.S. Senate investigating committee:

The CHAIRMAN. Does your organization [ACLU] uphold the right of a citizen or alien to advocate murder?

Mr. BALDWIN (director of ACLU). Yes.

The CHAIRMAN. Or assassination?

Mr. BALDWIN. Yes.

* * *

The CHAIRMAN. You do uphold the right of an alien to advocate the overthrow of the Government by force and violence?

Mr. BALDWIN. Sure, certainly.

On his eightieth birthday Baldwin received a very friendly message of congratulation from President Johnson. The ACLU's activities have several times received enthusiastic approbation from Presidents Truman and Kennedy.

measures have nothing to do with the repression of crime. Everybody recognizes that a criminal will always be able to get a weapon with which to kill, and everybody knows that, as Chicago's police superintendent said, to disarm the honest men is to arm the ruffians.

The idea of disarming the "silent majority" became an essential part of the program of leftist and new-leftist groups that have infiltrated government and legislative circles when it was realized that armed resistance by ordinary citizens, to whom the Constitution had given the right to bear arms, might perhaps — in case of a surprise *coup* by the radical Conspiracy — fill the place and play the role of a defaulting or defunct government. Conservative elements in the Senate introduced a mitigating measure exempting rifle and shotgun ammunition, except .22 caliber rimfire cartridges, from the requirements of the 1968 Gun Control Law concerning recording of sales of ammunition. This was passed by an overwhelming majority. Kennedy fought that very moderate exemption for more than three hours with what the papers called "a rare display of fury." The vociferous minorities of every description, tools of every demagogue in history, will not forget this at the proper moment.

From the numerous "letters to the editor" concerning the Dyke Bridge tragedy, both pro and con, that have passed under our eye, one of the most interesting, we think, is the following, sent to the *Manchester Union Leader* on July 27 by young Pierre Stuart:

> The youth of this country knows that there are powerful forces seeking to destroy Senator Edward Kennedy. Any accident, however tragic, serves their purpose. Those forces will receive the proper rebuff at the proper time.

The "powerful forces" mentioned by the young writer do not exist at the moment, whatever surprise the future may hold for us. The "youth of this country" to whom Pierre

Stuart alludes, the sort that have replaced the nice-looking, well-mannered, friendly, smiling college boys and girls of the pre-Rooseveltian era, and those infatuated nonentities, intellectual perverts, and enemy agents whom they have accepted as mentors, have nothing to fear so long as the millions of other young men and women and patriots of every age do not choose leaders different from those who have manipulated the destiny of the United States — and with it that of the world — for more than three decades.

If Edward Kennedy is the man Marcuse's and Aptheker's boys and girls have chosen, if the silent majority remains silent, the Senator will keep on trotting on his pinky nag toward the White House of his dreams, Poucha Pond or no Poucha Pond. Foolish is he who would write him off! This is said with all the more confidence because the forces that seem to have adopted him, including the giant international trust of the news media, *are perfectly able to create the dangerous political and military situation that will make the Presidency of the last of the Kennedy brothers, or of someone else of the same type, the only apparent alternative to a nuclear catastrophe for the U.S. population.*

In fact, just such a situation is being prepared by the withdrawal of United States forces from Europe and Asia — where they are present today primarily for the defense, not of Switzerland or Vietnam, but of the shores of their own country, against an irreconcilable enemy.

This newly enjoined isolationism is not that inherited from George Washington — the dignified detachment of a powerful and industrious country from the futile quarrels of others; it is rather flight and capitulation in the face of a continuously increasing danger. Its result will be, sooner or later, the emergence of a situation in which the United States will be forced to accept a crucial showdown at a moment chosen by the enemy, or a government chosen directly or indirectly by him.

It was the massing of Soviet troops on the Czecho-Slovakian borders that in 1946 brought a Communist government to Prague. It was the massing of Soviet troops inside Czecho-Slovakia, at West Germany's borders, that brought a Socialist government to Bonn in 1969, with the election of Willy Brandt.

There are several Willy Brandts in the United States. The inner revolutionary pressure is certainly greater here today than in West Germany; as for the military pressure, corresponding to the massing of divisions on Germany's borders, it is being prepared by the general withdrawal of American forces and influence from Europe and Asia — as recommended by Senator Kennedy and his cohorts — with all the military and political consequences that this withdrawal implies.

CHAPTER XVIII

The Truth Is Routed

On January 5, 1970, for the first time, after six months of open and undercover obstruction by Senator Edward M. Kennedy and his lawyers — months of tergiversations, appropriate proceedings, and special rulings by local, state, and federal authorities — the Senator, his companions at the cook-out party on Chappaquiddick Island, and other important witnesses were interrogated under oath about the time, the place, and the circumstances of the death of Mary Jo Kopechne on the night of July 18, 1969.

As is well known, the inquest took place secretly by order of the Massachusetts Supreme Court, and the only copy of the transcript of the proceedings and of the presiding judge's report, duly sealed and impounded, was filed with the clerk of the Dukes County Superior Court in Edgartown. In all likelihood, judging by previous proceedings, months would pass before the public would be informed about what happened, what was asked, and what was answered *in camera* at the Edgartown Court House. In all likelihood what the public would eventually learn from the 750 pages of transcript would be only a part of what it has the right to know concerning the violent death of any fellow citizen.

Even if the questions and answers asked and given by Senator Kennedy and his ten companions of the Lawrence cottage party were to be published in their totality, it seemed very unlikely that they would offer more to satisfy the legitimate inquisitiveness of the United States public than did

Senator Kennedy's two contradictory public explanations. Kennedy's highly efficient battery of lawyers had had almost six months to decide whether, in case of a formal inquest, their client should or should not stick to his former declarations. They very wisely decided that the Senator must stick to his TV account of Mary Jo's tragic death, hard as it was to believe, simply trying to harmonize it as well as possible with the police station report. No lawyer could have advised him to confess that he had never been in a state of shock at all, that he had never swum at night, prostrated and fully dressed, across the 500 feet of the Edgartown channel — thereby sacrificing definitively his political future. No lawyer could have asked him to confess that he was not in the car when it plunged into Poucha Pond — if this was indeed the truth — since so doing would have opened new and horrid vistas on the tragedy.

The Kennedy lawyers had also had half a year to teach male and female participants in the Lawrence cottage festivities, including their star client, what they had to remember, to forget, and to imagine — under oath indeed, but without the embarrassing and inhibiting presence of an observing and knowing public and a critical troop of newsmen. We may be sure that every possible question had been anticipated by the high-powered commando band of lawyers, and that every witness, from Kennedy to the last of the five charming girls, had been provided with proper and harmonious answers, and thoroughly rehearsed in their effective delivery. Six months and nine lawyers (not counting the special advisers) were more than enough for that important task. So that if Judge James Ambrose Boyle was accustomed to working with his tongue slightly protruding between his teeth, as many people do during artistic or literary effort, he must certainly have moved it into his cheek when he wrote, in his Statement on Inquest Rules, that "counsel are ordered not to discuss the testimony of one client with another client." This stipulation was all the more humorous because the five surviving girl participants in the Chappaquiddick expedition all had the same counsel, Attorney Paul Redmond, assisted by Attorney Daniel Daly, with whom, according to press reports, the girls had attended on weekends during the summer, real seminars on the subject of their demeanor, behavior, and statements during any official inquiry that might be held.

Thus, all the Edgartown inquest will ever produce will probably be what the full battalion of newsmen besieging the Edgartown Court House — grimly defended by a dense cordon of state troopers and by local and imported police, in pinchingly cold weather — were able to gather from the Court's open rulings; what they saw and what they did not see; and what they heard from the few witnesses who consented to leak some information, despite the orders of both higher and lower courts.

The first to violate those orders was Senator Kennedy himself. It was also in his favor that the strict rules on admission to the court's precincts were bypassed when Richard Drayn, the Senator's Washington press secretary, and James King, his administrative assistant in his Boston office, were permitted to enter and leave at will a courthouse which even the parents of Mary Jo, the victim, had been forbidden to enter.

Kennedy, who according to Massachusetts papers had spent much of the weekend "preparing for the start of the inquest with his lawyers in Boston," arrived at the courthouse shortly before 10:00 a.m., accompanied, as was usual in moments of stress, by his patient and faithful wife as moral support and permanent alibi, and by Bill Barry as bodyguard. He testified for two hours in a morning and an afternoon session. Emerging from the courthouse he volunteered the following statement to newsmen: "I am satisfied that I responded in the most complete manner possible to all

questions put to me by the district attorney and the Court."
Asked whether his story in general had paralleled his earlier
statements, he replied, "I would rather not characterize my
testimony, but substantially it did." He added that "at the
end I made a couple of points I thought might be useful to
add to the record." Many will ask themselves, with Ralph
de Toledano: "How many holes were punched into his
already perforated story of the circumstances of Mary Jo's
death?"

District Attorney Edmund Dinis — who after all was not
quite the menace an innocent public had believed — was still
more explicit in his extemporaneous remarks. He declared: "I
am satisfied to have put on the record all the witnesses
available to us," and informed the reporters that if the
examination under oath of those witnesses had been taken
immediately after the accident, the present inquest would
not have been necessary. This last statement would have been
rather enigmatic had it not been followed by the significant
confidence, made to those same reporters, that if Senator
Kennedy should run for re-election in the 1970 election, the
district attorney expected to vote for him. The *New York
Times* observed that Kennedy and Dinis would probably
appear together on the Democrat ticket.

As for the witnesses mentioned by District Attorney Dinis
— barring the possibility that some of them may have been
introduced into the courthouse so secretly that their presence
escaped the newsmen's vigilance, it seems that some who
were not called certainly would have been available had the
Court or the district attorney so desired — for instance, Mary
Jo's parents.

Dr. Donald R. Mills, who decidedly has a soft corner in his
heart for newsmen, also took the liberty of giving them some
information about what he had said at the secret inquest: his
testimony, he told them, "paralleled exactly that which he
gave at the autopsy hearing."

We were told nothing by the courtroom grapevine about the crucial testimony of John W. Farrar and Christopher Look except that it must not have differed from what those reliable witnesses gave at the autopsy hearing. About Farrar's testimony we were informed, by the same means, that Judge Boyle did not permit this witness to give his expert opinion on the possibility of removing Mary Jo from the car alive after a certain lapse of time, stating that such testimony was hearsay and that he was interested only in facts.

If this grapevine information was true, there were two substantial reasons to wonder at the judge's ruling: (1) Judge Boyle had stated correctly in his inquest rules that, an inquest not being an accusatory proceeding, the general rules for examination and cross-examination do not apply, the duty and the right of the Court being to seek and receive any testimony and information — *even hearsay* — "material to the question as to whether or not criminal conduct caused or contributed to the death of the victim"; (2) the fact that Kennedy and his two associates, Markham and Gargan, let hours pass without summoning the professional help that was immediately within their reach to rescue the girl — whom according to their own testimony they believed to have been still alive — might certainly have been a contributing factor in her death, and any expert information on this subject was certainly "relevant and pertinent" in a purely investigative procedure, *whatever the length of time during which the unfortunate Mary Jo may have struggled with the invading water.*

From the same source, the courtroom grapevine, it was learned that Markham and Gargan explained their failure to summon help that was available by asserting that they believed that Senator Kennedy — who was at that time in a state of paralyzing trauma — had already done it or was about to do it. As for the hazardous plunge of their prostrated friend, it was, they said, so quickly done that they had no time to prevent it, however great their desire to do so.

Something was also gathered by the shivering crowd with regard to subpoenaed and non-subpoenaed exhibits. In the first category there were those two doors of Kennedy's car brought by Dinis, which the Court did not find it necessary to examine. In the second category — that is, of exhibits that were not subpoenaed despite the clues they might have provided — were, to the best of the onlookers' knowledge, the clothing and shoes of the three aquatic performers, which were supposed to have been soaked six months before in the salt waters of Poucha Pond and the Edgartown channel. Chemical analysis would still have been possible, and to have had their identity and their vicissitudes testified to under oath would have been of great interest to a thorough and serious inquiry.*

So once more the most substantial information accessible to public opinion concerning Kennedy's role and responsibility in Mary Jo's death was that concerning the increasing secrecy maintained around them by every person and every agency concerned.

It appears that the precautions taken by the Massachusetts Supreme Court to ensure the secrecy of the Kennedy inquest did not seem to Judge Boyle proportionate to the gravity of what was to be hidden, or of what could be disclosed even in a well-controlled court. Either on his own initiative or acting upon higher orders, he found it necessary to reinforce those precautions.

The Supreme Court's ruling provided that:

---

*And this brings us to the matter of Senator Kennedy's driving license. This license, according to information gathered by Mr. Art Igan of the *Manchester Union Leader* from Registrar Richard E. McLaughlin of the Massachusetts Registry of Motor Vehicles, showed no sign of immersion. This fact obviously was of no probatory value; the Senator could always have claimed that he had not had his license with him, that tragic night. The real interest of the episode is in the illegal difficulties raised by the Massachusetts authorities when Mr. Igan sought formal confirmation of his telephone conversation with Mr. McLaughlin. The latter tried to deny that such a conversation had ever taken place.

The access to both the Judge's report and to the inquest transcript will be afforded only to the Attorney General, to the appropriate district attorney [Edmund Dinis, in this case], and to any person reported as actually or possibly responsible for Mary Jo Kopechne's death.

Further on:

The transcript of the inquest and the report of Judge Boyle shall be made available to the public only upon an order of a judge of the Superior Court and if one of the following conditions is met: (a) if the district attorney has filed with the Superior Court a written certification that there will be no prosecution; (b) that ... etc.

Those two rulings were of course legally connected. It would be against reason to ask the district attorney to make the important decision as to whether or not there would be prosecution, without putting into his hands a complete transcript of the inquest proceedings, amounting in this case to 750-odd pages, for study and consideration. Judge Boyle nevertheless ruled, either contrary to the order of the Supreme Court or following secret orders of that court:

Although the Judge is not bound by the rules of evidence that apply to criminal cases, it is as much the duty of the Court to decline to receive such improper testimony to the effect that persons innocent of any criminal involvement be not injured in reputation.

For the reason stated above and because this is not an adversary proceeding, *transcript testimony will not be furnished to the District Attorney,* or to counsel. [Emphasis added.]

Judge Boyle must have foreseen very important reasons indeed — important for the Kennedy side, of course — for taking upon himself the responsibility of aggravating the special secrecy ordered by the Supreme Court in favor of the Senator from Massachusetts, which had already horrified so many people in the United States and abroad. Such a move was all the more astonishing because it was Judge Boyle who had formerly ruled that all the seats available in the courtroom should be put at the disposal of the hundreds of newsmen who had crowded Edgartown in September.*

Judge Tauro of the Superior Court had also a word to say. He ordered that for greater security the transcript and Judge Boyle's report be transferred from the Dukes County Superior Court to the Suffolk County Superior Court in Boston. The transfer was conducted under the strictest security precautions, with state police supervision, by two officials of the Suffolk County court. Judge Tauro explained to the press that he was following the instructions of the Massachusetts Supreme Court, changing only the location of the impounded papers.

"All is quiet on the Kennedy front in Edgartown," said the *New York Times* on January 11, 1970, adding that the 1200 winter residents of this quaint little town "remained deeply skeptical of Kennedy's story, disbelieving his emotional report on national television last July 25 that shock and bewilderment kept him from reporting the accident for nine harrowing hours. They suspect he had devoted a considerable part of those nine hours to groping for some way of escaping responsibility."

As a last precaution, Massachusetts Attorney General Robert H. Quinn warned Mr. Leslie A. Leland, foreman of the Martha's Vineyard Grand Jury — upon which the population of the island relied, when all had been said and done by other courts and agencies, to discover what had really happened (or been perpetrated) in their county on the

---

*Judge Boyle's new attitude leads us to observe that it was just his rather provocative decision to fill his courtroom with reporters from all over the world that had given Kennedy's lawyers a priceless opportunity to appeal to the Massachusetts Supreme Court to save their star client from the deadly experience of a public hearing.

night of July 18 — that the grand jury had no right to call for an investigation on its own account without the authorization of the Massachusetts Attorney General, the district attorney, or a Superior Court judge. It did not seem likely that Mr. Leland would take the trouble to dispute this controversial admonition, knowing that the Massachusetts Supreme Court could always step in with another piece of impromptu legification.

The private tragedy of Mary Jo Kopechne ended when her body was smuggled away, by a Kennedy employee in a Kennedy-chartered plane, beyond the reach of any real legal examination. A public tragedy began at the same moment, parallel to the juridical manipulations which led to Kennedy's successful escape not only from any penalty but also from any public investigation.

"It should have been a national scandal when the court wrapped in secrecy the inquest into the death of Mary Jo," *says Ralph de Toledano.* The American tragedy is that, after all, it was not a national scandal. *The American tragedy is that it was demonstrated again, and in the ugliest and most discreditable manner, that thanks to the sternly directed collusion between the news media and too many administrative, judicial, and political organs, anybody,* if chosen by the Establishment, *can be hoisted and projected toward the highest position in the United States, without regard to his merits, his moral values, and the circumstances of his past, however dark.*

Don't cry over Camelot! Camelot is not dead. All the worthy knights are there, eagerly grouped around the Brotherhood's board, where lie heaped up tax-free foundations by the thousands, international and national sinecures by the hundreds of thousands, and counterfeit dollars by the billions, among the still throbbing remains of faith, patriotism, and sanity.

Yes, they are still there — Kennedy, Markham, and

Gargan, rescuers of fair ladies in distress; Goodwin, McNamara, Schlesinger, Sorensen, Galbraith, Bundy, Goldberg, Rostow, Yarmolinsky, and all their kind, awaiting only the proper moment to perch their new Arthur in the seat of command. This moment will be brought about by the right amount of pressure from the insurrection they are marshaling; by the increasing foreign menace they have promoted through unilateral disarmament and continuous withdrawal; and finally, by the imminence of the inevitable open or silent ultimatum to be delivered by Big Brother when the possibility of instantaneously pulverizing the United States "island" becomes an indisputable reality.

PART THREE

FINAL HOCUS POCUS
March 26, 1970 - November 3, 1970

CHAPTER XIX

Evisceration Of A Grand Jury

There were two surgeons, and the fact that the layout of the operation had been determined in advance by the Massachusetts Supreme Court and a dozen of the sharpest lawyers to be found in the American Bar Association does not at all diminish the commendation both deserve for having carried out successfully the difficult juridical feat they were expected to perform.

Let the *New York Times* introduce Judge Wilfred J. Paquet of the Suffolk County Superior Court, the Cerberean custodian of the impounded 764 pages of transcript of the top-secret January inquest, who had been designated to supervise the hearings of the Edgartown Grand Jury investigating the circumstances in which Mary Jo Kopechne met her death:

> Judge Paquet, who is 67 years old, is a tall, husky man with receding reddish brown hair. He is said by one lawyer to be a good judge in the sense of being a competent legal craftsman. The same lawyer added, "You have to be on your toes in his courtroom." Another puts it differently: "He runs a tight courtroom — there is no kidding with him." The judge is a Democrat; he is no longer politically active, but those who regard him as a less than distinguished jurist point at his long association with the Democrat governor who appointed him in 1951, the late Paul A. Dever.

About Judge Paquet's relationship with Edward R. Hanify, Kennedy's chief attorney in the case of Mary Jo Kopechne's death, the *New York Times* had the following to say:

163

About ten years ago Judge Wilfred J. Paquet of the Massachusetts Superior Court sentenced two convicted bookies to ten
years in jail. Two days later he ordered them released, and
explained he had decided the sentence was too severe . . . . Judge
Paquet's action and the issue were finally resolved in the Supreme
Judicial Court of Massachusetts. A Boston lawyer named Edward
R. Hanify argued in behalf of Judge Paquet. Mr. Hanify and
Judge Paquet will meet again in Edgartown: Mr. Hanify is
representing Senator Kennedy, Judge Paquet is presiding over the
hearings of the Dukes County Grand Jury.

The public and the press already knew District Attorney
Dinis, the second of the two jurists who were to be
responsible for the judicial incapacitation of the Dukes
County Grand Jury. Public and press could have guessed
which side of his ambivalent personality would emerge during
the closed-door hearing before the grand jury. They knew
that, at the end of the top-secret inquest in January,* Dinis
had declared that if Kennedy were the Democrat nominee in
the November election he "expected" he would vote for him;
and they learned later that Dinis was slated to figure on the
ticket with the Massachusetts Senator. They had heard the
district attorney declare, after hearing Kennedy's testimony
at the secret inquest, that he would have been satisfied with
it if it had been made under oath six months earlier.

Public and press had also learned that relations between
Kennedy and the district attorney were now on a "Ted" and
"Ed" basis, a long way from what they had seemed to be

---

*The inquest records and Judge Boyle's report, which had been removed, for
safety's sake, from the Edgartown Court registry to the registry of the Dukes
County Superior Court, and from there to the Suffolk County Superior Court
in Boston, were impounded but not sealed; at least not permanently sealed.
The Massachusetts Supreme Court had decided that every witness, accompanied by his or her lawyer, had the right to control the exact rendering of
his or her testimony by the Court stenographer. Edward Kennedy and his
chief lawyer, Edward Hanify, availed themselves of this right. We do not know
whether or not they were satisfied with their findings. Nor do we know
whether Judge Paquet was troubled by other witnesses wishing to exercise their
right of control.

when Dinis insisted, before Judge Brominski's court, that Mary Jo's body had been smuggled in haste out of his jurisdiction, in a Kennedy-chartered plane and by Kennedy's salaried staff, preventing thereby the routine autopsy he would have had performed to determine the exact cause of her death. All this may have explained the fact that not three hundred and forty American and foreign correspondents gathered in Edgartown for the grand jury hearing, as in January, but only a straggling group of about fifty.

No court of inquiry is armed with greater powers of investigation than a grand jury. The ten men and ten women who formed the Dukes County Grand Jury could have conducted a complete investigation of their own, using information already collected, and could have subpoenaed any witnesses they wished. But the exceptional and highly effective dispositions that had been made by the Massachusetts Supreme Court had only to be acted upon to deprive the grand jury of any means of information, and to provide the supervising judge and the prosecuting attorney with all the necessary legal — and illegal — means to control it, to muzzle it, to scare it, and to send it home without having been allowed to shed on the mysterious death of Mary Jo the light millions of the dead girl's fellow-citizens had the right to expect as a consequence of a grand jury's activities.

The Dukes County Grand Jury met on April 6 to decide whether or not Mary Jo Kopechne's death involved a criminal act by Kennedy or others. It was dispersed by the supervising judge and the prosecuting attorney on April 7. It had heard only four unimportant local witnesses, who had no direct connection with the case, *who had not been interrogated during the secret inquest in January*, and who seemed to have been brought there only to obscure somewhat the fact that the grand jury had been forbidden any significant activity.

Judge Paquet addressed the grand jury for ninety minutes.

It was the longest "charge" ever received by a grand jury, the newsmen said. Emphasizing almost violently the obligation of secrecy, the judge said to the jurors: "It would be violative of your oath *under God* if you reveal one single thing that happens in the jury room — your lips are sealed, and I don't mean for today, I mean forever." Judge Paquet insisted that among the "single things" he referred to, which the jurors would never be allowed to reveal, was *what the prosecuting attorney would tell them during their session,* in which he himself could not participate. The special importance of this injunction will be understood later.

Judge Paquet went back as far as 150 years to define by chosen precedents what he considered to be the only four legitimate sources of information at the grand jury's disposal:

1. Matters brought to its attention by the Massachusetts Supreme Court.

2. Matters introduced by District Attorney Dinis.

3. Matters that might come out unexpectedly in the course of the probe.

4. Matters known to jurors personally.

The grand jury could summon witnesses "*that are able to give useful information,*" said the judge, and could move to indict "if it found evidence of perjury or of attempts to influence its verdict."* This latter offense, he observed, was a very serious one of which he should be informed immediately. The course of the ensuing events showed the irony of those last remarks. No relevant witness was allowed to be heard by the Dukes County Grand Jury; no opportunity was given to it, therefore, to discover and indict anyone for perjury; and the almost terroristic influence that was exercised on it emanated from untouchable quarters, from the Supreme Court in Boston and from Judge Paquet himself.

---

*The grand jury would understand later what "able to give" meant.

Judge Paquet sternly reminded the grand jury that it was only an appendage of his court and could neither appeal to any higher judicial authority nor seek judicial review of his ruling, if he refused to permit the jurors to see the transcript of last January's inquest. It would have been embarrassing for him to add *in the open "charge" session* that he could legally forbid the jurors, for the same reasons of obligatory secrecy, to subpoena any of the witnesses (including Senator Kennedy) whose top-secret testimony was recorded in the impounded transcripts. Such a ruling, if openly given, could have been immediately and publicly challenged: *how had grand juries functioned in Massachusetts during the last 150 years,* and how would they function from now on?

The public "charge" session "was businesslike and even grim," said the newspapers. So intense was the determination of Judge Paquet to seal any possible exit for what might occur during the grand jury session that he decided to reinforce the grimness of the atmosphere he had created around the twenty jurors by the solemnity of a short religious performance. Not bothering about the "constitutionality" of this unprecedented and extraordinary move, *he brought with him and invited to his bench the Reverend Donald Cousa, pastor of St. Elizabeth's Church. Father Cousa offered a short prayer for "prejudice to be set aside and replaced by charity."*

Leslie H. Leland, the grand jury foreman, was a druggist from Vineyard Haven, aged 29. He had insisted upon the convocation of the grand jury, and had pompously declared that "the case was now the grand jury's responsibility" and that "the public has a right to know what is there and what is not there." All the other members of the grand jury were middle-aged or elderly persons. Their young foreman had received, the day before the opening session, several threatening telephone calls, and he was brought to court by an impressive escort of two Vineyard Haven police officers and three state troopers. The difference between his pre-session bombast and his pussyfooting behavior before the high-handedness of the supervising judge and the prosecuting attorney was proof enough that a better choice to lead the investigating grand jury could have been made among the honest and vigorous population of Martha's Vineyard, who were all more eager to clear up the mystery of a young girl's still unexplained death than to protect a Senator's political career.

Concerning what happened behind the closed doors of the grand jury room between the twenty jurors and District Attorney Dinis, we have the following sources of information:

1. That part of events that was of public knowledge, by judicial definition.

2. Circumstances unavoidably observable to the press and the public eye.

3. Facts that could be safely deduced from (1) and (2).

4. The reactions of the jurors after their abrupt dismissal by Judge Paquet and District Attorney Dinis.

Scanty as those elements of information were, they were fully sufficient to justify the opinion of the *Chicago Tribune:*

> This is the kind of thing that has hampered any effective investigation of the case from the beginning.

Mentioning the surprise ruling by which the Massachusetts Supreme Court — revising a 97-year-old statute ad hoc for Senator Kennedy's benefit — decided that the proceedings of the inquest on Miss Kopechne's death would be kept secret and their transcript impounded *until the prosecuting attorney certified that there would be no further action in the case,* the *Tribune* editorial continued:

> This remarkable ruling, depriving the Grand Jury of access to the record, amounted to a directive to the district attorney to pledge that there would be no prosecution of Senator Kennedy. The senator has been given special benefits and kid glove

treatment *from every court before which he has been repre-sented.* His only court appearance was to enter a plea of guilty to leaving the scene of the accident. He was let off with a two-month suspended sentence. From the start events in the case have been inexplicable .... Those events, with a certain amount of assistance from courts and public officials, have certainly conspired to protect Senator Kennedy at every turn of this strange sequence. *Now the sudden abandonment of the grand jury investigation indicates what has been a virtual certainty from the beginning: that the true facts of the episode will forever remain veiled.* [Emphasis added.]

It was Judge Paquet himself who made it known that he had denied to the grand jury the requested access to the secret inquest's records because of the Massachusetts Supreme Court ruling that those records were to be impounded until the moment the prosecutor informed the Court that there would be no further action in this case. What the court grapevine brought to light, and what fifty newspapermen could confirm by observing persons who emerged from the courthouse, was that *the grand jury was also forbidden to hear any of the witnesses who had been heard at the closed-door inquest.*

We will probably never know the exact words District Attorney Dinis employed to convince the jurors that only new and previously unheard witnesses could be called by them, since the lips of those jurors had been sealed by Judge Paquet and — quite unconstitutionally, we fear — by the Reverend Donald Cousa. We know, however, that the discussion between prosecutor and jurors lasted five hours, and that Dinis's chief argument was very much to the point: the witnesses heard by Judge Boyle at the closed inquest were all bound, by the same Supreme Court ruling, to absolute secrecy about all that they had said in Judge Boyle's court until the written records should have been released by order of the Supreme Court. So what would be the use of calling them before this release had been given?

The grand jury heard two witnesses the first day and two the second day. They spent a total of about twenty minutes in the courthouse. *None of them had appeared before Judge Boyle's closed court of inquiry. All of them were from Edgartown, none from Chappaquiddick.*

Miss Nina L. Trott, reservation manager at the Shiretown Inn, and Benjamin Hall, who lives near the hotel, were asked whether they had seen Kennedy in Edgartown the night of July 19, when, according to his police report, he had wandered through the streets for an indefinite length of time in his wet clothes and soaked shoes. They said they had not seen him, that they were sleeping at that time. Mr. Stephen Gentle, owner of a small private air-strip on the outskirts of Edgartown, who had rented the cottage for the cook-out party, was asked whether he knew anything about an airplane which allegedly had flown Senator Kennedy to the mainland and back to Martha's Vineyard at about 3:00 a.m. on July 19. He told reporters that he knew of no such flight. Mr. Joseph Carrel, former Democrat selectman and friend of Kennedy, who did fly Kennedy to the Hyannis Port retreat the day Mary Jo's body was discovered in Kennedy's car, was called; he remained in the courthouse only a few minutes, and there is no clue to what he may have said to the jury.

Neither Deputy Sheriff Christopher Look, who had seen the Kennedy car on dry ground an hour and a half after Kennedy declared it was at the bottom of Poucha Pond, nor scuba diver John Farrar, who removed Mary Jo's body from the submerged car, was summoned to testify. *Both were in Edgartown the day of the grand jury session; both had declared they were ready to testify; both had been heard previously at Judge Boyle's secret inquest.*

"When the jury assembled yesterday morning," Homer Bigart, the *New York Times* correspondent, reported next day, "Mr. Leland seemed convinced that the panel could begin a bold independent investigation even if Judge Paquet refused to let it see the inquest transcript." However, twenty-four hours later, when he was asked by Judge Paquet, "Have you any presentments [i.e., indictment] to make?" Leland answered — ill-humoredly and without rising — "No, I have no presentment to make." Maintaining the boorish attitude he had judged it proper to adopt toward the Dukes County Grand Jury from the beginning, Judge Paquet shouted at him: "Stand up! Not you! Has the jury any presentments to make?" Leland stood up, looking very unhappy, according to the press, and answered: "The grand jury has no presentment to make."

Paquet then thanked the jurors, reminding them once more that "secrecy must continue," and recessed the grand jury until a new panel could be sworn in, at which time, he added rather lugubriously to the already gloomy-looking jurors, "the heartbeats of this jury will cease." And after once more blasting the members of the press, who could not restrain themselves from some whispered comment on the precipitate ending of a case that for nine months had obsessed and plagued them and millions of other people in the United States and abroad, he departed for Boston with dignity and satisfaction.

Dinis looked happy and relieved when from the steps of the old Dukes County Court House he announced:

> The case is closed. I will file the appropriate certificate required by the Court to notify the clerk there is no proposed prosecution in this matter. That should clear the way to the release of the inquest transcript and the judge's report. *This is the end of the investigation into the death of Mary Jo Kopechne.* [Emphasis added.]

An unidentified juror made the following declaration to the *Manchester Union Leader* reporter concerning District Attorney Dinis's behavior during the two-day grand jury session:

The District Attorney offered us no help at all in our investigation. In fact Dinis did everything he could to discourage our probe into the case. I wish we could have had an unbiased district attorney leading us, and we might have accomplished something. The district attorney had all the facts and evidence before him long before the inquest. He could have acted, but instead he played politics with the whole situation.

It is, indeed, one of the strange features of the grand jury phase of the Kennedy-Kopechne affair that the prosecution was entrusted to a man who had declared five months earlier that he would seek re-election on the same ticket as the person chiefly involved in the death of the young girl. When one remembers that Judge Boyle had already sentenced Kennedy in this very case to the mildest penalty possible under Massachusetts law, and that Judge Paquet had previously been saved from what could have been a professional disgrace by Edward R. Hanify, the chief Kennedy attorney, one wonders at the number of jurists who might in all fairness have been expected to disqualify themselves and who had nevertheless remained in charge of the last effort to discover the truth about the circumstances in which Mary Jo Kopechne met her death.

When the same reporters asked Leslie Leland's opinion concerning the unnamed juror's allegation, he told them:

> We are supposed to have freedom of speech in this country, and yet by the judge's ruling I cannot ever speak my own personal opinion on the subject. To me this is a scare tactic. If I say one word about what transpired in the Grand Jury room, I can go to jail for two years . . . . I don't believe justice was served here . . . . One day some member of the Grand Jury will defy Judge Paquet's order *and tell all.* * [Emphasis added.]

---

*We venture to suggest that that member be Leslie Leland himself, and that day no later than tomorrow. This would be the only way to atone for the timidity and the incompetence he displayed as foreman of the Dukes County Grand Jury. Further, any future Dukes County Grand Jury could ask the Bedford County Superior Court to be relieved of any obligation of secrecy concerning the Kopechne inquiry, now that the transcript has been published. A negative answer would be sufficiently significant.

From *Human Events:*

> Dinis' performance in the Kennedy affair has been puzzling from the very start. In the days following the fatal accident, Dinis, a politically ambitious Democrat, stayed as far away from the case as he could. But as criticism mounted against his lack of action, Dinis pushed for an inquest and loudly — and futilely — demanded that Pennsylvania authorities permit Mary Jo's body to be exhumed. Behind the scenes Dinis did little to press the case . . . . When the Dukes County Grand Jury sought to reopen the case, to see if felony charges might be brought against Kennedy, Dinis fought their efforts behind closed doors. "He did not want us to look into the case," said one jury member. "He was adamant against prosecution. Without his assistance we were helpless."

To the same reporters the dismayed foreman of the bamboozled grand jury confided:

> Our hands were tied by legal manipulations. Judge Paquet stressed the fact that we were only to consider new evidence gained by our own knowledge, or presented by the district attorney. What chance did we have to learn of any new evidence on our own, either before or during the Grand Jury session?

The bullying of the grand jury had already started when, in January, Massachusetts Attorney General Robert H. Quinn warned foreman Leslie Leland that he could not act independently of the court of which the grand jury was an "appendage," or of the district attorney. As for the excision of the grand jury's organs of information, that was implied in the Massachusetts Supreme Court's ruling on the secrecy of the coming inquest; this is how it worked:

According to the Supreme Court ruling the transcript of the inquest and the report of Judge Boyle would be available to the public only after the district attorney had filed with the Superior Court a written certificate that there would be no prosecution in the case.

The jurors were informed that the Supreme Court ruling applied *not only to the general public but to them as well.* Until the written certificate had been filed they could neither have access to the inquest record nor call any of the witnesses who had been heard at the inquest.

In other words, they were to decide whether or not there should be further prosecution, but would be denied any significant means of information that would help them reach a decision until they had decided there should be none!

Judge Paquet tried to avoid letting the public learn of the interdiction against the calling of any relevant witnesses by warning the jurors that their lips were closed, before God and man, about whatever District Attorney Dinis would tell them. If publicized, this precedent would have prevented the rational functioning of any future grand jury in Massachusetts, the new secrecy "law" being supposedly general in application to all future inquests.

One is inescapably reminded of Frederick the Great's admiring exclamation: "There are judges in Berlin!" So are there judges in Boston!

CHAPTER XX

Deputy Sheriff Look's Testimony

The pages of Judge Boyle's report (reprinted in Appendix A) lead to the conclusion — expressed in the most moderate possible terms — that Senator Kennedy lied under oath about his actions on the night of July 18-19, 1969, when Mary Jo Kopechne met her death. Truth and justice must be grateful to Judge Boyle for having thus established legally what millions of his fellow citizens had already known since Kennedy's TV appearance of July 25. But the Massachusetts Senator owes him even greater gratitude for not having examined more deeply into the range and scope of the fraud, and for not having formulated recommendations corresponding to the offense.

"I infer that a reasonable and probable explanation of the totality of the above facts," wrote the judge, "is that Kennedy and Kopechne did *not* intend to return to Edgartown at that time; that Kennedy did *not* intend to drive to the ferry slip and his turn onto Dyke Road was intentional." (The emphasis here is Judge Boyle's.)

The twelve facts enumerated by Judge Boyle as proof that Kennedy had lied concerning his intentions when he left the cottage with Mary Jo were quite sufficient to justify not only such a "reasonable inference" but also a recommendation for further legal action. Said the *Chicago Tribune*:

> The terrible judgment on Senator Kennedy's conduct emphasizes the dereliction of Massachusetts authorities, from the

local police to the state's Supreme Court, in this extraordinary
case. Even Judge Boyle, whose courage was not lacking when he
submitted his report, did not recommend prosecution for perjury
or anything else. Neither did he cross-examine or permit the
district attorney to cross-examine Kennedy, who was treated with
the utmost gentleness, although his story could have been
discredited by any competent lawyer.

"Having reached this conclusion," the judge wrote further
in his report, "the question then arises if there was anything
criminal in his [Kennedy's] operation of the motor vehicle."
The question that arises is much more important than that. If
Kennedy did not leave the cottage at 11:15 with the
intention of catching the midnight ferry with Miss Kopechne,
what were his intentions? If they were no more reprehensible
than a ride to the beach with one of the six girls invited to
the cook-out — and if things really happened as Kennedy and
his companions told the acquiescent judge and the uninquisi-
tive district attorney — why all the prolonged and concerted
effort that followed to avoid, first, any examination, and
then, if that proved impossible, any public examination; and
why the concerted imposture?

A review of the examination of Kennedy and his companions by Judge Boyle and District Attorney Dinis seems to
show that this examination was aimed at limiting the issue to
the possibility of negligent or perhaps reckless driving. The
question of perjury had been taken care of by Judge Boyle's
precaution of declaring himself reasonably suspicious but not
convinced that Kennedy had lied. As for the failure of
Kennedy to appeal to the professional help that was within
his reach to save Mary Jo's life, the judge disposed of that
with the following words:

> The failure of Kennedy to seek *additional* assistance in
> searching for Kopechne, whether excused by his condition, or
> whether or not it would have been of any material help, has not
> been pursued because such failure, even when shown, does not

constitute criminal conduct. Since there was no evidence that any air remained in the submerged car, testimony was not sought or allowed concerning how long Kopechne might have lived had such a condition existed, as this could only be conjectured and purely speculative. [Emphasis added.]

Judge Boyle in his findings concluded that "death probably occurred between 11:30 p.m. on July 18, 1969, and 1:00 a.m. on July 19, 1969." That leaves a margin of one hour and a half. If testimony had been taken concerning the pocket of air that could have remained in the car during that hour and a half, the court might have decided that this testimony was not sufficient to prove anything; but testimony was not allowed. Scuba diver Farrar was not permitted to enter upon the subject. Imagine that, under exactly the same time-circumstances, the victim of a fatal traffic accident had been abandoned on the road by the operator of the car involved, for a period of an hour and a half or longer. Would not Massachusetts law, contrary to Judge Boyle's assertion, consider that this abandonment had wantonly and criminally contributed to the death of the victim and therefore constituted manslaughter, without special attention to the exact moment at which the victim might have breathed his last?

By talking of "additional assistance" Judge Boyle took it upon himself to give, for the second time in his report, the court's confirmation to the alleged rescue efforts of the three night prowlers. He did it the first time when in his report he informed the Superior Court that "he [Kennedy] summoned Gargan and Markham, without notifying the others, and they returned in the Valiant to the bridge, where Gargan and Markham unsuccessfully attempted to recover Kopechne." There is no other evidence concerning the heroic efforts of Kennedy, Gargan, and Markham than their own declarations: the declarations of a man convicted of lying under oath by

Judge Boyle himself, and of two of his friends who, like the rest of the Lawrence cottage party, had had six months to adjust their testimony to that of the lying Senator. Moreover, what strikes the reader of the seven hundred sixty-three pages of testimony is the fact that the most important result of the way the inquest was conducted was the official legal stamp of approval it gave to every statement, every assertion of the six males and five surviving females involved in what is still the Chappaquiddick mystery. Not that Judge Boyle did not realize that something was being hushed up by all the members of the Lawrence cottage party. *"As previously stated,"* said the judge toward the end of his report, *"there are inconsistencies and contradictions in the testimony, which a comparison of individual testimony will show. It is not feasible to attempt to indicate each one."* If the judge presiding over the secret inquest found it troublesome to spot and enumerate in the final report all the inconsistencies and contradictions sprinkled over the seven hundred sixty-three pages of transcript, how many of his fellow citizens will have the opportunity or the leisure to do so?

In fact, none of those contradictions and those inconsistencies were really challenged, or even really questioned. Sterner methods could have led the inquest to more significant issues than Kennedy's lies concerning the intent of his ride with Miss Kopechne; and *that was what was to be avoided.* In that respect, the most difficult moments of the inquest, for the presiding judge and the district attorney, were certainly those of Deputy Sheriff Christopher Look's testimony.

The autopsy scandal, and the juggling away of the evidence brought by Christopher Look, are the high points in the common effort of so many to conceal what really happened that tragic July night. We will never know what an autopsy would have brought to light. The only indication we have of what might have been its relevance and importance lies in all the trouble that was taken to prevent, first, a thorough, immediate post-mortem examination of the body, and later, an exhumation for the purpose of performing a belated autopsy. The Look testimony is another matter. It would have been, *and still is*, sufficient to tear apart the tangled web of all those seven hundred sixty-three pages of evidence and to prove that the testimony of the eleven surviving members of the "strictly for fun" party had only one purpose — not to contradict, and even to support, a central imposture, whose unmasking might have provided and might still provide the key to the mystery of Mary Jo Kopechne's death.

Even before the towing of the Kennedy car from the Chappaquiddick tidal pond onto dry ground, Dukes County Deputy Sheriff Christopher F. Look Jr. had given Patrolman Robert Brougier the description of a car he had seen the night of the accident at the junction of the Chappaquiddick main road and the road to Dyke Bridge. The moment he saw the car as it emerged from the water, he exclaimed without hesitation: *"That's the same car I saw last night."* We may note that at that time none of the persons gathered at the site of the accident knew to whom the car belonged or that Senator Kennedy was involved. Christopher Look's testimony is, therefore, from the very beginning, without political implications — something that can hardly be said of much of the testimony that was accepted without objection by the presiding judge and the district attorney during the closed inquest.

Look's testimony under oath before Judge Boyle's court of inquiry was as categorical on the chief points involved as his deposition, also under oath, before Judge Brominski. We find it useful, however, to record it the way Judge Boyle wanted to hear it. According to the transcript of testimony in the closed court in Edgartown, Look saw, at about 12:45 a.m. on July 19, a "dark-colored" car with two persons in the front seat, "and also either another person or an object of clothing, a handbag or something, sitting on the back."

Look explained in detail the circumstances under which he observed the car:

> . . . the car passed directly in front of me about 35 feet away from my car, my headlights were on this car, and right across and then stopped. I continued around the corner and stopped and I noticed the car lights were backing up, and I said to myself, Well, they probably want some information; so I stopped my car and got out and started to walk back to them on Cemetery Road. I got about 25 or 30 feet when the car was backing up and backed toward the ferry landing on the macadamized road, and then it drove down the Dyke Road.

He said, as he had said to Officer Brougier, that the dark car had a Massachusetts registration number that "began with an L and had a 7 at the beginning and one at the end." The license number of Kennedy's black Oldsmobile sedan was L78-207.

Reporting before Judge Boyle on the scene when Kennedy's car was taken from the water the next morning, Look testified:

> As soon as they started to pull it out and it became visible, I walked over and told Officer Brougier, gee, that is the same car I saw last night . . . I didn't examine it that closely. I just looked quickly and decided in my own mind that was the same one I had seen and I walked over and mentioned it to Officer Brougier.

As the time question involved in Christopher Look's testimony is of the utmost importance in connection with the truth about the tragic night and the efforts that were, or were not, made to discover this truth, we do not hesitate to be repetitive. Here is Judge Boyle's rendering of Look's testimony:

Christopher F. Look Jr., a deputy sheriff, then living on Chappaquiddick, was driving easterly on Chappaquiddick Road to his home at about 12:45 a.m. on July 19. As he approached the junction of Dyke Road, a car crossed in front of him and entered Cemetery Road, stopped, backed up, and drove easterly on Dyke Road. He saw two persons in the front seat and a shadow *on the shelf back of the rear seat* which he thought could have been a bag, article of clothing, or a third person. The car was dark-colored with Massachusetts registration plate L7 − 7. He was unable to remember any other number or *how many there were intervening.* Later that morning he saw the Kennedy Oldsmobile when it was towed to shore, *but he cannot positively identify it as the same car he saw at 12:45.* [Emphasis added.]

We observe that the number of intervening figures was implicit in what Look called his photographic image of the numbers. However, Judge Boyle, as we shall see, did not permit him to insist upon this fact.

Judge Boyle did not fail to realize the importance of Look's testimony.

His report continues:

During the inquest, an investigation was initiated through the Registry of Motor Vehicles to determine whether a tracking of the location on July 18 and 19, 1969, of all dark-colored cars bearing Massachusetts plates with any and all combinations of numbers beginning with L7 and ending in 7 would be practicable. The attempt disclosed that it would not be feasible to do this since there would be no assurance that the end result would be helpful *and, in any event, the elimination of all other cars within the registration group (although it would seriously affect the credibility of some of the witnesses) would not alter the findings in this report.* [Emphasis added.]

In these days of systematic card-indexing and computers, police have been able to solve more difficult problems than the elimination of the possible presence of any car but one, of all those which (1) bore Massachusetts plates, (2) had L7 − 7 plates, (3) were dark in color, (4) were four-door sedans, and (5) were, that night, on the road leading to the Dyke Bridge on Chappaquiddick Island. But Judge Boyle, who lived on Martha's Vineyard not far from the police station and the ferry slip, should have known that such an investigation, even if worthwhile for those who were not afraid of the truth, was not necessary.

According to the police investigation and the ferry men's statements, no other car, whether corresponding with Christopher Look's description or not, had crossed from Chappaquiddick to Edgartown on the ferry after 12:45 a.m. on July 19; and none corresponding to the description had been seen crossing from Chappaquiddick to Edgartown the next morning while everyone's attention was concentrated on the accident and its strange circumstances. So if a double of the Kennedy car had crossed to Chappaquiddick on Friday or any previous day by ferry (the only way of getting there), it would still have been on the island on Saturday, and could not have gone unnoticed by the officials who were gathered there and by the island's inhabitants. It should in fact still be on Chappaquiddick Island!

What is very difficult to understand is the flagrant contradiction in Judge Boyle's final comment on Look's testimony, quoted above. If the validation of this testimony "would seriously affect the credibility of some of the witnesses," beginning with Edward Kennedy himself, how could the Judge assert that "it would not alter the findings of the report?"

The fact is that any serious investigation concerning Look's very positive statement would have proved its truthfulness, and by the same token would have proved that the totality of Kennedy's statements and those of his companions — all irrevocably predicated upon the time of the accident testified to by Kennedy under oath — were mendacious and therefore perjured. This would have forced Judge Boyle to recommend further action by any proper judicial means, a criminal trial included, and it would very likely have brought finally to light the true story of the Chappaquiddick tragedy.

But that was what everyone concerned — the parents of Mary Jo included — seemed to be determined to avoid.

To all the elements of proof which convinced Judge Boyle that Kennedy had lied when he stated under oath that his intention in leaving the cottage with Mary Jo was to reach the ferry slip before midnight, the judge could have added a clinching argument by observing what the Senator had declared at the police station: "I was driving a car on the high road in order to reach the ferry to Edgartown. I was not familiar with the road and I turned to the right instead of turning to the left." But the next week he did not dare to give the same explanation to his TV audience, and contented himself with this modest description of the situation: "A little over one mile away the car that I was driving on an unlit road went off a narrow bridge which had no guard rails and was built on a left angle to the road."

It seems that Judge Boyle had, unfortunately for the cause of justice, adopted a rule of not permitting the district attorney or his substitute to confront Kennedy and other witnesses with the contradictions between their earlier statements and those they offered in his court. Here are some instances:

> District Attorney DINIS. With regard to the statement you made at the police station, Senator. You wind up by saying, "When I fully realized what happened this morning, I immediately contacted the police." Now, is that what you did?

That was not at all what the Senator did, as was amply proved by known facts and sworn testimony, and it was evident that Kennedy had lied that time also. Had Dinis been permitted to insist, Kennedy would have been forced to admit and explain the discrepancy between his two stories. But Judge Boyle spared him this painful necessity.

> The COURT (interrupting). Mr. Dinis, are you going to ask that the statement be put on the record?
> Mr. DINIS. Yes, your honor.
> The COURT. Mr. Kennedy has already said that this was a copy of the statement he made. He already testified as to all his movements. *Now, won't you let the record speak for itself?*
> Mr. DINIS. All right, your honor. [Emphasis added.]

A few minutes later another opportunity to pinpoint a *crucial contradiction* between Kennedy's two statements presented itself:

> Mr. DINIS: Well, did you at that time ask anyone to take you back directly to Edgartown?
> Senator KENNEDY. No, I asked Mr. Gargan to go to the scene of the accident.
> Mr. DINIS. But you did not ask anyone to take you back directly to Edgartown?
> Senator KENNEDY. I asked them to take me to Edgartown after their diving.
> Mr. DINIS. After the diving?
> Senator KENNEDY. After the diving.
> Mr. DINIS. I show you, Mr. Kennedy, what purports to be a copy of the televised broadcast which you made approximately a week after the accident. Would you read the statement and tell me whether or not that is an exact copy of what you said.
> Senator KENNEDY. Yes, I would say that it is accurate.

At the police station Kennedy had declared: "I sat in the rear seat and asked someone to drive me again to Edgartown." The whole story of the second drive to the Dyke Bridge, and of Markham and Gargan's heroic efforts to save Mary Jo, was offered to the public only a week later, and here was an opportunity to extract an explanation of the differences between the two from the Senator. But Dinis could do nothing but conform with the Court's instructions. There was no confrontation of Kennedy with the contradictory statements; his statements at the police station and on TV were simply passed as Exhibits No. 2 and 3, according to the transcript.

There was still another opportunity to probe by direct interrogation the authenticity of this second trip to the bridge, and of those alleged rescue attempts. Judge Boyle understood its importance immediately, and promptly quashed it.

Mr. Ross W. Richards is a friend of Senator Kennedy and a fellow yachtsman. He had won the regatta of July 18, had occupied rooms adjacent to Kennedy's at the Shiretown Inn, and had had a long talk with him the morning of the accident, between 7:30 and 8:00 a.m. The following is an excerpt from Mr. Richards' examination by Assistant District Attorney Fernandes:

> Mr. FERNANDES. You said the Senator discussed the possibility of joining you at breakfast later?
> Mr. RICHARDS. Later.
> Mr. FERNANDES. And then you say Mr. Markham and Mr. Gargan came to the deck?
> Mr. RICHARDS. Yes, sir.
> Mr. FERNANDES. And could you please describe to the Court what observation you made of those two gentlemen at the time?
> Mr. RICHARDS. They were ruffled looking. I would say they looked damp. Their hair had not been combed in some time.
> Mr. FERNANDES. And when you say damp, what do you mean?
> Mr. RICHARDS. Well, just what I said, that they appeared that they might have been wet from the night dew or fog or something.
> Mr. FERNANDES. Well, let me refresh your recollection, Mr. Richards. Did you have a conversation with Lieutenant Dunn in your office?
> Mr. RICHARDS. Yes, sir.

Mr. FERNANDES. And do you recall telling him that they were both soaking wet? Did you use those words with Lieutenant Dunn?

Mr. RICHARDS. *I don't remember.*

Mr. FERNANDES. Well, let me see if this refreshes your recollection. Shortly before the 8 o'clock bell rang . . .

The COURT. Just a moment, I am not going to allow —

Mr. FERNANDES. I am just refreshing his recollection.

The COURT. I am not going to allow impeachment!

Mr. FERNANDES. If your Honor please, I don't offer it for impeachment, only to refresh his recollection.

The COURT. No, I am not going to allow it. [Emphasis added.]

Judge Boyle's violent interruption is understandable. At the moment of Mr. Richards' conversation with Lieutenant Dunn, and for a week longer, nobody knew that Markham and Gargan were supposed to have immersed themselves that night, either in the nude or fully clothed and shod. What Fernandes was aiming at — six months after the fact — was, very likely, to learn what *or who* had given Mr. Richards the idea of anticipatively accrediting an incident which, if it really happened, was known at that time only to Kennedy, Markham, and Gargan.

The mentioned instances should help in understanding why Judge Boyle did not like Deputy Sheriff Look's testimony either, and why he took the trouble to reduce it to the uncertainty of hearsay, by suave, persuasive, authoritative cross-examination:

The COURT. Could you be any more definite about the color of the car, other than that it was a dark color?

Deputy Sheriff LOOK. No, sir, that it was *either black or dark blue* —

The COURT. Or dark green, any color? You could not identify it as being definitely of the same color as the car you saw taken out of the water?

Deputy Sheriff LOOK. No, sir.

The COURT. And you recognized or you saw a letter, a 7, and then another 7 at the end?

Deputy Sheriff LOOK. Yes, sir.

The COURT. Do you remember how many numbers, letters and numbers, there were on the plate?

Deputy Sheriff LOOK. *Since that time —*

The COURT. *No, no, I mean then.*

Deputy Sheriff LOOK. No, sir.

The COURT. So that when you saw this number on the car that came out of the water, you can't identify that as being the same identical number that you saw the previous night?

Deputy Sheriff LOOK. *In my opinion —*

The COURT. *No, I am talking about the positive identification.*

Deputy Sheriff LOOK. No, I can't.

The COURT. You can't identify the exact color?

Deputy Sheriff LOOK. No, sir.

The COURT. Or the exact plate number?

Deputy Sheriff LOOK. No, sir. [Emphasis added.]

This was one of the moments when Court and lawyers must have congratulated themselves on the absence of three hundred forty watchful and critical international newsmen from the courtroom.

Hanify, indeed, could not have done better. But Judge Boyle went perhaps a little too far when he tried — successfully — to introduce the idea of *a shelf* into Look's testimony, so that he could insert it into his report later:

The COURT. Now, I am speculating a little bit, but it looks as though this car has in the rear, as many cars do, sort of a little shelf?

Deputy Sheriff LOOK. Yes, sir.

The COURT. And I take it it was on that shelf where you saw what you thought might be a person, or a bag, or some clothing?

Deputy Sheriff LOOK. Clothing on that side of the car, yes.

So what Christopher Look really saw could not have been a person. A person does not lie or sit on a shelf. *Quod erat demonstrandum.*

Judge Boyle had no more right to introduce the idea of a "shelf" into his report as having originated with Christopher Look than he had to declare that "later that morning he [Look] saw the Kennedy Oldsmobile when it was towed to shore, but he cannot positively identify it as the same car he saw at 12:45." The "shelf" was Judge Boyle's idea, and Look did identify Kennedy's car positively and without any hesitation, when it was towed from Poucha Pond waters the next morning, as the same car he had seen at 12:45 a.m.

The following colloquy between Judge Boyle, District Attorney Dinis, and Fernandes could only increase our perplexity about the final disregard of Look's crucial testimony in the judge's report:

> The COURT. Mr. Dinis, did you make any investigation through the Registry of Motor Vehicles to determine how many cars in Massachusetts are registered with the L7 hm-hm-hm 7?
> Mr. DINIS. No, your Honor, we did not.
> The COURT. *I think it is so important that I will even postpone the inquest. Now, I don't know, it may turn out that there is no other car that has L7 and an ending, or it could be that any other combination could be a white car.* [Emphasis added.]
> Mr. DINIS. We could have that in an hour, I think.
> Mr. FERNANDES. Your Honor, we will start it right away. I will get on it with the Lieutenant.

In the inquest transcript we find no trace of any results of the investigation that Dinis and Fernandes intended to start immediately and to conclude in an hour. The FBI once, after studying 180,000 applications in the New York State Motor Vehicle Registry, identified the kidnaper of a baby by the peculiar way he formed his T's. No such effort would have been necessary in the search for a car corresponding to Look's description that (a) could have been at that Chappaquiddick crossroad at 12:45 a.m. on July 19 and (b) was not the Kennedy car.

Mathematically speaking, there could be 1110 cars with Massachusetts registration numbers beginning with L7, ending with 7, and having three intermediate numerals. But even by admitting only that part of Look's description that was admitted by Judge Boyle — a four-door sedan of very dark color — the number of cars to consider would have been considerably reduced. Indeed, a careful look into any crowded parking lot will show that there are at least ten times more light-colored cars than dark-colored ones, and at least twice as many two-door models as four-door models. These very conservative figures alone would reduce the number of necessary investigations to *fifty-five*. And taking into account the number of cars of all types — station wagons, convertibles, two-tone jobs, and foreign, compact, and sport cars — that Look could not possibly have mistaken for Kennedy's Oldsmobile, it is clear that the number of Massachusetts cars whose whereabouts would have had to be determined for the night of Mary Jo's death would have again been sharply reduced.

Dinis and Fernandes knew this very well when they assured Judge Boyle that they could have the required results "in one hour." Then why did not the Court order the investigation that could have proved Kennedy right and Look wrong, and why did not Kennedy's lawyers demand it? The answer is obvious: they knew that the results of such an investigation would have been disastrous to the Senator.

CHAPTER XXI

Judge Boyle's Report
And Other Neglected Points

The two points involved here and the corresponding testimony, although concerned with two different moments of the sunken car chronicle, both have the same orientation value, in the study of the seven hundred sixty-three pages of transcript. The first concerns the verisimilitude of some of the most important statements offered to Judge Boyle; the second puts a finishing touch to what we have called the autopsy scandal.

As was to be expected, the most reliable testimony in the Chappaquiddick tragedy came from local people who had no personal connection with any of the cottage guests, and no personal involvement in the tragedy. The following excerpt is from the testimony of Mr. Jared Grant, owner and operator of the Chappaquiddick ferry, who was interrogated by Assistant District Attorney Fernandes:

> Mr. FERNANDES. Were you available for calls if someone wanted the ferry that night [the night of the accident]?
> Mr. GRANT. I was.
> Mr. FERNANDES. Was this standard procedure with your ferry operation in the summertime at that time?
> Mr. GRANT. Year round we are on call twenty-four hours a day.
> Mr. FERNANDES. And is there a public telephone that you are aware of also on Chappaquiddick?
> Mr. GRANT. Yes.
> Mr. FERNANDES. When do you normally close down?

191

Mr. GRANT. Usually we close down at 12:00 and we get out of there usually around 12:30.

Mr. FERNANDES. And if someone wanted you after 12:00, where would they call?

Mr. GRANT. My house.

Mr. FERNANDES. Are those numbers posted on either side of the ferry?

Mr. GRANT. Yes.

Mr. FERNANDES. And did you receive any calls that night?

Mr. GRANT. No.

Mr. FERNANDES. If I am at Chappaquiddick and I want a ferry and you are not there at the landing, how do I find you? If I use a telephone, where does this call get me, to your home?

Mr. GRANT. Yes.

Mr. FERNANDES. A switchboard of some kind?

Mr. GRANT. No, there is a regular dial system and my number is posted.

Mr. FERNANDES. If I am on Chappaquiddick, the Chappaquiddick ferry area, and I want your attention, and I want you to come and pick me up, how do I do that?

Mr. GRANT. There is a bell on the side of the building over there.

Mr. FERNANDES. If you are not there I would use the telephone and as a result of the call you would arrive?

Mr. GRANT. Yes. Usually what people do is drive up to the ramp with their lights on, and leave them on, and we come and get them. If they should happen to walk down, if you don't see anybody, it being dark over there, they ring the bell to come across.

So it was well established that if the eight persons remaining at the cottage had wanted to reach Edgartown that night they could have done so by ferry any time they wished, and the three persons who that night faced the fast-running water at the ferry slip had at their disposal not only the telephone but also a bell and the necessary directions for calling the ferry operator to come and take them across. Why did they not do so? Why did they choose instead to let one of their number swim across? As long as no acceptable explanation for that extraordinary behavior is given, there will be only two possible answers to that question: one is that Kennedy in fact crossed the channel in a less hazardous way, but that for some reason important to his version of the accident he did not care to divulge it; the other, that his reason for leaving Chappaquiddick Island urgently and secretly was so imperative that he actually took the risk of crossing the dangerous channel in the way he described.

Both Gargan and Markham were asked to explain their behavior at the ferry landing. Both evaded the question completely and filled the emptiness of their answers with the emotional farrago characteristic of the Kennedy defense and the Kennedy defenders.

> Mr. DINIS. So you arrived at the ferry shortly after leaving Dyke Bridge?
>
> Mr. GARGAN. I wouldn't say shortly after. *I just don't know the answer to that question* because whether or not we drove around or went directly to Dyke Bridge, to tell you the truth *my memory is a blank.* I do remember arriving at Dyke Bridge and that we did have a conversation there for some ten minutes at the ferry slip but during this period of time we were conversing about the fact, number one, I said to him that we had to report the accident.
>
> The second thing I suggested to him was that he had to call Dave Burke immediately and that he ought to call Burke Marshall *before he reported to the police.* That was my suggestion. [Emphasis added.]

So we are informed once more by one of that trio of experienced lawyers that the delay in informing the proper authorities of the accident was caused by their urgent desire to get the assistance and advice of still more experienced attorneys, in view — as Senator Kennedy put it — of the myriad complications they could foresee. After identifying Dave Burke as the Senator's administrative assistant in Washington, Mr. Gargan went on:

Mr. GARGAN . . . . my suggestion was to call Dave Burke for one particular reason, Mr. Dinis, and that is that I had been present when Mrs. Kennedy, his mother, had received the call from the South Pacific when the president was missing. I know that Mrs. Kennedy had heard on the radio that her son had been shot. I know that, thirdly, she heard that Bob had been shot and I suggested to the Senator he call Dave Burke before he went to the police station, let the family know that he was all right [although Mary Jo was not], that this had happened, and then report it to the police, and I thought he should call Burke Marshall because Burke Marshall, so far as I know, was the best lawyer that I know.

Mr. DINIS. So you made no effort to call the family yourself?

Mr. GARGAN. I did not. I thought he should do it.

Was Mr. Markham, the former Massachusetts Attorney General, more helpful? The following is his account of the conversation with the Senator as the three confederates drove away from the scene of the accident:

Mr. DINIS. So I understand it, you and Mr. Gargan suggested that you get help and report it?

Mr. MARKHAM. That is correct. Report the accident.

Mr. DINIS. All right. When the suggestion about assistance, getting help, was that followed through in any way in the sense that someone said, "Let's get to the telephone, let's get the police"?

Mr. MARKHAM. At that time we were back in the car and Mr. Gargan was back driving the car. We came back down the road.

Mr. DINIS. Which road?

Mr. MARKHAM. The dirt road. We came up the dirt road.

Mr. DINIS. Before telling us about the conversation on the dirt road, did you notice any light or any house?

Mr. MARKHAM. *I did not, no, sir.*

Mr. DINIS. *Either lights or houses?*

Mr. MARKHAM. *No, sir.**

---

*It was obviously impossible for Markham and Gargan to have spent about forty-five minutes at the Dyke Bridge without seeing the Dyke House. Judge Boyle and District Attorney Dinis, who were familiar with the locality, knew this very well. Why did they let Markham get away with such an evident imposture? The other houses on the Dyke Road, too, were as visible to any passer-by as the Dyke House, even though they were not lighted.

Mr. DINIS. What conversation was going on, on the dirt road as you were driving? By the way, where were you going to?

Mr. MARKHAM. *I don't know.* We were just going back to the main road. The Senator again became very emotional. He was sobbing and on the verge of actually breaking down crying. He said, "This couldn't have happened, I don't know how it happened." I said, "Well, it did happen and it has happened." He said, "What am I going to do, what can I do?" "There is nothing you can do," and there was some suggestion between Joe and the Senator, about calling a Mr. Burke Marshall and also letting the family know . . . .

Mr. DINIS. Did you know where you were going? Did anyone say, "Take me to the ferry"?

Mr. MARKHAM. After this he said, "Okay, take me back to the ferry," and we got back to the ferry landing. By this time there were no ferries.

Mr. DINIS. Were you aware that the ferry could be summoned by using the telephone?

Mr. MARKHAM. *I don't know if I was aware or not.* [Emphasis added.]

The way Mr. Markham describes the Senator's swim is also not without interest.

Mr. DINIS. Did you watch him swim?

Mr. MARKHAM. Yes.

Mr. DINIS. For how long?

Mr. MARKHAM. Well, as far as we could see. Probably halfway across.

Mr. DINIS. Could you tell if he had continued on where he would come out of the water?

Mr. MARKHAM. On the other side.

Mr. DINIS. Where approximately, the ferry landing?

Mr. MARKHAM. Yes.

Mr. DINIS. Directly across?

Mr. MARKHAM. *I don't recall where the other ferry landing was.* I don't know if I could see it at that point.

Mr. DINIS. In time, Mr. Markham, approximately how long did it take you in observing him in the water?

Mr. MARKHAM. Approximately three or four minutes or so.

Mr. DINIS. Were you concerned with the fact of whether or not he would arrive safely on the other side?

Mr. MARKHAM. *No, I wasn't.* [Emphasis added.]

Before abandoning these two gentlemen we must observe that Mr. Markham seems to invoke the darkness of the night, as did Senator Kennedy and Mr. LaRosa for other reasons, to explain why he could not see the other ferry slip at a distance of 500 feet, or follow the Senator in his natation farther than approximately 250 feet. But according to the most reliable witness and to the calendar, the night of July 18-19 was a clear, bright night. From Assistant District Attorney Fernandes' interrogation of Jared Grant, the ferrymaster:

Mr. FERNANDES. Now, would you tell us what kind of a night was that? Do you remember the weather conditions?

Mr. GRANT. It was a beautiful night, very calm, the water was like glass. That is the reason I stayed there, because it was a humid night and it was too hot to sleep . . . .

* * *

Mr. FERNANDES. And you stayed at Edgartown until *20 minutes past one?*

Mr. GRANT. Yes.

Mr. FERNANDES. Are you pretty certain of the time?

Mr. GRANT. I am pretty certain within about five minutes . . . .

* * *

Mr. FERNANDES. Did you see anyone in the area when you left?

Mr. GRANT. There were a lot of people in the area.

Mr. FERNANDES. On what side?

Mr. GRANT. On the Edgartown side. It was the night of the regatta. *There were people on the dock; there were some people fishing off the dock; there were boats running back and forth in the Harbor.* [Emphasis added.]

Half-past one was the time at which, according to Mr. Gargan's testimony, he and Senator Kennedy and Mr.

Markham reached the ferry slip on the Chappaquiddick side, and about the time the Senator started his swim.

From Christopher Look's testimony:

> The COURT. There has been testimony that it was an extremely dark night.
> Deputy Sheriff LOOK. My recollection, sir, it would be a moonlit night.
> The COURT. You feel quite positive about this?
> Mr. LOOK. Yes, sir, at this particular time. From the time I got off work until I went home [the time he met LaRosa and the two girls] and I went to bed, it was a moonlit night.
> The COURT. Do you remember if the whole night was a moonlit night?
> Mr. LOOK. Yes, I think it was, sir.

On the fourth day of the inquest, Mr. Hanify included several affidavits as exhibits on behalf of Senator Kennedy. They consisted of: (1) an affidavit of Robert D. Watt, M.D., the Kennedys' family doctor; (2) a certificate of an x-ray examination from the Cape Cod Medical Center; (3) another x-ray certificate from the same source; (4) a medical certificate from Milton Brougham, M.D.; and (5) a certificate from the Boston Neurological Laboratory. These documents describe in about 2500 words the state of Senator Kennedy's health after the accident. The conclusion to be drawn from the diagnosis is, as Judge Boyle mentions in his report, that this state of health was consistent with "impairment of judgment and confused behavior." Anyone who has read the inquest transcript may decide for himself whether or not this diagnosis was consistent with the Senator's behavior — as testified to by himself, his friends, and reliable witnesses — from the moment of the accident until the moment he appeared in the police station at Edgartown and submitted to Chief Arena the unsigned report written by Mr. Markham.

Concerning Mary Jo's death, the transcript and its medical

annexes are less rich in information. There is, however, one bit of testimony concerning Mary Jo's death certificate, obtained by Assistant District Attorney Fernandes from Dr. Mills, to which the Court failed unaccountably to give the attention it deserved.

First, let us consider the examination of Dr. McHugh, the state police chemist, by Assistant District Attorney Fernandes and the Court:

> Mr. FERNANDES. Would you instruct the Court as to what is this benzidine test?
>
> Dr. McHUGH. A test that indicates the presence of blood on the material. This test had shown positive over certain areas of the submitted white shirt.
>
> The COURT. I think for the record you ought to say where it is, such as the back of the neck or the inside or something of that kind.
>
> Dr. McHUGH. If I might, I have it noted here. Let's see. Yes, sir. To continue, on gross examination of this item under visible and ultra-violet light disclosed the presence of reddish-brown and brown washed-out stains principally on the back and left sleeve surface. Most of these stains gave positive benzidine reaction indicating the presence of residual traces of blood.

Let us observe that those stains were visible to the eye, and that neither Dr. Mills nor the morticians in their report and testimony had mentioned them. As Mary Jo's body had been submerged in running water for about ten hours, it is no wonder the stains were "washed out"; and the fact that they were present at all seems to indicate that they had been present on the material *before its immersion.* Expert opinion on the subject would have been sought in any accusatory proceeding, such as, for instance, a grand jury hearing.

Further on, we read:

> The COURT. Would you point to those areas now?
>
> Dr. McHUGH. *This would be the back of the shirt, this whole area in here* gave positive benzidine tests. (Indicating.) To

continue, the back of both sleeves and the back of the right sleeve of the submitted shirt reacted positive, right sleeve in particular reacted positive to the benzidine test. It is the back of these two sleeves, extending down here. (Indicating.) *Unusually strong benzidine tests* were obtained on the outside rear collar area of the shirt. That would be along this area right here. (Indicating.) [Emphasis added.]

We are far here from the slightly blood-tinged foam reported initially by Dr. Mills.

Asked by the Court if the presence of blood on Mary Jo's garment was consistent with his diagnosis of death by drowning, Dr. Mills answered that it was.

> Mr. FERNANDES. Could you explain to the Court the reason why you formed that opinion.
> Dr. MILLS. In a drowning case — when a person drowns — there is what we call an exacerbation of blood or a putting out of blood from the lungs in the violent attempt to gain air, and blood, I believe usually perhaps more often than not, may be evidenced in the mouth and the nose of the decedent. Such blood might, in the effort, the physical effort to avoid drowning, might spread, I suppose almost everywhere to the person's clothing.

Again one feels the lack of complementary expert opinion concerning the possibility that the "very small amount" of blood released — to use Dr. Mills' own expression — would spread, if it spread at all, in such a submerged and agitated environment, otherwise than homogeneously and in extreme dilution. But the real interest of Dr. Mills' testimony lies in the precision of his answers concerning the wording and signing of the death certificate, which permitted, *retrospectively,* the embalming of Mary Jo's body and its subsequent transportation, under the supervision of a Kennedy secretary, out of the jurisdiction of the Massachusetts authorities:

The COURT. I have no further questions.

Mr. FERNANDES. Just one more. Did you at any time sign a death certificate?

Dr. MILLS. Yes.

Mr. FERNANDES. Will you tell us when and where?

Dr. MILLS. Yes, Mr. Guay and Mr. Gifford came to my office that afternoon when I was attempting to hold office hours.

Mr. FERNANDES. Do you know what time that was, approximately?

Dr. MILLS. 2:30 to 3:00 o'clock, *with a certificate for me to sign, which I did.*

Mr. FERNANDES. And you understood Mr. Gifford to be Mr. Kennedy's legislative assistant?

Dr. MILLS. That is right. He introduced himself to me.

Mr. FERNANDES. And you signed it at that time?

Dr. MILLS. I signed it at that time.

Mr. FERNANDES. And the death certificate indicated the cause of death?

Dr. MILLS. As asphyxiation by immersion. In other words, by drowning. [Emphasis added.]

That an official medical examiner should sign without hesitation a death certificate presented to him, and presumably drafted, by a secretary of the individual chiefly concerned in the death of a victim of a presumed accident, is strange enough. But stranger still, we believe, is the attitude of the responsible court, which seems not to have attached any importance to this extraordinary procedure.

CHAPTER XXII

The Phony Inquest: I

Senator Kennedy had only eleven hours, according to his timetable, to meditate on the report he dictated to Markham in the Edgartown police station. He had seven days to prepare, with the help of his lawyers, friends, and speech writers, the script for the TV performance. The eleven surviving members of the Chappaquiddick cook-out party were allowed six months to compose and coordinate their sworn testimony, to anticipate the questioning, and to polish their answers with the assistance of the cleverest professionals available.

The eleven companions of Mary Jo Kopechne who appeared before Judge Boyle can be divided into two groups: (1) the outer group, Kennedy, Markham, and Gargan, who on that July night, according to their own statements, came into direct contact with the place of the accident; and (2) the inner group, the five girls and three other men who, according to their statements, left the cottage that night only for some short or longer walks, and, if we must believe them, were unaware of what had happened at Poucha Pond until sometime the next morning.

Coordination of testimony was of course much easier among three than among eight. Kennedy, Markham, and Gargan had only to stick to Kennedy's first two statements, unreliable and inconsistent as they were, and to prop them up with as many suitable particulars as imagination could invent and a swarm of lawyers and consultants would

201

approve. As can be ascertained from the inquest transcript, the strategy recommended to the inner group was that of evasion, vagueness, confusion, and defiant and brazen loss of memory.

What the inner circle had to explain was chiefly: how did they fail to notice the time when Kennedy and Miss Kopechne left the party — or if they did notice it, why did they not inquire or worry about the prolonged absence of the pair? They had to explain most particularly their lack of curiosity, their indifference, concerning the disappearance of both of the two cars, the extended absence of Markham and Gargan, and their return, "exhausted, disheveled, red in the face" (as some but not all of the party described them), and stammering about an extraordinary thing that had happened. Raymond La Rosa, who, according to the Senator's account, had been the first to see Kennedy when he approached the cottage, staggering with exhaustion and soaked from hair to shoes (if that really was the condition of the Senator at that moment), had to explain either his lack of curiosity or, if he had been informed about what had happened, the reason why he had not offered the Senator immediately the personal *assistance and advice that he, as an experienced scuba diver, could have given better than anyone else in the party.*

Besides talking in general of contradictions and inconsistencies, Judge Boyle did not insist in his report on the shiftiness of both the girls and the men of the party, and on their obvious intention of hiding at least a part of what they knew.

The two Lyons sisters, Maryellen and Ann, both testified that they met Christopher Look while they were walking toward the cottage about 12:40 a.m., accompanied by Mr. La Rosa. This verified at least a part of the testimony of Deputy Sheriff Look, who affirmed that he saw Kennedy's car on dry ground a few minutes before he met the Lyons girls and LaRosa. If the Kennedy timetable, confirmed by La Rosa, was correct; if the latter had in fact seen the Senator discomposed and drenched to the skin three-quarters of an hour *before* this night walk, is it likely that La Rosa would have walked calmly with the two girls, both friends and companions, without telling them of this unusual occurrence? Does it not seem much more probable either that whatever happened, happened *after* that meeting with Christopher Look, *or that the whole story was quite different from that related by Kennedy and his two companions?* In any case, this meeting was a strong argument for the adoption of the Look timetable — already accepted by the Edgartown police.

Questioned about the equanimity with which they accepted the disappearance of the two cars, which forced them to spend the night in the cottage although such had not been their intention, and about their strange indifference when at about 2:00 a.m. they were vaguely told that Mary Jo had driven alone back to the motel, Miss Ann Lyons testified that she had thought nothing of Kennedy's and Mary Jo's departure. "Wouldn't it have been surprising to you," Judge Boyle asked her, "if they were leaving the party permanently without saying a word to anybody?" — "Yes, sir," she replied. Earlier she had also testified that no one was particularly concerned about returning to the mainland, saying, "We just assumed that at an appropriate time we would go back to the island [Martha's Vineyard]."

Typical answers given by all members of the party during questioning were: Who was there at that moment? *I don't remember.* — Did anyone else hear that? *I don't know.* — Who told you that? *I have forgotten.* The inflexible rule evidently was not to involve another witness, since, not being present in the court, he could not know what you had said, and his answers might contradict yours. The training seems to have been almost perfect.

When Markham and Gargan returned, "exhausted,

disheveled, and red in the face," at about 2:00 a.m., the girls got the curious impression, without remembering who told them, that Miss Kopechne had caught the ferry and had driven back alone to the motel, *and that the Senator, not having been able to find a boat, had swum the channel.* "I just assumed that for some reason he decided he didn't want to [go with Miss Kopechne]," said Maryellen Lyons. None of the other girls had wondered more than had Miss Lyons about the reason why Kennedy and Miss Kopechne had separated. We, however, must wonder why Gargan or Markham (the girls do not remember which it was) had fabricated that clumsy version of the night's events — always assuming that any credence at all can be given to the girls' prattle.

The testimony of Miss Esther Newburgh (who was rooming with Miss Kopechne at the Katama Shores Motel in Edgartown) contained several interesting points. When she testified that she had found Miss Kopechne's handbag under a table in the living room of the cottage, Assistant District Attorney Fernandes asked her whether the key to the motel room she shared with Miss Kopechne was in it:

> Miss NEWBURGH. *I don't think* the key to the room was in it. *I think* I had it.
> Mr. FERNANDES. How did she [expect to] get into her room?
> Miss NEWBURGH. I don't know. Normally in a motel you can get extra keys to a room. [Emphasis added.]

Judge Boyle sought clarification of some points in Miss Newburgh's story.

Her chat with the judge was as follows:

> The COURT. So far as you know nothing is said by her to you, her roommate, or to anyone else, as to where she is going?
> Miss NEWBURGH. Right.
> The COURT. Now, you make an assumption?
> Miss NEWBURGH. Yes.

The COURT. That she is not going back to the motel?

Miss NEWBURGH. No, I didn't make that assumption . . . . I had the assumption that it was a long day watching that race, she was exhausted, and the Senator was probably driving her back to the motel so that she could get some rest.

The COURT. Without her saying a single word to you or to anyone else in the party.

Miss NEWBURGH. That is right.

At one point, however, Miss Newburgh gave some precise information. She had noticed Mary Jo and Kennedy leaving the cottage at exactly 11:30 p.m. She was certain about the time because "I had a large watch that I wear all the time and I looked at it." This very interesting precision had been recently adopted by all the girls in discussing anything related to the fundamental discrepancy between Christopher Look's testimony and that of the Kennedy team about the moment at which the Senator's car was last seen on dry ground. In July and later, all the girls who talked about it to newspapermen had declared that they did not know at what time Kennedy and Mary Jo had left the party, but realized only later that they were missing. Here, for instance, is what Louise Hutchinson of the *Chicago Tribune* Press Service reported on April 29, 1970, about an interview with Miss Newburgh on July 23, 1969:

> Last July 23, five days after the Chappaquiddick party, Miss Esther Newburgh, in an interview in her Virginia apartment, told two *Tribune* reporters she did not know when Kennedy and Miss Kopechne left the party.
>
> She also was vague about the time of events that evening, because, she said, she was wearing a psychedelic watch "that you couldn't read."
>
> Yet at the inquest, she said she saw Kennedy leave the party cottage at 11:30 p.m., and was certain of the time because "I had a rather large watch that I wear all the time and I looked at it."
>
> Although she told reporters that "at no time were we aware of

the time" and "I think everyone forgot the only way to get over (to Edgartown) was the ferry," her inquest testimony was different.

Even before Kennedy left, she told the (inquest) court, there was talk of having to catch the midnight ferry or make arrangements to hold the ferry.

"There was some concern about whether we could make the ferry," she told the court.

As *Time* magazine observed:

> Most confusing and contradictory in the transcript was the testimony about what happened back at the cottage after Markham and Gargan, damp and disheveled, staggered in about 2 a.m. Judge Boyle himself appeared to grow rather testy at the suggestion that nobody really questioned the pair closely about what had happened to Kennedy or Mary Jo, although the girls they left behind said there had been speculations for hours about where everybody had gone.

Questioned about her reaction, or rather her lack of reaction, when, according to Markham's testimony, he returned from his long absence and fell exhausted on the bed where Miss Newburgh was resting, telling her, "You are not going to believe what happened," Miss Newburgh responded: "Nobody volunteered any information at this time . . . . I didn't question Mr. Gargan, who didn't seem to want to talk in detail about what happened .΄. . . We assumed that Mary Jo was back in that motel room." We must not forget that Miss Newburgh knew, all through that agitated night, that the key to Mary Jo's room at the motel was in her own purse, and that Mary Jo's purse had been left in the cottage.

Miss Susan Tannenbaum's contribution to the confusion particularly irritated Judge Boyle, who questioned her about the general unconcern over the unceremonious departure of their host, the disappearance of both cars, and the missed ferry:

The COURT. Were you not surprised . . . ?
Miss TANNENBAUM. Yes, I was surprised.
The COURT. And were the other girls surprised?
Miss TANNENBAUM. *I don't know.*
The COURT. Was there not some discussion about it between you?
Miss TANNENBAUM. I had no discussion *that I can remember.*
The COURT. You are not accustomed to being deserted in that fashion, are you?
Miss TANNENBAUM. No. [Emphasis added.]

Miss Rosemary Keough had to explain the mystery of her handbag's presence in the submerged car. That handbag had simply been returned to her by an unknown person who appeared for it at the Edgartown police station. Miss Keough said she had left it in Kennedy's car on Friday evening when driving with another member of the party back to Edgartown to get a radio from the Shiretown Inn. Mary Jo's handbag, forgotten at the cottage, was returned by mail to Mrs. Kopechne, who said she did not believe her daughter could have forgotten it if she had really been leaving to go to her motel.

The testimony of the well-trained girls had been nothing but a prolonged taunting of the court's patience, and it is very doubtful that such behavior would have gone unchallenged by judge and prosecutor in an open court or before a grand jury. Those contemptuous and evasive statements having been kept strictly secret — as were the rest of the doings of the inquest — until the Dukes County Grand Jury had been successfully dispatched, the five girls are now secure from any legal action for perjury or contempt of court.

The male members of the inner group were not much more helpful than the girls in assisting justice to discover the truth about Mary Jo Kopechne's death. Raymond La

Rosa, who is a member of a scuba-diving club, was in a way, like Christopher Look, a key witness. He was the first of the ten members of the party remaining at the cottage after the departure of Kennedy and Mary Jo to see Kennedy when he returned to the cottage on foot. His testimony should have been of the utmost importance because (1) he was the only one besides Markham and Gargan who could have described the state and appearance of the Senator after his alleged immersion in Poucha Pond; (2) having seen the Senator in that state, he would surely not have failed to ask him what had happened and to advise him, not only as a friend but as almost a professional in diving and rescue work; and (3) as he passed the rest of the night with the other members of the party, he must have given them some information about what he had learned — and his testimony to this effect could have belied the total ignorance those others professed in all their sworn replies to questioning.

The following excerpts from Senator Kennedy's testimony will serve as a fitting introduction to Mr. LaRosa's characteristic dodging of District Attorney Dinis's questions:

> Mr. DINIS. Was Mr. La Rosa aware of the accident?
> Senator KENNEDY. No, he hadn't heard — no, I don't believe so.
>
>   *   *   *
>
> Mr. DINIS. How long had you known Mr. La Rosa prior to this evening?
> Senator KENNEDY. Eight years, ten years, eight or ten years.
> Mr. DINIS. Were you familiar with the fact or — strike that — did you have any knowledge that Mr. La Rosa had some experience in skin-diving?
> Senator KENNEDY. *No, I never did.* [Emphasis added.]

And here are extracts from Mr. La Rosa's examination by District Attorney Dinis, without much commentary:

Mr. DINIS. Had you planned to stay overnight [at the cottage]?

Mr. LA ROSA. No, sir.

Mr. DINIS. Did something happen to cause you to stay there overnight?

Mr. LA ROSA. Yes, sir.

Mr. DINIS. What happened?

Mr. LA ROSA. Both — we had no transportation.

Mr. DINIS. Well, there were two automobiles, were there not?

Mr. LA ROSA. Both cars were gone.

Mr. DINIS. Both cars were gone?

Mr. LA ROSA. Yes, sir.

Mr. DINIS. When did you make this discovery?

Mr. LA ROSA. Well, we realized it when Mr. Gargan and Mr. Markham left.

Mr. DINIS. Left in the white Valiant?

Mr. LA ROSA. Yes, sir.

Mr. DINIS. With Senator Kennedy?

Mr. LA ROSA. Yes, sir.

The refusal to explain why they accepted without any surprise or irritation the fact that they were marooned on Chappaquiddick Island that night was common to all the members of the cottage party. Mr. La Rosa, however, had to dodge an even more precise and crucial question:

Mr. DINIS. Did Senator Kennedy have any conversation with you around 11:15 that night?

Mr. LA ROSA. Not directly, no.

Mr. DINIS. Or 12:15?

Mr. LA ROSA. I'm not sure about the time, but I was sitting out in front of the cottage alone and *I heard a voice*, which I recognized as Senator Kennedy's, call my name out twice, and *I only vaguely saw a form,* and it was extremely dark, and I was looking into a light, as I recall, that is out in front of the cottage.

Mr. DINIS. Did you see the Senator?

Mr. LA ROSA. Vaguely. *Not so that I could recognize him,* but I recognized his voice.

Mr. DINIS. Did he speak with you?

Mr. LA ROSA. He only called my name.

Mr. DINIS. Was there any further conversation beyond your name?

Mr. LA ROSA. Yes, sir. He asked me to get Mr. Markham and Mr. Gargan.

Mr. DINIS. And did you do that?

Mr. LA ROSA. Yes, I did.

* * *

Mr. DINIS. And did they leave with Mr. Kennedy?

Mr. LA ROSA. *I don't know that for sure.* They left the cottage. I didn't see them leave. I didn't see them drive away. [Emphasis added.]

As Mr. La Rosa testified later, he realized that Senator Kennedy — whom he saw only as a form despite the light in front of the cottage — had come back without his car. The curiosity of Mr. La Rosa was not aroused, despite this remarkable circumstance, and Kennedy's request for Markham and Gargan, and the mystery of the voice coming out of the night from a person who obviously wished not to be seen; and his lack of curiosity persisted until 7:00 o'clock next morning, despite the disappearance of four of his fellow guests, the long and tedious wait, and the fact of being forced to sleep on the floor instead of in a comfortable bed at the Shiretown Inn.

Mr. DINIS. And you did not see either Mr. Markham or Mr. Gargan again that night?

Mr. LA ROSA. Not until the next morning.

Mr. DINIS. And when they arrived, how were they dressed?

Mr. LA ROSA. *I don't understand that.* You mean at 7:00 o'clock?

Mr. DINIS. At 7:00 o'clock, when you first saw them, they were dressed, were they not? They had clothing on?

Mr. LA ROSA. Yes, sir.

Mr. DINIS. What condition was the clothing in?

Mr. LA ROSA. I didn't notice anything unusually different.

* * *

Mr. DINIS. So you say in effect that after they left at 12:15, when you heard Senator Kennedy's voice, they did not return all evening?

Mr. LA ROSA. I only know that they did return. I didn't see them. *I had gone to sleep.*

Mr. DINIS. It had been reported to you that they did return?

Mr. LA ROSA. No, I only had heard.

Mr. DINIS. What did you hear?

Mr. LA ROSA. I heard some voices which I recognized, but I was in a room with the door closed, and *I went back to sleep.*

* * *

Mr. DINIS. Were you aware of any difficulties occurring during the night?

Mr. LA ROSA. *No, sir.*

Mr. DINIS. You were not.

Mr. LA ROSA. No, sir.

Mr. DINIS. Now, you said earlier you hadn't planned to spend the night at Chappaquiddick?

Mr. LA ROSA. That is right.

Mr. DINIS. Were you interested in finding a way back to Edgartown, to the Shiretown Inn?

Mr. LA ROSA. *I just assumed that we would go back.*

* * *

Mr. DINIS. What time did you retire — what time did you go to bed?

Mr. LA ROSA. *That is very difficult, but it was sometime after 2:00 or 3:00,* somewhere in that neighborhood.

Mr. DINIS. Do you know whether or not there was some inquiry for the whereabouts of Mary Jo Kopechne by any of the members of your party?

Mr. LA ROSA. Not directly.

Mr. DINIS. Well, what do you know?

Mr. LA ROSA. There was a mention of, "I wonder if anything happened."

Mr. DINIS. And who said that?

Mr. LA ROSA. *I don't recall.*

Mr. DINIS. Well, in response to that question was there any answer?

Mr. LA ROSA. *No, there was no answer.*

* * *

Mr. DINIS. Why was that question asked?

Mr. LA ROSA. I don't know.

Mr. DINIS. And you have no recollection as to who asked it?

Mr. LA ROSA. No.

Mr. DINIS. What time did you hear the voices of Mr. Markham and Mr. Gargan?

Mr. LA ROSA. I really don't know what time it was because I had fallen asleep. [Emphasis added.]

To properly appreciate La Rosa's profound indifference to the fate of his friend and host and of Miss Kopechne, and the apathy with which it was accepted by the Court, we must remember that La Rosa was the man who not only had heard that mysterious voice coming out of the dark, but who, despite his denial, must have seen Kennedy soaked to the bone — if the Senator was indeed telling the truth, if the whole story was not an enormous fabrication to which eleven persons had been allowed to contribute.

There was, however, a moment when Mr. La Rosa could not have known for certain whether the clever thing to do was to remember or to forget the time things had occurred. That moment would have determined the proper sequence of events between the two walks he said he had taken with some of the girls on the road past the cottage, and the departure of the soaked Kennedy with Markham and Gargan toward the Dyke Bridge, driving their car along the same road. The Court, which several times had shown that it preferred not to be faced with such awkwardness as contradictions between witnesses or between statements by the same witness, helped him in a fatherly manner out of the necessity of giving a precise answer.

Mr. DINIS. Was that some time around quarter of 1:00?

Mr. LA ROSA. I am not sure about the time, but I am sure it might have been about that time.

Mr. DINIS. Was it after 12:30?

Mr. LA ROSA. I will say so.

Mr. DINIS. Now, had Mr. Markham and Mr. Gargan already left with Senator Kennedy?

Mr. LA ROSA. Yes, sir, they were gone before we went out for the walks.

The COURT. On both these walks?

Mr. LA ROSA. On both.

Mr. DINIS. What time was the first walk? [This was the knotty question.]

The COURT. *Now please don't guess. A guess is just of no value at all. If you can give an estimate, if you will, that is reasonably accurate, then that would be helpful to us, but no wild guess.*

Mr. LA ROSA. I really don't know. It wasn't too long after they had left. [Emphasis added.]

District Attorney Dinis, understandably puzzled, did give La Rosa the opportunity to describe a second time his dramatic encounter with a shadow and a voice, which seemed to him to be that of the Senator.

Mr. DINIS. Now when you saw the Senator out under the light when he called to you —

Mr. LA ROSA. The Senator was standing out near the street.

Mr. DINIS. Yes —

Mr. LA ROSA. Beyond the light. I was looking into that light, *because I was seated on the ground near it and looking into it, I saw him standing out by a fence, as far as I can recall: a shadow, a form. I recognized the voice more than I recognized the object that I saw.*

Mr. DINIS. You did not go near him?

Mr. LA ROSA. No, sir, I did not. [Emphasis added.)

* * *

Mr. DINIS. Did you have any — did you see the Senator's car at that time when he called to you?

Mr. LA ROSA. No, sir.

Mr. DINIS. No further questions, your Honor.

The COURT. I don't think we need this witness again, do you, Mr. Dinis?

Mr. DINIS. Not unless something should develop, your Honor.

The COURT. All right, you are excused. You may leave the island.

The Court was thus asked to believe that not even the Senator's return without his car and without his passenger, and his urgent summons to his two friends, caused La Rosa to suspect that something had happened. The Court could not possibly have believed it, could not have failed to conclude that all this evasion, this fabrication, and this effrontery had only one purpose: *to conceal some damning truth.*

CHAPTER XXIII

The Phony Inquest: II

Christopher Look's testimony would have offered a starting point for any serious investigation, since it discredited all the statements made under oath by the members of the Lawrence cottage cook-out party. In rejecting it, Judge Boyle accredited all those statements except Kennedy's explanation of his failure to take the right turning when trying to reach the ferry slip that night.

The importance of Look's testimony was that, once it was admitted, it would have become necessary to admit also that the circumstances in which Mary Jo met her death were quite different from those related or confirmed by Kennedy and his friends. Among those circumstances, one of the most disputable was Senator Kennedy's escape from the submerged car, which was inseparably connected with the timetable adopted by the Senator and all his companions — the timetable belied by Look's statement.

The Senator offered three successive descriptions of his escape, which were progressively more complete and detailed.

At the police station he said:

> The car turned over and sank into the water and landed with the roof resting on the bottom. I attempted to open the door and window of the car *but have no recollection of how I got out of the car.* [Emphasis added.]

A week later, on TV, he said:

> The car overturned in a deep pond and immediately filled with water. I remember thinking as the cold water rushed in around my head that I was for certain drowning. Then water entered my lungs and I actually felt the sensation of drowning. But somehow I struggled to the surface alive.*

We see that no mention was made here of the Senator's efforts to open the door or the window. However, full and contradictory details on this point were given by him at the inquest:

> District Attorney DINIS. After you realized it was an unpaved road and that you were driving at twenty miles an hour, what happened then?
> Senator KENNEDY. I went off Dyke Bridge, or I went off a bridge.
>
> * * *
>
> Mr. DINIS. What happened after that, Senator?
> Senator KENNEDY. Well, I remember the vehicle itself just beginning to go off the Dyke Bridge, and the next thing I recall is the movement of Mary Jo next to me, the struggling, perhaps hitting or kicking me, and I, at this time, opened my eyes and realized I was upside down, that water was crashing in on me, that it was pitch-black. I knew that and I was able to get half a gulp, I would say, of air before *I became completely immersed in the water.* I realized that Mary Jo and I had to get out of the car.
> I can remember reaching down to try and get the door knob of the car and lifting the door handle and pressing against the door and it not moving. I can remember reaching what I thought was down, which was really up, to where I thought the window was and feeling along the side to see if the window was open *and the window was closed,* and I can remember the last sensation of being completely out of air *and inhaling what must have been half a lungful of water* and assuming that I was going to drown and the full realization that no one was going to be looking for us that night until the next morning and that I wasn't going to get

---

*Full text of police station statement is quoted in Chapter Three. Full text of TV statement is quoted in Appendix B.

out of that car alive and then somehow I remember coming up to the last energy of just pushing, pressing, and coming up to the surface.

* * *

Mr. DINIS. And you say that at that time you had a thought to the effect that you may not be found until morning?

Senator KENNEDY. I was sure I was going to drown.

Mr. DINIS. Did you make any observation of the condition of Miss Kopechne at that time?

Senator KENNEDY. Well, at the moment I was thrashing around I was trying to find a way that we could both get out of the car, and at some time after I tried the door and the window I became convinced I was never going to get out.

Mr. DINIS. Was the window closed at that time?

Senator KENNEDY. *The window was open.*

Mr. DINIS. On the driver's side?

Senator KENNEDY. That's correct.

Mr. DINIS. And did you go through the window to get out of the car?

Senator KENNEDY. *I have no idea in the world how I got out of the car.* [Emphasis added.]

What can we make of these two contradictory statements, made almost in the same breath? Was the window open or closed? What happened between the moment when the Senator, feeling along the side of the car, found the window closed, and the moment he found it open and presumably went through it? Two things must be observed: (1) one point is paramount in all three descriptions of the Senator's escape — that he has no idea how he got out of the car, he remembers everything but that; and (2) there is a strange reluctance to talk about the windows and their condition. Even after informing the Court that at the last moment the window was mysteriously open, he does not venture to say that he got out of the car that way. This reluctance first manifested itself when, early in his interrogation, Judge Boyle asked him if it was a warm night. Kennedy answered:

I would think it was cool at that hour, but I really have no
personal knowledge as to which windows were open or closed. I
have read subsequently which ones were open or blown open, but
at that time I really don't recall.

It is a pity that it did not occur to the top-secret court, as
it certainly would have done to an accusatory court, to have
actual experiments made to gain certain knowledge of the
time it would take a man of Kennedy's bulk to get out
through the driver's window from an identical upturned car,
even on dry ground, even unencumbered by a back brace.*

As for the description of the Senator's agony while
struggling in the sunken car, we recommend, to anyone who
has had normally disagreeable experiences while swimming or
diving, a careful reading of that part of Kennedy's account
just following the moment when, after getting "half a gulp"
of air ("I would say"), he became "completely immersed in
the water." A professional Indian Ocean pearl diver could
perhaps have done all he did and emerged alive.

The members of the Dyke Bridge group — Kennedy,
Markham, and Gargan — were inseparably joined in a
common responsibility in which the cottage group did not
directly share. These three had to explain: (1) Kennedy's
failure to summon professional help immediately; (2) the
failure of the whole group to summon such help, which was
as near as the fire station across from the cottage, although

---

*The only interesting sight to which the newspaper men gathered at the doors
of the Edgartown courthouse were treated, besides the corporate smile of the
five eligible young girls, was the detached door of a car which could not have
been anything else than the left front door of the Kennedy Oldsmobile,
brought there, presumably, as an important exhibit. It was, however, finally
decided not to introduce the door into evidence in Court, and the opportunity was thereby lost to answer not for the Senator only, but also for the
Court and millions of the Senator's fellow-citizens, the nagging question:
Could the Senator, given his corpulence and the circumstances, have gotten
out of the submerged car by the only exit available to him, this door's
window?

by their own statements they believed that Mary Jo might be still alive; and (3) their failure to inform the police until (according to their own timetable) about eleven hours after the accident took place.

Kennedy had already made, in Judge Boyle's court, a plea of guilty to these failures and to leaving the scene of the accident, and had received a two-month suspended prison sentence for it. It was, therefore, up to him to do his best to exonerate his two friends of the accusation of inhuman and perhaps criminal conduct. They, in their turn, had to help Kennedy, first of all, to confirm — against Look's unshakable testimony — the time the Senator gave for the accident, on which the whole structure of his explanation had to rest; second, to convince the Court of the truthfulness of his statements concerning his escape from the submerged car and his swim across the channel to Edgartown; and finally, to certify his state of impaired judgment and his confused behavior, belied by all his self-confessed activities during the critical hours of the night and morning of the tragedy.

Let us note once more that Judge Boyle in his report expressed doubt about the veracity of Kennedy's statements only as they concerned his intentions when he left the cottage with Miss Kopechne, and his assertion that he took the Dyke Bridge road by mistake. The judge's disbelief stopped there; he showed no other skepticism concerning the statements of Kennedy, Gargan, or Markham. The course of the examination, and particularly the text of Judge Boyle's report, gives, on the contrary, the sanction of an official legal seal to Kennedy's and his friends' assertions. Questions were generally put in such a way as to give Kennedy and his two companions every opportunity to stress their points, and they were never pushed much harder than a defense lawyer would push his client or his witnesses to answer unambiguously the questions of the attorney or the Court.

The exoneration of Gargan and Markham by the key witness, Senator Kennedy, therefore proceeded very easily. The first precaution taken was to give Kennedy opportunity to explain that Gargan and Markham had not yet been informed of the exact nature of the accident *at the moment they passed the Chappaquiddick fire station on their way to the bridge.* The questioning by District Attorney Dinis went as follows:

> Mr. DINIS. And now, did Joe [Gargan] come to you?
> Senator KENNEDY. Yes, he did.
> Mr. DINIS. And did you have conversation with him?
> Senator KENNEDY. Yes, I did.
> Mr. DINIS. Would you tell us what the conversation was.
> Senator KENNEDY. I said, you had better get Paul [Markham], too.
> Mr. DINIS. Did you tell him what happened?
> Senator KENNEDY. At that time I said, better get Paul, too.
> Mr. DINIS. What happened after that?
> Senator KENNEDY. Well, Paul came out, got in the car. I said, there has been a terrible accident, we have got to go, and we took off down the road, the Main Road there.
>
> * * *
>
> Mr. DINIS. Now, before you drove down the road, did you make any further explanation to Mr. Gargan or Mr. Markham?
> Senator KENNEDY. Before driving? No, sir. I said, there has been a terrible accident, let's go, and we took off.

So the Court was informed that neither Gargan nor Markham knew that Kennedy's Oldsmobile was at the bottom of Poucha Pond with Mary Jo in it, until they reached Dyke Bridge. After their efforts to save the trapped girl — who a few minutes earlier they had thought to be alive — they did not use the telephone at the Dyke House or at any of the nearby cottages, but went to the ferry slip with, we must suppose, the intention of using the public phone booth there to summon assistance and inform the police, or to summon the ferry, which they knew was available. They did not do so, and here is the explanation offered by Senator Kennedy and accepted by the Court:

> Mr. DINIS. Was there any effort made to call for assistance?
> Senator KENNEDY. No, other than the assistance of Mr. Gargan and Mr. Markham.
> Mr. DINIS. I know, but they failed in their efforts to recover —
> Senator KENNEDY. That is right.
> Mr. DINIS. — Miss Kopechne?
> Senator KENNEDY. That is correct.

Then, before the Senator had given any real answer to Dinis's question — concerning the reason why no other assistance had been summoned — one of those well-timed interruptions for "off the record discussion" took place, meant, one cannot help feeling, to provide opportunity for properly adjusting the dialogue between Court and witness. After this interruption, which was of unstated length, Dinis resumed his examination:

> Mr. DINIS. I believe, your Honor, before the witness left the courtroom the question was whether or not any assistance had been asked for.
> The COURT. I think the answer had been No.
> Mr. DINIS. And now may I ask you, Mr. Kennedy, was there any reason why no additional assistance was asked for?
> Senator KENNEDY. Was there any reason?
> Mr. DINIS. Yes, was there any particular reason why you did not call either the police or the fire department?
> Senator KENNEDY. Well, I intended to report to the police.
> The COURT. That is not quite responsive to the question.
> Mr. DINIS. Was there any reason why it did not happen at that time?
> The COURT. Call for assistance.
> Senator KENNEDY. I intended to call for assistance and to report the accident to the police within a few short moments after going back to the car.
> Mr. DINIS. I see, and did something transpire to prevent this?
> Senator KENNEDY. Yes.

Mr. DINIS. What was that?

Senator KENNEDY. With the Court's indulgence [promised, perhaps, during the off-the-record discussion?], to prevent this, if the Court would permit me I would like to be able to relate to the Court the immediate period following the time that Mr. Gargan and Markham and I got back into the car.

The COURT. I have no objection.

Mr. DINIS. I have no objection.

Senator KENNEDY. Responding to the question of the District Attorney —

Mr. DINIS. Yes.

As anybody could ascertain by reading Kennedy's full testimony, the District Attorney and the Court never did get the answer they were awaiting to this fundamental question. They never got it from Kennedy, and they did not get it from Markham and Gargan when their turns came to explain their ruthless remissness.

But let us focus our attention for the moment on Kennedy's twisted explanations, even more replete with emotional gibberish than the first Sorensen version, presented on TV in July.

Senator KENNEDY. At some time, I believe it was about 45 minutes after Gargan and Markham dove, they likewise became exhausted and no further diving appeared to be of any avail and they so indicated to me and I agreed. [Why did they not, then at least, run to the Dyke House and phone for expert rescue and medical assistance?] So they came out of the water and came back into the car and said to me, Mr. Gargan and Mr. Markham at different times as we drove down the road toward the ferry, that it was necessary to report this accident.

There was an important question concerning this trip toward the ferry slip. Judge Boyle stressed it in his report, but nobody pressed it during the inquest. Judge Boyle stated:

The three drove back to the ferry landing. After much discussion it was decided that Kennedy would return to Edgartown (*no mention how*) to telephone David Burke, his administrative assistant, and Burke Marshall, an attorney, and then report the accident to the police. [Emphasis Judge Boyle's.]

Yes, how *did* they intend to manage Senator Kennedy's passage to Edgartown? Had they decided already, after those long discussions, that the Senator should swim across? And if so, why did they all agree to settle for such a reckless method? The Court did not insist on an explanation.

Senator Kennedy referred movingly to his very understandable reluctance to telephone the tragic news to Mrs. Kopechne, to his own mother and father, and to his wife, although nobody had questioned him about that. Once more, as he was to do several times during the inquest, he avoided giving any reasonable answer by reminding the Court that at that time he was simultaneously convinced *that Mary Jo was alive, and that she was dead* — two mutually exclusive hypotheses by which he wanted his two companions, who were not in a state of impaired judgment, to benefit also. His statement continued:

A lot of different thoughts came into my mind at that time about how I was going to really be able to call Mrs. Kopechne at some time in the middle of the night to tell her that her daughter was drowned, to be able to call my own mother and my own father, relate to them, my wife, and I even — even though I knew that Mary Jo Kopechne was dead and believed firmly that she was *in the back of that car* [why did he think she was in the *back* of the car?], I willed that she remained alive.

As we drove down that road I was almost looking out the front window and windows trying to see her walking down that road. I related this to Gargan and Markham and they said they understood this feeling, but it was necessary to report it. And about this time we came to the ferry crossing and I got out of the car and we talked there just a few minutes.

I just wondered how all this could possibly have happened. I also had a sort of a thought and the wish and desire and *the hope that suddenly this whole accident would disappear*, and they reiterated that this has to be reported and I understood at the time that I left that ferry boat, left the slip where the ferry boat was, that it had to be reported and I had full intention of reporting it, and I mentioned to Gargan and Markham something like, "You take care of the girls, I will take care of the accident." — that is what I said and dove into the water. [Emphasis added.]

Was there any reason for the Court to believe in the authenticity of this "now you see it now you don't" memory stunt? At the Edgartown police station on July 19, 1969, this is how Kennedy, dictating to Markham, reported that part of the night's tribulations:

I remember returning, walking, to the place where my friends were eating. There was one car before the cottage. I sat in the rear seat and asked someone to drive me again to Edgartown. I remember walking about for a long while before returning to the hotel. When this morning I realized what had happened, I got immediately in touch with the police.

Not a word about the trio's rescue expedition. When Assistant District Attorney Fernandes asked Markham whether Kennedy had made any mention of those rescue attempts at the police station, his answer was:

Mr. MARKHAM. No. The Senator that morning, I think when we were at the telephone booth, or sometime that morning before we went to the police station, he told us, he said, "Look, I don't want you people *put in the middle of this thing. I'm not going to involve you. As far as you know you didn't know anything about the accident that night.*" [Emphasis added.]

Markham had, as we know, written the police report at Kennedy's dictation, had accepted that important omission, and therefore must have contemplated participating in an important bit of deception, at least until after consultation with Burke Marshall, the lawyer the three comrades had feverishly but vainly tried to contact that morning before reporting to the police. This opens two questions: (1) What trust can one have in the testimony of that former Assistant U.S. Attorney for Massachusetts, knowing of his connivance at one such piece of deception? (2) What was the "thing" in which both Gargan and Markham would have preferred not to be involved? Their efforts at rescue surely would have provoked only praise from Police Chief Arena, the newsmen present, and the U.S. public in general, the more so because Mr. Gargan's "arm was all bloodied and bruised" and "scraped all the way from his elbow," as Senator Kennedy testified, in this dangerous attempt.

Not a word was said at the police station, and not one question was asked by Police Chief Arena, about how Kennedy reached Edgartown that night. At the hearing for trial on July 25, before Judge Boyle, not one word was said or asked about the rescue attempts made by Markham and Gargan under Kennedy's direction, or about the means by which Kennedy got from one island to the other. Yet it would seem that both prosecutor and judge had the obligation to demand this essential elucidation before sending Kennedy home *magna cum laude,* and letting him give to millions of listeners, that very night on TV, the fanciful explanation that he had not cared, and indeed would not at that time have dared, to give in public and under oath.

Neither in his police report nor in his TV speech did Kennedy say anything about having promised his two companions that he would report the accident to the police when he reached Edgartown (nor have his companions ever explained how they expected the Senator to reach that city). All that he said on TV was that he had "instructed" Gargan and Markham "not to alarm Mary Jo's friends that night." When Dinis asked him during the secret inquest what prompted him to give this instruction to his two friends, this is the best explanation the Senator was able to produce after six months of reflection:

Senator KENNEDY. I felt strongly that if those girls were notified that an accident had taken place and that Mary Jo had in fact drowned, which I became convinced of by the time that Markham and Gargan and I left the scene of the accident, that it would only be a matter of seconds before all of those girls who were long and dear friends of Mary Jo's to go to the scene of the accident and dive themselves and enter the water and with, I felt, a good chance that some serious mishap might have occurred to any one of them. It was for that reason that I refrained — asked Mr. Gargan and Mr. Markham not to alarm the girls.

Remarkably considerate for a man in a state of shock!

At that moment the Court interfered and mercifully put an end to that part of the interrogation, so that nobody had the opportunity to remark that it would have taken only seconds, had the five girls and three men remaining in the cottage group been informed of the accident, for at least one member of the group to decide to summon professional assistance immediately, whether by telephoning to the police or by any other means — for instance, ringing the alarm bell at the Chappaquiddick fire station, just across from the cottage, where a light was always burning, or knocking at the door of their neighbor, the captain of the Chappaquiddick fire company. This was exactly what Kennedy did not want done, whatever it was that had happened at the Dyke Bridge, before he got in touch with his lawyers.

Kennedy's assertion that he did not inform Markham and Gargan of what had really happened until they reached the bridge, was not confirmed by Gargan in answering Dinis's questions:

District Attorney DINIS. And you say the Senator was leaving with Miss Kopechne later alone?

Mr. GARGAN. Well, where he was going, again I don't know. I assumed he was going to the ferry. He went out the door. That is all I can tell you, Mr. Dinis. I did not see him after that.

Mr. DINIS. When did you next see the Senator?

Mr. GARGAN. I next saw the Senator in the back seat of the Valiant.

Mr. DINIS. At what time?

Mr. GARGAN. I would say approximately between 12:15 and 12:30 [a.m.] .

Mr. DINIS. And what did he say to you at that time?

Mr. GARGAN. The first thing he said to me was, "Get Paul Markham."

Mr. DINIS. And what did he say after that?

Mr. GARGAN. Well, I got into the car and Paul Markham got into the car. The Senator said to me, "The car has gone off the bridge down by the beach and Mary Jo is in it." With that I backed up the car and went just as fast as I could towards the bridge.

* * *

Mr. DINIS. Did he tell you any more than that about the accident?

Mr. GARGAN. No, that is all he said.

Whatever uncertainty existed about the time at which Gargan and Markham were fully informed concerning the accident, there was no disagreement between them and Kennedy about the moment when, after long discussion, the Senator told them that he himself would take care of informing the police. It was at the moment before he jumped into the fast-running waters, leaving his companions so hurriedly that they could not stop him. Gargan explained that he did not worry about the Senator's ability to reach the other shore because he knew that the Senator was a strong swimmer. The fact that Kennedy was fully dressed and had not even removed his shoes, as any experienced swimmer would have done, and the fact that both Gargan and Markham — according to their own statements — knew that the Senator was exhausted and in a state close to absolute irrationality and even delirium, does not seem to have caused them to have any misgivings. Again according to their own statements, they could follow him with their eyes, in the night and the dark waters, for no more than half the stretch of 500 feet. Surely any rational person, in the circumstances described by the Senator and confirmed by his two companions, would have found in his rash plunge yet another reason to telephone for help; namely, to assist the already exhausted Senator, who might have been carried far down the channel by the powerful current. But Gargan and Markham did not do so.

They did, however — according, once more, to their own testimony — again return to the ferry, before they went back to the cottage. Their avowed intention in so doing was to jump into the water too, and swim to Edgartown to see whether Kennedy had made it across the channel. Here again the question should have been put to them (but was not): Why did they not use any of the telephones that were at their disposal, at the ferry landing, at the Dyke House, at one of the other neighboring cottages, or at the Chappaquiddick fire house? *What was it they wanted to hide?*

Together with the people of Chappaquiddick Island and of Martha's Vineyard, we do not believe that Kennedy reached Edgartown by swimming the channel. How he did reach his bed that night we may never know, now that he has successfully crossed his last judicial hurdle. But if, contrary to the belief of so many, Kennedy really did take the unnecessary risk of that crazy jump, and if his two friends let him take it, the mystery that surrounds the death of Mary Jo Kopechne is deeper than ever. *What was the compulsion that forced Senator Kennedy to leave secretly and hurriedly at night, at the greatest personal risk, the place where Mary Jo Kopechne had met her death?*

Another question Gargan and Markham were never seriously asked to answer was why they consented to prolong the black-out of information even after 8:30 a.m. on July 19, when they joined Kennedy at the Shiretown Inn, until the moment when, after crossing again by ferry to Chappaquiddick, they heard that the car with the trapped girl had been discovered — and why even then they did not make up their minds to go to the police until their efforts to reach a renowned lawyer in Washington had proven in vain.

Senator Kennedy, moreover, gave not one but two explanations of his and his friends' failure to inform the proper authorities until 10:00 a.m. the next day. That part of his examination was so characteristic of the methods adopted by what we will call "the defense" that it seems desirable to reproduce it here for the edification of those who do not have access to the transcript:

Mr. DINIS. Now, what time [on the morning of July 19] did Mr. Markham and Mr. Gargan arrive [at the Shiretown Inn]?

Senator KENNEDY. About a few — I would think about 8:30 . . . .

* * *

Mr. DINIS. Did you have any conversation with Mr. Markham or Mr. Gargan or both at that time?

Senator KENNEDY. Yes, I did.

Mr. DINIS. Can you give the Court what the conversation was?

Senator KENNEDY. Well, they asked, had I reported the accident, and why I hadn't reported the accident; and *I told them about my own thoughts and feelings as I swam across that channel* and how I was always willed that Mary Jo still lived; how I was hopeful even as that night went on and as I almost tossed and turned, paced that room and walked around that room that night that somehow when they arrived in the morning they were going to say that Mary Jo was still alive. I told them how I somehow believed that when the sun came up and it was a new morning that what had happened the night before would not have happened and did not happen, *and how I just couldn't gain the strength within me, the moral strength, to call Mrs. Kopechne at 2:00 o'clock in the morning* and tell her that her daughter was dead. [Emphasis added.]

Mr. DINIS. Now, at some time you actually did call Mrs. Kopechne?

Senator KENNEDY. Yes, I did.

Mr. DINIS. And prior to calling Mrs. Kopechne, did you cross over on the Chappaquiddick ferry to Chappaquiddick Island?

Senator KENNEDY. Yes, I did.

Mr. DINIS. And was Mr. Markham and Mr. Gargan with you?

Senator KENNEDY. Yes, they were.

Mr. DINIS. Now, did you then return to Edgartown after some period of time?

Senator KENNEDY. Yes, I did.

Mr. DINIS. Did anything prompt or cause you to return to Edgartown once you were on Chappaquiddick Island that morning?

Senator KENNEDY. Anything prompt me to? Well, what do you mean by prompt?

Mr. DINIS. Well, did anything cause you to return? You crossed over to Chappaquiddick?

Senator KENNEDY. Other than the intention of reporting the accident, the intention of which had been made earlier that morning.

Mr. DINIS. But you didn't go directly from your room to the police department?

Senator KENNEDY. No, I did not.

Mr. DINIS. Did you have a particular reason for going to Chappaquiddick first?

Senator KENNEDY. Yes, I did.

Mr. DINIS. What was that reason?

Senator KENNEDY. It was to make a private phone call to one of the dearest and oldest friends that I have and that was to Mr. Burke Marshall. I didn't feel that I could use the phone that was available, the public phone that was available outside of the dining room at the Shiretown Inn, and it was my thought that once I went to the police station, that I would be involved in a myriad of details and I wanted to talk to this friend before I undertook that responsibility.

* * *

Mr. DINIS. You did not reach him?

Senator KENNEDY. No, I did not.

So we are told that one of the reasons why the Senator did not inform the police that night and that morning was that until the moment his friends joined him at 8:30 a.m. he was

still under the delusion that Mary Jo Kopechne was alive; and
that the other reason was that he wanted to consult an
experienced jurist before "undertaking that responsibility."

When Judge Boyle tried very kindly to extricate him from
those involved and painfully embarrassing explanations, the
Senator did not hesitate to try to have it both ways by
brazenly contradicting himself once more concerning his
strange delusion about Mary Jo's fate:

> Judge BOYLE. I think we can put in the record this question:
> Why did you not seek further assistance after Mr. Markham and
> Mr. Gargan had exhausted their efforts in attempting to reach
> Mary Jo? *Now, you give the answer.*
> Senator KENNEDY. It is because *I was completely convinced
> at that time that no further help and assistance would do Mary
> Jo any good.* I realized that she must be drowned and still in
> the car *at this time* and I appeared — the question in my mind
> at that time was, what should be done about the accident?
> [Emphasis added.]

Of the two explanations offered by Kennedy, only the
second could be reasonably considered valid: the Senator
and his two companions wanted to avoid talking with
anybody about the circumstances that brought about the
death of Mary Jo until they could consult some more
experienced lawyer. This of course would not have been
necessary if their sole intention had been to tell immediately, exactly, and completely what really happened. Had a
grand jury been permitted to function, it would not have
let pass such evasive and contradictory testimony as was
offered by the eleven members of the Lawrence cottage
party without recommending prosecution, which could have
brought fully to light the reason for all these calculated
evasions and contradictions. But we already know about
the cleverly prepared ambush by which, nine months after
Mary Jo's mysterious death, the Edgartown Grand Jury was
prevented from functioning, and that the results of Judge

Boyle's white-washing inquest were kept secret until after the grand jury's summary dismissal.

With characteristic effrontery Senator Kennedy has protested that he had always wanted an open inquest, and wanted it as early as possible, and that it was only in order to protect his "constitutional rights" that his lawyers asked for a closed court.

There has been a lot of bawling since the sunken car tragedy for the constitutional rights of everybody from Senator Kennedy to Mr. John B. Crimmins. But nothing has been heard about the constitutional rights of Mary Jo Kopechne. There was not one lawyer, not one friend, to protect those rights in the Massachusetts courts, in the Pennsylvania courts, or at Judge Boyle's secret inquest.

CHAPTER XXIV

The Phony Inquest: III

There were some unpleasant situations to be faced by the members of the Lawrence cottage party during their examination. They weathered them or dodged them according to their talents and capacities. One centered on the moment when La Rosa shouted to Gargan from the front door, and Gargan to Markham, that Kennedy was back and wanted them. This was an event difficult to forget; anyone who heard La Rosa's call, or Gargan's, had one more reason — and a very good one — to wonder and worry about what was going on. It also offered the Court an opportunity to test the sincerity of the witnesses' professed ignorance. Did they or did they not know that Kennedy had returned, without both the car and Mary Jo?

Take this excerpt from Paul Markham's examination:

Mr. MARKHAM. I was inside the cottage. Mr. La Rosa came in and said, "Paul, the Senator wants to see you."

Mr. DINIS. Can you stop there for a second? Mr. La Rosa came in and asked for you?

Mr. MARKHAM. He didn't ask for me. He was at the door. He said, "The Senator wants you."

Mr. DINIS. Who else was present at that time?

Mr. MARKHAM. *I don't know.*

Mr. DINIS. Do you know if the activity was concentrated [at that time] more inside the cottage than outside?

Mr. MARKHAM. *I really couldn't say.*

Mr. DINIS. Do you know if there were other people present?
Mr. MARKHAM. Yes, there were.* [Emphasis added.]

Charles Tretter had simply not been there at the time. He had left with Miss Keough, he said, at 11:30 for a first walk in the direction of the ferry slip. They returned at about 12:15. So, no problem for them. When they reached the cottage, he said, everybody "seemed to be gone."

The COURT. Who did you actually see? Anyone?
Mr. TRETTER. No.
The COURT. You saw nobody?
Mr. TRETTER. *Not that I can recall.* [Emphasis added.]

So they left for a second walk.

The two Tretter-Keough walks lasted either from 11:30 p.m. (according to Tretter) or from 11:55 p.m., 12:15; or 12:30 (according to Miss Keough's various timetables) until 2 a.m. (according to both). They can be considered as one long walk of about two to two and a half hours, interrupted by an alleged return to the cottage — where both agreed that they stopped only for a moment, saw no one, and were seen by no one. The entire period of the walks was spent, according to both witnesses, on the portion of the main road between the cottage and the fork where the road turns left to the ferry landing and right to the Dyke Bridge.

It was over this same stretch of road and during the same

---

*It is obvious from the interrogation of the eleven cottage guests that there was between them a general understanding not to impair anyone else's freedom to answer any question as best suited him, or her. Markham of course could not have failed to identify at least some of the persons who were present in the cottage when he returned with Gargan from their night expedition; but how could he know what Tretter or Miss Keough, for example, would find it appropriate to answer when asked whether they had seen him and Gargan returning to the cottage? The transcript of the Kopechne-Kennedy inquest abounds in answers as obviously mendacious as this profession of total ignorance by the former Assistant United States Attorney for Massachusetts. The Court does not seem to have attached much importance to this fact, which was nevertheless in itself an indication that there was something the witnesses had jointly decided to hide.

interval of time (a) that Senator Kennedy trudged back to the cottage from the scene of the accident; (b) that five other members of the cook-out party also took their night strolls; (c) that Markham, Gargan, and Kennedy hurried back to the scene of the accident in the white Valiant; (d) that Markham and Gargan, in the same car, drove back to the cottage from the ferry slip; and (e) that Christopher Look, after seeing the Kennedy car at the crossroads, was driving over when he passed and offered a lift to La Rosa and the Lyons girls. *Nevertheless, during those two and a half hours nobody met Tretter and Miss Keough, and they met nobody.* After some insistence by the Court, they did suggest that they might perhaps have been passed by the white Valiant without recognizing it.

Here are some excerpts from Tretter's testimony:

Assistant District Attorney FERNANDES. And how long a time would you say this walk lasted?

Mr. TRETTER. Oh, it must have been an hour — an hour and a half.

Mr. FERNANDES. Do you know what time you returned to the cottage?

Mr. TRETTER. I think it was around 2:00 o'clock.

Mr. FERNANDES. And you tell the Court that when you returned after the second walk, Mr. Gargan, Mr. Markham, and Mr. La Rosa, and various other people, some of the girls, were present.

Mr. TRETTER. Yes.

* * *

The COURT. When you returned to the cottage and found all the group there, with the exception, I think you said, of Mr. Kennedy and Miss Kopechne — is that right? They weren't there?

Mr. TRETTER. *To the best of my knowledge.*

* * *

The COURT. Did you inquire as to what had happened, where they had gone, why they had gone leaving you two alone?

Mr. TRETTER. *I may have,* but my impression or my

memory is of my coming into the cottage and Mr. Gargan saying, "Jack, it is late, let's get some sleep." And I could hear the two Lyons sisters, who I know very well, saying, "It's late, let's get some sleep." [Emphasis added.]

Miss Keough apparently showed some curiosity:

> District Attorney DINIS. Now, had you heard any conversation concerning the whereabouts of Mary Jo and Senator Kennedy?
> Miss KEOUGH. I did ask Mr. Gargan.
> Mr. DINIS. And what did he tell you?
> Miss KEOUGH. He said not to worry about it, that Mary Jo and the Senator had *probably* taken the ferry.
>
> * * *
>
> Mr. DINIS. Now, did anyone else hear Mr. Gargan tell you that?
> Miss KEOUGH. *I don't believe so. I was talking directly to Mr. Gargan.* [Emphasis added.]

Miss Keough's final "corrected" timetable opens a new vista on the moment when Gargan, Markham, and Kennedy left together for the Dyke Bridge. Here is her questioning on this point by Assistant District Attorney Fernandes:

> Mr. FERNANDES. Well, you say that you went for your first walk around 11:45?
> Miss KEOUGH. Yes, it was after twenty of 12:00.
> Mr. FERNANDES. It was after Mr. Kennedy left with Mary Jo Kopechne?
> Miss KEOUGH. Yes, sir.
> Mr. FERNANDES. And you left for a walk and you were gone for about 45 minutes?
> Miss KEOUGH. Yes.
> Mr. FERNANDES. Why do you say —
> Miss KEOUGH. Can I correct myself?
> Mr. FERNANDES. Yes.
> Miss KEOUGH. I didn't have a watch, but the last time I remember it was twenty of 12:00 which I looked at Miss Tannenbaum's watch that I went to the front of the cottage and *sat for fifteen minutes.* So it would be more like a quarter after 12:00 or 12:30 when I left.

Mr. FERNANDES. When you left the second time?

Miss KEOUGH. The first time.

Mr. FERNANDES. The first time?

Miss KEOUGH. Yes, sir.

Mr. FERNANDES. How many cars were in the yard at that time, do you know?

Miss KEOUGH. *I didn't notice the cars.*

Mr. FERNANDES. You didn't notice at all?

Miss KEOUGH. No.

Mr. FERNANDES. Do you know if Mr. Markham or Mr. Gargan were still there?

Miss KEOUGH. When I left, they were still there.

Mr. FERNANDES. They were still there at 12:30?

Miss KEOUGH. *Yes, sir, they were still there when I left, whatever time it was.* [Emphasis added.]

Miss Keough sat for fifteen minutes in front of the cottage without observing how many cars were there, or whether in fact there was any car at all. This was a matter that ought to have interested her at the time — around midnight — since she knew that the last scheduled ferry was due to leave about then.

If she left for this first walk at 12:00 or 12:15, while Markham and Gargan were still at the cottage, she and Tretter ought inevitably to have met the Senator dragging himself along in his wet clothes. If the later time limit has to be taken into account — that is, if she and Tretter left about 12:30 and Markham and Gargan were still at the cottage then — a meeting with the Senator would still, one must suppose, have been unavoidable. But according to Senator Kennedy's testimony, based on the clock in the Valiant, at 12:20 he, Markham, and Gargan were already back at the Dyke Bridge trying to rescue the trapped girl. (It is of special interest that these two contradictory bits of testimony are among the very few allegedly confirmed by someone consulting a timepiece.) The confusion here is such that one cannot help thinking of Christopher Look's obviously unbiased testimony and accepting his timetable as the only authentic one.

Miss Maryellen Lyons did see Mr. La Rosa come in but did not hear him say that the Senator was there. La Rosa told her that, much later.

> Mr. DINIS. Did you see Mr. Gargan and Mr. Markham leave at any time?
> Miss LYONS. I would say after the Senator and Miss Kopechne were gone, sometime after that, Mr. La Rosa came into the cottage where I was at that time and called for Mr. Markham and Mr. Gargan just asked him to come outside, and after that I didn't see them again. I mean, didn't, you know, they were gone.

Miss Esther Newburgh had a still better answer. She did not hear anything; she only saw La Rosa come in.

> Assistant District Attorney FERNANDES. What did he [La Rosa] say?
> Miss NEWBURGH. I didn't see him say anything. I saw him motion to Mr. Markham and Mr. Gargan.
> Mr. FERNANDES [evidently sketching a gesture]. What did he do? Show the judge.
> Miss NEWBURGH. You mean how he motioned?
> Mr. FERNANDES. What did he do?
> Miss NEWBURGH. He did essentially what you did.
> Mr. FERNANDES. He just waved his arm and asked him [them?] to come out?
> Miss NEWBURGH. Essentially.

But let us go back to Miss Maryellen Lyons' statement, which becomes more interesting when she refers to the moment when Markham and Gargan returned from their night expedition.

> Mr. DINIS. Well, were there others present with you, or was it a private conversation with you?
> Miss LYONS. No, it was a general; it was in the main room of the cottage.
> Mr. DINIS. They told everyone how the Senator dove into the channel?

Miss LYONS. *I don't know if everybody was listening.* I only know that —

Mr. DINIS. Well, you knew that at 2:00 in the morning that the Senator had gone back to Edgartown?

Miss LYONS. Yes, I did.

Mr. DINIS. And that he had jumped into the water and swam across the channel and they also told you they jumped in with him?

Miss LYONS. Yes, they did — no, he dove in and they were with him and saw him dive in *and I believe they said* that because of his back, you know, they sort of instinctively just dove in after him.

Mr. DINIS. Well, what about his back?

Miss LYONS. Well, he has a bad back. I assume that when he dove into the water to swim, that they were concerned.

Mr. DINIS. Did they tell you more? Did you ask them any questions about this particular episode of the Senator going back and swimming back to Edgartown?

Miss LYONS. Did I ask them any more questions?

Mr. DINIS. Yes.

Miss LYONS. We, you know, when they arrived, we asked them, you know, where they had been, what had happened. Oh, it was just, Oh, don't even ask us, *we have been looking for boats.* It was confused.

Mr. DINIS. *That they had been looking for boats,* they said that?

Miss LYONS. That was one of the things they said, and that somebody else had said Miss Kopechne was back at Katama Shores, and that the Senator was back at Edgartown.

* * *

Mr. DINIS. Did you ask why the Senator decided to dive in, or swim across the channel?

Miss LYONS. *No, I didn't.*

Mr. DINIS. Did anyone ask that at all?

Miss LYONS. No. [Emphasis added.]

Miss Ann Lyons confirmed her sister's statements and volunteered a valuable additional piece of information:

Mr. FERNANDES. You say [you walked] up the street?

Miss LYONS. Up the street towards the ferry.

Mr. FERNANDES. Towards the ferry?

Miss LYONS. Yes, and we didn't walk very far because I don't really enjoy walking, and *I think we got about to the fire station and then we came back* . . . .

* * *

Mr. FERNANDES. Sometime thereafter did Mr. Markham and Mr. Gargan arrive?

Miss LYONS. Well, *I went to bed at that point.* [Emphasis added.]

The nearness of the fire station was therefore not unknown to the group.

Miss Susan Tannenbaum shared the general indifference and lack of curiosity:

Mr. DINIS. Now you say that Mr. Gargan and Mr. Markham had already left. Did you see them return?

Miss TANNENBAUM. I was in the cottage when they returned.

Mr. DINIS. Did you have a conversation with Mr. Gargan?

Miss TANNENBAUM. *Simply to ask if things would quiet down.*

Mr. DINIS. What did you mean by that?

Miss TANNENBAUM. I was sleeping in the front room. I was trying to sleep. [Emphasis added.]

Mr. John B. Crimmins, who generally has the custody of Senator Kennedy's car, was an interesting witness. It was from him that the Senator got the keys of the Oldsmobile when he left with Mary Jo, and it was he, according to his statement, to whom the Senator mentioned that he was tired, that Miss Kopechne did not feel well, and that both wanted to return to Edgartown to their respective hotels.

The COURT. What was the reason you didn't drive Mr. Kennedy and Miss Kopechne down to the ferry [or to Edgartown] and then bring the car back?

Mr. CRIMMINS. I don't know. He asked me for the keys. It was his automobile and I gave them to him. I didn't question him.

The COURT. Well, you were staying at this reasonably isolated cottage on Chappaquiddick, which is several miles from the ferry?

Mr. CRIMMINS. That is right.

The COURT. On which island there is no public transportation. Now, by taking that car this left you without transportation, didn't it?

    Mr. CRIMMINS. I was staying there[?].

The COURT. I say it left you without transportation, didn't it?

    Mr. CRIMMINS. There was another car.

* * *

The COURT. The Valiant is a compact, is it not?

    Mr. CRIMMINS. *I don't remember.*

The COURT. I asked if the Valiant was not a compact car.

    Mr. CRIMMINS. It was a small car.

The COURT. So that nine people were going to be left with one small car, and you who had this Oldsmobile transportation as more or less your own was going to be left without transportation? [Emphasis added.]

Did Crimmins hear La Rosa call Gargan and Markham and tell them that Kennedy wanted them? Had he admitted that he heard him, he would have had to explain why he did not go out and ask his employer what the trouble was — with the car or with the Senator. But by another of those much to be deplored coincidences he had not heard La Rosa; he had already fallen asleep.

About the time he retired Crimmins gave three different versions:

    Mr. FERNANDES. And were there others inside the cottage?

    Mr. CRIMMINS. In and out.

    Mr. FERNANDES. In and out. And could you tell us how long you stayed at the cottage?

    Mr. CRIMMINS. I went to sleep. I went to bed.

    Mr. FERNANDES. What time?

    Mr. CRIMMINS. 12:00 or after.

    Mr. FERNANDES. And did you sleep till early morning?

    Mr. CRIMMINS. Early morning.

* * *

    Mr. FERNANDES. And where were the other people at that time, as you best remember, when at least you went to retire, where were they?

Mr. CRIMMINS. There were some in and some out.

Mr. FERNANDES. Who was there at that time that you remember?

Mr. CRIMMINS. *I don't know.*

Mr. FERNANDES. Do you know who was not there at that time?

Mr. CRIMMINS. *I don't know.*

Mr. FERNANDES. Do you remember seeing Mr. Markham and Mr. Gargan at that time?

Mr. CRIMMINS. Yes, I did.

Mr. FERNANDES. And this is approximately 12:00 o'clock?

Mr. CRIMMINS. No, before that.

Mr. FERNANDES. I am talking just before you retired now.

Mr. CRIMMINS. We were all there before I retired. [He had said previously that Gargan and Markham had left before he went to bed.]

Mr. FERNANDES. And you are certain you retired at 12:00 o'clock?

Mr. CRIMMINS. Thereabouts, 12:00, 12:30, 1:00 o'clock, I don't know.

Mr. FERNANDES. So, now, it could have been 1:00 o'clock?

Mr. CRIMMINS. Anywhere from 12:00 to 1:00. [Emphasis added.]

* * *

Mr. FERNANDES. Could you tell us where you were between 11:15 and 12:45 that night, 11:15 p.m. and 12:45 a.m.? [11:15 is the time Kennedy says the accident occurred; 12:45 is the time Look saw his car still on dry ground. Mr. Fernandes has here a nice point.]

Mr. CRIMMINS. In the cottage.

Mr. FERNANDES. Sleeping?

Mr. CRIMMINS. No, I was not sleeping. I don't know what time I went to bed, I'm not sure of the time.

Crimmins' further contribution to the Court's information was the explanation that the liquor he had brought from Boston to Hyannis Port, and from Hyannis Port to the cottage on Chappaquiddick (three half gallons of vodka, four fifths of scotch, two bottles of rum, and two cases of canned beer) was not primarily for consumption at the party but was to be taken back to Hyannis Port where "I had a little house behind Mr. Gargan's and have a drink at the house if anybody dropped in to say hello."

How and when did the cottage guests finally learn that Mary Jo was dead?

La Rosa learned it as follows:

> Mr. DINIS. Mr. Gargan on the 19th told you at 9:30 a.m. that Mary Jo was missing?
>
> Mr. LA ROSA. That is right.
>
> Mr. DINIS. Was there further discussion about the disappearance of Mary Jo Kopechne?
>
> Mr. LA ROSA. As I recall there were a lot of hurried questions, *but I don't recall any of the specifics.* [Emphasis added.]
>
> *   *   *
>
> Mr. DINIS. When did you learn that Mary Jo Kopechne's body had been found?
>
> Mr. LA ROSA. I learned the details of that when I arrived back at the Shiretown [about 10:00 a.m.].
>
> Mr. DINIS. How did you learn that?
>
> Mr. LA ROSA. I began to ask some questions of my young associates who were there.
>
> Mr. DINIS. What associates?
>
> Mr. LA ROSA. Mr. Tretter was there.

At about 10:00 a.m. Mr. Tretter had learned at the girls' motel, from one of the girls (he could not recall which), that there had been an accident.

> Assistant District Attorney FERNANDES. And then you had a conversation with Mr. Gargan at the Dunes? [The Dunes is the common local name for Katama Shores Motor Hotel, the girls' motel.] Well, let me strike that. Let me rephrase it. When and how did you find out that she had died?
>
> Mr. TRETTER. *I don't really understand the question.*
>
> Mr. FERNANDES. Well, when was the first time — you say at 10:00 o'clock you understood there was an accident?
>
> Mr. TRETTER. Yes.

Mr. FERNANDES. At that time did anyone say she had drowned?
Mr. TRETTER. No.
Mr. FERNANDES. Or she was hurt or in the hospital?
Mr. TRETTER. No.
Mr. FERNANDES. Just that there was an accident?
Mr. TRETTER. Right.
Mr. FERNANDES. And then there came a time when you knew that something more serious had happened?
The COURT. Well, there came a time when you learned she died?
Mr. TRETTER. Yes.
Mr. FERNANDES. When and how? Who told you?
Mr. TRETTER. Mr. Gargan.
Mr. FERNANDES. Where, at the Dunes?
Mr. TRETTER. At the Dunes, yes.
Mr. FERNANDES. I think you said approximately 11 o'clock?
Mr. TRETTER. It would be after, I believe. [Emphasis added.]

Mr. Tretter's testimony seems here to contradict that of Mr. La Rosa, who said it was at about 10:00 and at the Shiretown Inn that he and Mr. Tretter learned, presumably from Gargan, who he "thinks" was present at the time, the details of the accident that resulted in Mary Jo's death.

There is a more important discrepancy between some of Mr. Markham's statements and Mr. Tretter's description of the information Mr. Gargan, in Mr. Tretter's presence, gave the five girls at the Katama Shores, sometime between 10:00 and 11:00 o'clock. According to Mr. Tretter, Gargan's narration included all the details of the rescue attempts by himself and Markham and of Kennedy's swim across the channel. Yet, according to the testimony offered to the Court the next day by Mr. Markham, in trying to explain why none of these particulars had been reported at the police station, it had been decided between Kennedy, Markham, and Gargan at the ferry landing at about 9:30 a.m. — half an hour before the girls, in Mr. Tretter's presence, were told the story of the rescue attempts — that Gargan and Markham were not to be "put in the middle of this thing." In Kennedy's words as reported by Markham: "As far as you know, you didn't know anything about the accident." *That was the attitude taken at the police station, and as far as the public knows, that attitude was maintained by the three men until Kennedy's appearance on TV.*

Miss Newburgh's statement about this particular moment partially confirmed Mr. Tretter's. All the girls were present at Katama Shores, she said, when Mr. Gargan told them of Mary Jo's death and Kennedy's rescue efforts. When pressed for more details, Miss Newburgh could not give them:

> Assistant District Attorney FERNANDES. Was anything else said?
> Miss NEWBURGH. And then you had five girls who just lost a friend *who can't remember very much at that point.* [Emphasis added.]

Maryellen Lyons, who was one of the five girls who, according to Mr. Tretter and Miss Newburgh, were supposed to have heard of Mary Jo's death for the first time from Mr. Gargan at the motel, gave quite a contradictory version. At the cottage, she said, Mr. Gargan had told the girls only that "there has been an accident and Mary Jo is missing." She explained further that Mr. Gargan took them only as far as the ferry, and they took the ferry over and "took a cab from the other side to Katama Shores and we were there, you know, by ourselves."

> District Attorney DINIS. When Mr. Gargan was asked about what happened, what did he say?
> Miss LYONS. He just said he didn't know. He just said that there was an accident and she was missing.
> Mr. DINIS. And did you later talk with Mr. Gargan about 10 o'clock at Katama?
> Miss LYONS. I think it was after 10 o'clock.
> Mr. DINIS. When did you learn that Mary Jo had died?

Miss LYONS. I think pretty soon after we got back to Katama Shores.

Mr. DINIS. And who told you?

Miss LYONS. I believe it was Mr. Gargan.

Mr. DINIS. Didn't you question him about his earlier story that Mary Jo had taken the automobile and gone back to Katama the night before?

Miss LYONS. Well, when we got back to Katama and we went to Mary Jo's room to see if she was there, we did ask. We asked, you know, what had happened, you know, why weren't we told; was the Coast Guard called; all of those questions.

Mr. DINIS. What was the answer?

Miss LYONS. *He didn't know the answer.*

Mr. DINIS. He said he didn't know? Mr. Gargan said he didn't know, is that correct?

Miss LYONS. Yes.

Mr. DINIS. Now, when did you actually learn that Mary Jo was dead?

Miss LYONS. As far as knowing, I don't think I really knew or felt it until we learned that the skin-diver had been down.

Mr. DINIS. Who brought you that information?

Miss LYONS. I think this was on the phone from either Mr. Gargan or somebody. I didn't take the call. *I think it was the phone.*

Mr. DINIS. Didn't Mr. Gargan at Katama Shores after you arrived and went into Mary Jo's room, didn't he take you aside and tell you what happened?

Miss LYONS. He didn't come back with us to Katama Shores originally. He drove us to the ferry and we took the ferry over and took a cab from the other side back to Katama Shores and we were there, you know, by ourselves. [Emphasis added.]

* * *

Mr. DINIS. And Mr. Gargan did not tell you anything at Katama Shores about how Mary Jo died?

Miss LYONS. No.

Even when the girls left Martha's Vineyard for the mainland on Saturday afternoon, they ignored the details of Mary Jo's death:

Mr. DINIS. Was there any conversation on the boat about what happened?

Miss LYONS. We were just stunned. I don't remember any conversation.

Mr. DINIS. Didn't you talk about it at all?

Miss LYONS. Well, we didn't know what had happened. This was the big thing and at that time I felt *— I didn't know that Mr. Gargan and Mr. Markham had been at the scene until just prior to the Senator's address on television because Mr. Markham and Mr. Gargan came back to the cottage and appeared very normal. Nothing was wrong.* [Emphasis added.]

The testimony of this more artless witness on this important point does not agree at all, therefore, with that of Mr. Tretter. According to Mr. Tretter's statement Mr. Gargan told the girls at Katama Shores, in his presence, the whole story of the accident and the rescue efforts by Kennedy, himself, and Mr. Markham. According to Miss Newburgh the girls were also told of the accident and Senator Kennedy's attempts to rescue the trapped girl.

Miss Ann Lyons' testimony agrees with her sister's:

Mr. DINIS. Now, was anything said about what had happened, at Katama, by Mr. Gargan or anyone else?

Miss LYONS. As I said, we kept questioning him [Gargan] and he kept telling us that he had no details. I think at the Katama he told us that the Senator had been driving the car and had already reported it to the police.

Mr. DINIS. Were there any details as to how it happened?

Miss LYONS. *No, sir.*

Mr. DINIS. Or when it happened?

Miss LYONS. *No, sir.* [Emphasis added.]

We prefer to believe the two Lyons girls for three reasons: (1) Of all the girls, they were Mary Jo's closest friends; one of them roomed with her in Washington. (2) They had no visible reason, at that point, not to tell the truth, whereas Mr. Tretter and Miss Newburgh could have been seeking to show that the Senator's version, as he told it on TV and repeated it at the inquest, was spontaneous and genuine and known to many before the TV performance. (3) Neither Kennedy nor Markham had told the police, that morning, about the Gargan and Markham rescue attempts, or about Kennedy's swim across the Edgartown channel. Why should those details, kept secret from the police, have been told to everyone else?

Miss Keough's statement on this particular point was as follows:

> Mr. DINIS. Now, what time did you learn that Mary Jo had this accident?
> Miss KEOUGH. When I returned to Katama, which I approximate between quarter of 11:00 and 11:15. I don't know.
> Mr. DINIS. Did Mr. Gargan tell you of the accident at Katama?
> Miss KEOUGH. I didn't hear it from Mr. Gargan. I learned it from Maryellen, Nance and Esther.

One could not say that Miss Susan Tannenbaum's statement was much help to the Court in reconciling the obvious inconsistencies and contradictions implied in determining the moment at which the full Kennedy version of the accident was formulated for the first time:

> Mr. FERNANDES. When did you know Mary Jo had died?
> Miss TANNENBAUM. Mid-morning.
> Mr. FERNANDES. What time?
> Miss TANNENBAUM. Approximately 11:00.
> Mr. FERNANDES. Where were you?
> Miss TANNENBAUM. I returned to the Katama Shores.
> Mr. FERNANDES. Who told you?
> Miss TANNENBAUM. Mr. Gargan.
> Mr. FERNANDES. Was anyone present when Mr. Gargan told you that she died?
> Miss TANNENBAUM. Correction. *I only learned that Mary Jo was missing.*
> Mr. FERNANDES. At what time?

Miss TANNENBAUM. 10:30, 11:00, at the Katama Shores.

Mr. FERNANDES. What time did you leave Chappaquiddick?

Miss TANNENBAUM. Approximately 7:30.

Mr. FERNANDES. And from 7:30 to 10:00 you heard nothing about the whereabouts of Mary Jo?

Miss TANNENBAUM. That is correct.

Mr. FERNANDES. May we have that again?

Miss TANNENBAUM. That is correct.

Mr. FERNANDES. Then you heard she was missing, and then later Mr. Gargan told you she had died. Did he tell you how she died?

Miss TANNENBAUM. *I do not remember exactly, I think.* [Emphasis added.]

At the risk of being repetitive we will give another example of the witnesses' consistent evasiveness when faced by a pertinent question. It would have been interesting to know the state and condition in which Gargan and Markham appeared to be when they returned to the cottage after their long absence. Here are the answers gathered by the Court from the various witnesses interrogated on this subject:

La Rosa. — "I did not see them. I had gone to sleep."

Tretter. — About Gargan: "He looked like I did, I guess . . . ." About Markham: "I couldn't really see. There were no lights in the cottage, as I recall."

Crimmins (who does not seem to have observed anything special). — "I remember getting up and saying something and going right back to bed."

Maryellen Lyons. — "Mr. Gargan and Mr. Markham came back to the cottage and appeared very normal."

Esther Newburgh. — "Mr. Gargan came in and collapsed." Later, when asked about Markham: "I was concerned mostly in trying to get to sleep and I was not looking at them [Markham and Gargan] very specifically." Did she remember what clothes Gargan was wearing? "I was not looking that close."

Ann Lyons. — Asked if she had occasion to observe Gargan

on his return to the cottage, she said, "No, sir, I wear glasses and I did not have them on." So she was not questioned at all about Markham.

Rosemary Keough. — She talked to both Gargan and Markham after their return but does not seem to have observed anything remarkable in their appearance or behavior.

Susan Tannenbaum. — "I overheard Mr. Markham say he was very tired." Did he appear excited? "No, he seemed tired." Did she make any observation about Gargan's appearance? "No."

Ross W. Richards. — This friend of Kennedy's, who saw Markham and Gargan in the morning of Saturday, July 19, declared to Lieutenant Dunn that "they were both soaking wet." Challenged in court by Assistant District Attorney Fernandes, Richards didn't remember having used these words to Lieutenant Dunn, and reduced his sensational assertion to: "They looked damp . . . they appeared that they might have been wet from the night's dew or fog or something."

One is tempted to agree with Ralph de Toledano that the members of the Lawrence cottage party "appear by their testimony to be the most stupid, the most unconscious, or the most cynical people in these United States." Not all of them, of course, were all of that. Before passing a general judgment on the "neutral" attitude of Mary Jo's companions concerning what is still the mystery of her death, we must take into account the brainwashing, the pressures, the suggestions to which some, at least, of the girls were subjected for so many months.

As concerns the judicial authorities involved, it is obvious that the influence of the Kennedy clan obtained passage of the law that ordered secrecy for the inquest into Mary Jo's death, and that the same influence governed and limited the examination of Kennedy and of his companions, despite some honest efforts on the part of Assistant District Attorney Fernandes and the less and less persistent efforts of District Attorney Dinis.

It is left to the imagination of everybody to decide what the felonious circumstances were that so many people concurred in ignoring and conspired to conceal. But the real tragedy of the Chappaquiddick affair is that it is only part and parcel of the great American tragedy; as there is no more alarming signal of moral decline in a human community than the apathy, the prejudice, and the corruption of its courts.

CHAPTER XXV

What Happened To Nancy Burns?

This girl was saved! She was saved in circumstances similar to those in which Mary Jo Kopechne met her death, but more difficult. She was saved because the people around her were unselfish, responsible, cool, and courageous, and thought of nothing but immediately doing everything in their power to assist another human being in peril of death.

It happened on February 21, 1970, forty-five days before the convocation of the Dukes County Grand Jury, which had to decide whether there was enough probability that criminal omission or commission had contributed to the death of Miss Kopechne to justify further legal proceedings. The grand jury, therefore, could have taken into consideration this new element of information — had its activities not been stringently curtailed, thanks to the learned precautions taken by the Massachusetts Supreme Court.

Here is the story, as told by the magazine *Popular Mechanics* and brought later to general public knowledge by the *Reader's Digest* of August 1970.

Miss Nancy Burns, aged 17, wanting to use the radio of the car in which she was seated — a sleek, fast-back Mustang — turned on the ignition instead of the accessory key. The car, which inadvertently had been left in low gear, was propelled over the seawall that fronts the Miami River, six feet below, and the girl was submerged with it in fifteen feet of murky water.

Her companion, young Mark Smith, also seventeen, who

at the time had been washing the car, was able to get the left-hand door open and tried to put his foot on the brake. His foot got caught, and he was dragged down into the river, hooked to the car. He freed himself with great difficulty and dove down immediately several times, trying vainly to get one of the car's two doors open. His father, who was working on his yacht nearby, did not lose a moment: he ran to a telephone and made the proper calls, and in a few minutes professional help was on the way.

The rescue was not easy. The car was lying on its right side in fifteen feet of muddy water. The driver's door had been slammed back by the pressure of the water and could not be opened. The passenger's door was open "the width of two hands," but after six exhausting dives, Fireman Larry Norton — an experienced lifeguard who had once saved three children from drowning — could open it only two feet more, because of the muddy bottom upon which the car was almost resting. It was by this narrow and dangerous access that Norton entered the car, which at any moment could have crushed him against the river bottom.

Let *Reader's Digest* tell the rest:

> Holding the doorpost with his left hand, he groped with the right up the driver's seat back to the tall head rest. High against the ceiling, his hand touched an object: a small sandaled foot.
>
> Twenty seconds have passed.
>
> Fighting exhaustion, Norton worked with furious speed. He got a firm grip on Nancy's right ankle, and began to pull hard. The girl came floating down into the front seat. He circled her slim waist with his right arm. And suddenly he knew he was through. His lungs could take no more. And in that moment he felt a hand ever so slowly wrapping itself around his right arm.
>
> The touch electrified him . . . . He braced his feet against the hard steel of the half-open door and gave the girl a powerful shove. She shot upward. A second or two later she surfaced, her long hair streaming on the water; the next moment Norton shot up beside her.

Nancy had been submerged for close to fifteen minutes.

Young Mark and his father; David Harley, a British yachtsman who with extraordinary presence of mind had dived with a rope and tied the door handle of the car to the piling of the seawall to prevent it from settling further; and Firemen Bob Lane, Dan Green, Sam Givens, Paul Daman, and Larry Norton, who had answered the call for help, had all behaved like responsible, honest human beings. The difficulties they were facing were certainly greater than would have been met by Farrar and his crew if Kennedy and his companions, instead of wasting long hours in mysterious amateur endeavors in the impenetrable darkness of the Chappaquiddick tragedy, had summoned professional assistance immediately from the Dyke House, or fifteen minutes after the accident, from the Chappaquiddick fire station. Senator Kennedy informed the Court of Inquiry that it took him only fifteen minutes to walk from the bridge to the cottage.

The difficulties confronting Larry Norton and the danger faced by Nancy Burns were manifestly greater than those that would have faced rescuers and victim at the Dyke Bridge; first, because the Mustang was submerged in fifteen feet of water rather than twelve; second, because the form of the two-door Mustang, which has the rear window close to the horizontal, and the car's position in the water, and its dimensions, suggest that the air pocket was shallower and less voluminous than might have formed in the submerged Oldsmobile; and third, because Norton dived without mask and oxygen tank, whereas Farrar and his men, who would have been at Dyke Bridge in no more and probably less than twenty minutes, were equipped with full scuba gear.

John Farrar, with eighteen years' experience in scuba diving and rescue work behind him, thought the chance of saving Mary Jo would have been good if he had been called promptly, and he introduced in support of his opinion, among other impressive considerations, cases in which persons had lived up to five hours in the air pockets of submerged cars.

But the important thing to consider in the Dyke Bridge tragedy is not how great was the possibility of a successful professional rescue, but the fact that this possibility did exist — as proven once more by Nancy Burns' rescue from the Miami River — and that Mary Jo was deliberately deprived of it by Senator Kennedy and his two companions.

As for the alleged aquatic exploits of the three around the submerged Oldsmobile, we have only their allegations about these, and the long-rehearsed confirmations, riddled with contradictions, inconsistencies, and discrepancies, of the other revelers at the Lawrence cottage party.

Conclusion

It might be asked —

When Pearl Harbor, Yalta, Operation Keelhaul, the handing over of China to the Communist beast, the betrayal of the Hungarian patriots, the Katanga infamy, the Bay of Pigs, the establishment of the Soviet stronghold in Cuba, the protection of traitors and criminals, unilateral disarmament, the no-win wars in Korea and Vietnam, have been accepted —

When systematic corruption of teenagers and younger children by pornographic literature and so-called sex education in the schools; the invasion of the streets by looters, arsonists, and snipers; confinement in a mental institution by simple administrative decision or the arbitrary ruling of a judge; the public defilement of the national flag and the glorification of that of the enemy; the outlawing by the courts of the land of the name of God and of the display of the Cross, are looked at with indifference —

Why make such a fuss about the death of a girl, a simple secretary, found in a submerged car in a tidal pond, whatever the circumstances of the accident?

Yes, this might be asked.

Yet, in the inmost recesses of their consciences, their feelings, their presentiments, millions have understood, at least for a while, that between the moment when the body of that young girl was found in that car, in the tidal waters of that remote island, and the moment when Edward Moore Kennedy was reelected to the United States Senate by the

257

electorate of the State where the accident occurred, something had happened in this country commensurate with the outrages recalled above.

Millions have understood, at least for a while, that what had happened had plunged the American community still deeper into the zone of callous insensibility, of mental and moral asphyxiation, where it could not live much longer without coagulating into a faceless mass of political robots, broken to the harness of a satanic and lethal power — a power which, since the very beginning of the Roosevelt era, has been driving the United States, and with it the whole world of Western civilization, toward surrender and perdition.

Judge Boyle's Report

COMMONWEALTH OF MASSACHUSETTS

Dukes County, ss
District Court
Inquest re Mary Jo Kopechne
Docket No. 15220

REPORT
James A. Boyle, Justice

I, James A. Boyle, Justice of the District Court for the County of Dukes County, in performance of the duty required of me by Section 12 of Chapter 38 of the General Laws of Massachusetts, in the matter of the inquest into the death of Mary Jo Kopechne, holden at Edgartown January 5, 1970 to January 8, 1970 inclusive, herewith submit my report.

There are 763 pages of transcript and 33 numbered exhibits. Although most testimony was given orally, some was accepted by affidavit and included as exhibits.

It is believed that, to aid in understanding this report, certain names and places should first be relatively located and some measurements shown;

(1) The Town of *Edgartown,* which is one of six towns on Martha's Vineyard, includes a small, sparsely settled island named *Chappaquiddick.* (Map, Exhibit 32)

(2) The *mainland* of Edgartown is separated from Chappaquiddick by Edgartown Harbor, the distance between being approximately five hundred feet, and transportation of vehicles and persons is provided by a small motor ferry which plies between two ferry slips or landings. The ferry slip on the Edgartown side is near the center of town. (Exhibit 19)

(3) Chappaquiddick has few roads. At the ferry slip, begins a macadam

paved road called *Chappaquiddick Road,* the main road of the island, with a white center line which is partly obliterated at the Curve. The road is approximately twenty feet wide, running in a general easterly direction for two and one-half miles, whence it Curves south and continues in that direction past the Cottage to the southeast corner of the island. Chappaquiddick Road is sometimes referred to in the testimony as *Main Street* and, after it Curves, as *School Road* or *Schoolhouse Road,* because a school-house formerly stood on that portion of it. (Exhibits 16, 19)

(4) At the Curve, and continuing easterly, begins *Dyke Road,* a dirt and sand road, seventeen to nineteen feet wide, which runs a distance of seven-tenths miles to Dyke Bridge, shortly beyond which is the ocean beach. (Exhibits 15, 16, 17)

(5) *Dyke Bridge* is a wooden structure, ten feet six inches wide, has timber curbs on each side four inches high by ten inches wide, no other guard rails, and runs at an angle of twenty-seven degrees to the left of the road. There are no signs or artificial lights on the bridge or its approach. It spans Poucha Pond. (Exhibits 7, 8, 9, 10)

(6) The *Kennedy Oldsmobile* is eighteen feet long and eighty inches wide. (Exhibits 1, 33)

(7) *Poucha Pond* is a salt water tidal pond, and has a strong current where it narrows at Dyke Bridge. (Exhibits 10, 18)

(8) *Cemetery Road* is a single car-width private dirt road, which runs northerly from the junction of Chappaquiddick and Dyke Roads. (Exhibits 16, 22)

(9) The *Lawrence Cottage* (herein called Cottage) is one-half mile from the junction of Chappaquiddick and Dyke Roads and approximately three miles from the ferry slip. (Exhibit 20)

(10) Proceeding northerly from the Cottage, on the east side of Chappaquiddick Road, a distance of one-tenth mile before the Curve, is a metal sign with an arrow pointing toward the ferry landing.

(11) *Katama Shores Motor Inn* (called Katama Shores) is located approximately two miles from the Edgartown ferry slip.

(12) *Shiretown Inn* (called Shiretown) is a very short distance from the Edgartown ferry slip, approximately one block.

Although the testimony is not wholly consistent, a general

summary of the material circumstances is this: A group of twelve persons, by invitation of Edward M. Kennedy, a United States Senator from Massachusetts, were gathered together at Edgartown to attend the annual sailing regatta held on Friday and Saturday, July 18 and 19, 1969. They were

John B. Crimmins	Rosemary Keough
Joseph Gargan	Mary Jo Kopechne
Edward M. Kennedy	Ann (also called Nance) Lyons
Raymond S. LaRosa	Maryellen Lyons
Paul F. Markham	Esther Newburgh
Charles C. Tretter	Susan Tannenbaum

(All hereafter referred to by surnames)

The six young women, in their twenties, had been associated together in Washington, D.C. and were quite close friends. Kopechne shared a Washington apartment with Ann Lyons. Reservations had been made for them to stay at Katama Shores, in three double rooms. Kopechne roomed with Newburgh. Crimmins, chauffeur for Kennedy when he was in Massachusetts, drove Kennedy's black Oldsmobile sedan from Boston to Martha's Vineyard on Wednesday, July 16. He brought a supply of liquor with him and stayed at the Cottage. Tretter, who brought some of the young women, arrived late Thursday and stayed at Shiretown. LaRosa, who brought his Mercury car, came Thursday and shared the room with Tretter. Gargan and Markham sailed Kennedy's boat to Edgartown on Thursday and roomed together at Shiretown. Kennedy arrived by plane on Friday, July 18, was met by Crimmins at the airport, and was driven to the Cottage. Kennedy shared a room at Shiretown with Gargan. The Lyons sisters arrived Friday morning and were driven by Gargan to Katama Shores. Markham, who stayed at Shiretown Thursday night, moved to the Cottage to stay with Crimmins for Friday and Saturday nights. Kennedy, with Gargan, was entered to sail his boat in the regatta on Friday and Saturday.

The Cottage became headquarters for the group and a cook-out was planned for Friday night. Three cars were available for general transportation; LaRosa's Mercury, Kennedy's Oldsmobile 88, and a rented white Valiant.

Thursday night, those present, including Kopechne, visited the Cottage; Friday morning, they, including Kopechne, traveled over Dyke

Bridge to the beach to swim; Friday evening, they, including Kopechne, traveled to the Cottage for the cook-out. Kennedy, who arrived at 1:00 *P.M.* Friday and was driven by Crimmins to the Cottage, was then driven by Crimmins over Dyke Road and Dyke Bridge to the beach to swim; he was driven back to the Cottage to change, to the ferry to sail in the race and, after the race, was driven back to the Cottage. There were other trips between Edgartown and the Cottage but not including Kopechne or Kennedy. These are set forth to indicate the use of, and increasing familiarity with, the roads on Chappaquiddick.

The Cottage is small, contains a combination kitchen-living room, two bedrooms and bath, has an open yard, no telephone, and is near to and visible from Chappaquiddick Road, which had little traffic. The entire group of twelve had assembled there by approximately 8:30 *P.M.* on Friday. Two cars were available for transportation on Chappaquiddick, the Oldsmobile and Valiant. LaRosa's Mercury was at the Shiretown. Activities consisted of cooking, eating, drinking, conversation, singing, and dancing. Available alcoholic beverages consisted of vodka, rum, scotch, and beer. There was not much drinking and no one admitted to more than three drinks; most only to two or less.

During the evening, Tretter, with Keough, drove to Edgartown in the Oldsmobile to borrow a radio. Keough left her pocketbook in the vehicle on that trip.

Only Crimmins and Markham planned to stay the night at the Cottage. The others intended to return to their respective hotels in Edgartown. It was known that the last ferry trip was about midnight, but that a special arrangement for a later trip could be made.

Between 11:15 and 11:30 *P.M.* Kennedy told Crimmins (but no other person) that he was tired, wanted to return to Shiretown to bed, that Kopechne did not feel well (some conflict here — see pages 32 and 346) and he was taking her back to Katama Shores, requested and obtained the car keys to the Oldsmobile, and both he and Kopechne departed. Kopechne told no one, other than Kennedy, that she was leaving. Kopechne left her pocketbook at the Cottage.

Kennedy stated he drove down Chappaquiddick Road toward the ferry, that when he reached the junction of Dyke Road, instead of bearing left on the Curve to continue on Chappaquiddick Road, he mistakenly turned right onto Dyke Road, realized at some point he was on a dirt road, but thought nothing of it, was proceeding at about twenty miles per hour when suddenly Dyke Bridge was upon him. He braked but the car went off the bridge into Poucha Pond and landed on its roof. The driver's window was open and he managed to reach the surface and swim to shore. It was extremely dark, there was a strong current, and repeated efforts by him to extricate Kopechne from the car were unsuccessful. Exhausted, he went to shore and, when recovered, walked back to the Cottage, not noticing any lights or houses on the way. He summoned Gargan and Markham, without notifying the others, and they returned in the Valiant to the bridge, where Gargan and Markham unsuccessfully attempted to recover Kopechne.

The three drove back to the ferry landing. After much discussion, it was decided that Kennedy would return to Edgartown (no mention how) to telephone David Burke, his administrative assistant, and Burke Marshall, an attorney, and then report the accident to the police. Kennedy advised Gargan and Markham to return to the Cottage, but not to tell the others of the accident. Suddenly and unexpectedly, Kennedy left the car, dove into the harbor and swam across to Edgartown. Gargan and Markham finally returned to the Cottage, but did not then tell the others what had occurred.

After Kennedy and Kopechne had left the Cottage, their purported destination unknown to anyone except Crimmins, the social activities gradually diminished. The absence of Kennedy and Kopechne was noticed but it was presumed they had returned to Edgartown. Some persons went walking. Only LaRosa saw Kennedy return at about 12:30 *A.M.* and he, at Kennedy's request, summoned Gargan and Markham, who went to Kennedy, seated outside in the rear seat of the Valiant, and they took off. When Markham and Gargan returned about 2:00 *A.M.*, some were sleeping and the others, realizing they would not return to Edgartown that night, then slept or tried to. There not being sufficient beds, some slept on the floor.

In the morning, those in the Cottage returned to Edgartown at different times. The young women eventually reached Katama Shores and were then told what had happened, although some of them had previously been made aware that Kopechne was missing.

Kennedy, after swimming across to Edgartown, went to his room, took off his wet clothes, lay on the bed, then dressed, went outside and complained to someone (later identified as the innkeeper, Russell Peachey) of noise and to inquire the time. He was told it was 2:24 *A.M.* He returned to his room and remained there until 7:30 *A.M.* when he went outside, met Richards, a sailing competitor; chatted with him for one-half hour, when Gargan and Markham appeared and the three retired to Kennedy's room. When Kennedy informed them he had failed to report the accident, they all went to Chappaquiddick to use the public telephone near the ferry slip and Kennedy called David Burke, his administrative assistant, in Washington. (But Exhibit 4, list of calls charged to Kennedy, does not show this call.) Gargan returned to the Cottage to tell those there about the accident. Kennedy and Markham went to the Edgartown Police Station, and were later joined by Gargan.

At about 8:20 *A.M.* Police Chief Arena, receiving notice of a submerged car at Dyke Bridge, hurried to the scene, changed into swim trunks, and made several futile attempts to enter the Oldsmobile. Farrar, a scuba diver, was summoned, found and recovered the body of Kopechne from the car, and also found in the car the pocketbook of Keough. The car was later towed to shore.

Dr. Donald R. Mills of Edgartown, Associate Medical Examiner, was summoned and arrived about 9:15 *A.M.*; examined the body and pronounced death by drowning; turned it over to Eugene Frieh, a mortician, who took the body to his establishment at Vineyard Haven. The clothing and a sample of blood from the body were turned over to the State Police for analysis. No autopsy was performed and the body was embalmed and flown to Pennsylvania on Sunday for burial.

When Kennedy and Markham arrived at the Police Station, Chief Arena was at Dyke Bridge. He returned to the station at Kennedy's request. Kennedy stated he was the operator of the car and dictated a statement of the accident as Markham wrote it down. Chief Arena then typed the statement which Kennedy said was correct but did not sign. (Exhibit 2)

On July 25, 1969, Kennedy pleaded guilty in this Court to, and was sentenced on, a criminal charge of "leaving the scene of an accident after causing personal injury, without making himself known." That same night, Kennedy made a television statement to the voters of Massachusetts. (Exhibit 3)

A petition by District Attorney Edmund Dinis in the Court of Common Pleas for Lucerne County, Pennsylvania, for exhumation and autopsy on the body of Kopechne, was denied after hearing. Expert evidence was introduced that chemical analysis of the blouse worn by Kopechne showed blood stains, but medical evidence proved this was not inconsistent with death by drowning. (Exhibit 31)

Christopher F. Look, Jr., a deputy sheriff then living on Chappaquiddick, was driving easterly on Chappaquiddick Road to his home about 12:45 *A.M.* on July 19. As he approached the junction of Dyke Road, a car crossed in front of him and entered Cemetery Road, stopped, backed up, and drove easterly on Dyke Road. He saw two persons in the front seat, a shadow on the shelf back of the rear seat which he thought could have been a bag, article of clothing, or a third person. The car was dark colored with Massachusetts registration plate L7 – 7. He was unable to remember any other numbers or how many there were intervening. Later that morning, he saw the Kennedy Oldsmobile when it was towed to shore, but he cannot positively identify it as the same car he saw at 12:45 *A.M.* During the inquest, a preliminary investigation was initiated through the Registry of Motor Vehicles to determine whether a tracking of the location on July 18 and 19, 1969, of all dark colored cars bearing Massachusetts plates with any and all combinations of numbers beginning with L7 and ending in 7, would be practicable. The attempt disclosed that it would not be feasible to do this since there would be no assurance that the end result would be helpful and, in any event, the elimination of all other cars within that registration group (although it would seriously affect the credibility of some of the witnesses) would not alter the findings in this report.

A short distance before Dyke Bridge, there is a small house called "Dyke House," then occupied by a Mrs. Malm and her daughter. (Exhibit 18) Both heard a car sometime before midnight but are not sure of its direction. The daughter turned off her light at midnight. (Page 593 et seq.)

Drs. Watt and Brougham examined Kennedy on July 19 and 22. Diagnostic opinion was "concussion, contusions and abrasions of the scalp, acute cervical strain. Impairment of judgment and confused behavior are consistent with this type of injury." (Exhibit 27)

Eugene D. Jones, a professional engineer, testified by affidavit as to the condition of Dyke Road and Dyke Bridge and concluded that the site is well below approved engineering standards and particularly hazardous at night. (Exhibits 29, 30)

Donald L. Sullivan, an employee of Arthur D. Little, Inc., testified by affidavit as to a road test conducted on or about October 10, 1969 describing the factors involved in a motor vehicle, on high beam light, approaching Dyke Bridge at night, with film showing the results of such test. (Exhibit 28)

State Police Chemist McHugh, who analyzed the blood sample taken from the body of Kopechne, testified the alcoholic content was .09 percent, the equivalent of three and one-half to five ounces of eighty to ninety proof liquor consumed by a person, weighing about one hundred ten pounds, within an hour prior to death, or a larger amount if consumed within a longer period.

This concludes, in substance, the material circumstances as testified to by the witnesses.

The failure of Kennedy to seek additional assistance in searching for Kopechne, whether excused by his condition, or whether or not it would have been of any material help, has not been pursued because such failure, even when shown, does not constitute criminal conduct.

Since there was no evidence that any air remained in the immersed car, testimony was not sought or allowed concerning how long Kopechne might have lived, had such a condition existed, as this could only be conjecture and purely speculative.

As previously stated, there are inconsistencies and contradictions in the testimony, which a comparison of individual testimony will show. It is not feasible to attempt to indicate each one.

I list my findings as follows:

I. The decedent is Mary Jo Kopechne, 28 years of age, last resident in Washington, D.C.

II. Death probably occurred between 11:30 *P.M.* on July 18, 1969 and 1:00 *A.M.* on July 19, 1969.

III. Death was caused by drowning in Poucha Pond at Dyke Bridge on Chappaquiddick Island in the Town of Edgartown, Massachusetts, when a motor vehicle, in which the decedent was a passenger, went off Dyke Bridge, overturned and was immersed in Poucha Pond. The motor vehicle was owned and operated by Edward M. Kennedy of Boston, Massachusetts.

The statute states that I must report the name of any person whose unlawful act or negligence *appears* to have contributed to Kopechne's death.

As I stated at the commencement of the hearing, the Massachusetts Supreme Court said in its decision concerning the conduct of this inquest "the inquest serves as an aid in the achievement of justice by obtaining information as to whether a crime has been committed." In *LaChappelle* vs. *United Shoe Machinery Corporation*, 318 Mass. 166, decided in 1945, the same Court said "It is designed merely to ascertain facts for the purpose of subsequent prosecution" and " . . . . . the investigating judge may himself issue process against a person whose *probable* guilt is disclosed." (Emphasis added)

Therefor, in guiding myself as to the proof herein required of the commission of any unlawful act, I reject the cardinal principle of "proof beyond a reasonable doubt" applied in criminal trials but use as a standard the principle of "probable guilt."

I have also used the rule, applicable to trials, which permits me to draw inferences, known as presumption of facts, from the testimony. There are several definitions and I quote from the case of *Commonwealth* vs. *Green*, 295 Pa. 573: "A presumption of fact is an inference which a reasonable man would draw from certain facts which have been proven. The basis is in logic and its source is probability." Volume 29 American Jurisprudence 2nd Evidence Section 161 states in part, "A presumption of fact or an inference is nothing more than a probable or natural explanation of facts . . . and arises from the commonly accepted experiences of mankind and the inferences which reasonable men would draw from experiences."

I find these facts:

A. Kennedy was the host and mainly responsible for the assembly of the group at Edgartown.

B. Kennedy was rooming at Shiretown with Gargan, his cousin and close friend of many years.

C. Kennedy had employed Crimmins as chauffeur for nine years and rarely drove himself. Crimmins drove Kennedy on all other occasions herein set forth, and was available at the time of the fatal trip.

D. Kennedy told *only* Crimmins that he was leaving for Shiretown and requested the car key.

E. The young women were close friends, were on Martha's Vineyard for a common purpose as a cohesive group, and staying together at Katama Shores.

F. Kopechne roomed with Newburgh, the latter having in her possession the key to their room.

G. Kopechne told *no one*, other than Kennedy that she was leaving for Katama Shores and did not ask Newburgh for the room key.

H. Kopechne left her pocketbook at the Cottage when she drove off with Kennedy.

I. It was known that the ferry ceased operation about midnight and special arrangements must be made for a later trip. No such arrangements were made.

J. Ten of the persons at the cook-out did *not* intend to remain at the Cottage overnight.

K. Only the Oldsmobile and the Valiant were available for transportation of those ten, the Valiant being the smaller car.

L. LaRosa's Mercury was parked at Shiretown and was available for use.

I infer a reasonable and probable explanation of the totality of the above facts is that Kennedy and Kopechne did *not* intend to return to Edgartown at that time; that Kennedy did *not* intend to drive to the ferry slip and his turn onto Dyke Road was intentional. Having reached this conclusion, the question then arises as to whether there was anything criminal in his operation of the motor vehicle.

From two personal views, which corroborate the Engineer's statement (Exhibit 29), and other evidence, I am fully convinced that Dyke Bridge constitutes a traffic hazard, particularly so at night, and must be approached with extreme caution. A speed of even twenty miles per hour, as Kennedy testified to, operating a car as large as this Oldsmobile, would at least be negligent and, possibly, reckless. If Kennedy knew of this hazard, his operation of the vehicle constituted criminal conduct.

Earlier on July 18, he had been driven over Chappaquiddick Road three times, and over Dyke Road and Dyke Bridge twice. Kopechne had been driven over Chappaquiddick Road five times and over Dyke Road and Dyke Bridge twice.

I believe it probable that Kennedy knew of the hazard that lay ahead of him on Dyke Road but that, for some reason not apparent from the testimony, he failed to exercise due care as he approached the bridge.

IV. I, therefor, find there is probable cause to believe that Edward M. Kennedy operated his motor vehicle negligently on a way or in a place to which the public have a right of access and that such operation appears to have contributed to the death of Mary Jo Kopechne.

February 18, 1970

JAMES A. BOYLE
Justice

Senator Kennedy's TV Speech

My fellow citizens:

I have requested this opportunity to talk to the people of Massachusetts about the tragedy which happened last Friday evening.

This morning I entered a plea of guilty to the charge of leaving the scene of an accident. Prior to my appearance in court it would have been improper for me to comment on these matters.

But tonight I am free to tell you what happened and to say what it means to me.

On the weekend of July 18, I was on Martha's Vineyard Island participating with my nephew, Joe Kennedy, as for 30 years my family has participated in the annual Edgartown Sailing Regatta. Only reasons of health prevented my wife from accompanying me. On Chappaquiddick Island, off Martha's Vineyard, I attended on Friday evening, July 18, a cookout I had encouraged and helped sponsor for a devoted group of Kennedy-campaign secretaries.

When I left the party around 11:15 p.m., I was accompanied by one of these girls, Miss Mary Jo Kopechne. Mary Jo was one of the most devoted members of the staff of Senator Robert Kennedy. She worked for him for four years and was broken up over his death. For this reason and because she was such a gentle, kind and idealistic person, all of us tried to help her feel that she still had a home with the Kennedy family.

There is no truth, no truth whatever, to the widely circulated suspicions of immoral conduct that have been leveled at my behavior and hers regarding that evening. There has never been a private relationship between us of any kind. I know of nothing in Mary Jo's conduct, on that or any other occasions — and the same is true of the other girls at that party — that would lend any substance to such ugly speculation about their character. Nor was I driving under the influence of liquor.

Little over one mile away, the car that I was driving on an unlit road went off a narrow bridge, which had no guard rails and was built on a left angle to the road.

The car overturned in a deep pond and immediately filled with water. I remember thinking as the cold water rushed in around my head that I was, for certain, drowning. But somehow I struggled to the surface alive. I made immediate and repeated efforts to save Mary Jo by diving into the strong and murky current, but succeeded only in increasing my state of utter exhaustion and alarm.

My conduct and conversations during the next several hours, to the extent that I can remember them, make no sense to me at all.

Although my doctors inform me that I suffered a cerebral concussion as well as shock, I do not seek to escape responsibility for my actions by placing the blame either on the physical and emotional trauma brought on by the accident or on anyone else.

I regard as indefensible the fact that I did not report the accident to the police immediately.

Instead of looking directly for a telephone after lying exhausted in the grass for an undetermined time, I walked back to the cottage where the party was being held and requested the help of two friends — my cousin, Joseph Gargan, and Paul Markham — and directed them to return immediately to the scene with me — this was sometime after midnight — in order to undertake a new effort to dive down and locate Miss Kopechne.

Their strenuous efforts, undertaken at some risk to their own lives, also proved futile.

All kinds of scrambled thoughts, all of them confused, some of them irrational, many of them which I cannot recall, and some of which I would not have seriously entertained under normal circumstances, went through my mind during this period. They were reflected in the various inexplicable, inconsistent and inconclusive things I said and did — including such questions as whether the girl might still be alive somewhere out of that immediate area, whether some awful curse did actually hang over all the Kennedys, whether there was some justifiable reason for me to doubt what had happened and to delay my report, whether somehow the awful weight of this incredible incident might, in some way, pass from my shoulders.

I was overcome, I'm frank to say, by a jumble of emotions: grief, fear, doubt, exhaustion, panic, confusion and shock.

Instructing Gargan and Markham not to alarm Mary Jo's friends that night, I had them take me to the ferry crossing. The ferry having shut down for the night, I suddenly jumped into the water and impulsively swam across, nearly drowning once again in the effort, and returned to my hotel about 2 a.m. and collapsed in my room.

I remember going out at one point and saying something to the room clerk.

In the morning, with my mind somewhat more lucid, I made an effort to call a family legal adviser, Burke Marshall, from a public telephone on the Chappaquiddick side of the ferry, and then belatedly reported the accident to the Martha's Vineyard police.

Today, as I mentioned, I felt morally obligated to plead guilty to the charge of leaving the scene of an accident. No words on my part can possibly express the terrible pain and suffering I feel over this tragic incident.

This last week has been an agonizing one for me and for the members of my family. And the grief we feel over the loss of a wonderful friend will remain with us for the rest of our lives.

These events, the publicity, innuendo and whispers which have surrounded them, and my admission of guilt this morning, raise the question in my mind of whether my standing among the people of my State has been so impaired that I should resign my seat in the United States Senate.

If at any time the citizens of Massachusetts should lack confidence in their Senator's character or his ability, with or without justification, he could not, in my opinion, adequately perform his duties, and should not continue in office.

The people of this State — the State which sent John Quincy Adams and Daniel Webster and Charles Sumner and Henry Cabot Lodge and John Kennedy to the United States Senate — are entitled to representation in that body by men who inspire their utmost confidence.

For this reason I would understand full well why some might think it right for me to resign. For me, this will be a difficult decision to make.

It has been seven years since my first election to the Senate. You and I share many memories; some of them have been glorious, some have been very sad.

The opportunity to work with you and serve Massachusetts has made my life worthwhile.

And so I ask you tonight — the people of Massachusetts — to think this through with me. In facing this decision, I seek your advice and opinion. In making it, I seek your prayers.

For this is a decision that I will have finally to make on my own.

It has been written a man does what he must, in spite of personal consequences, in spite of obstacles and dangers and pressures.

And that is the basis of all human morality. Whatever may be the sacrifices he faces if he follows his conscience — the loss of his friends, his fortune, his contentment, even the esteem of his fellow men — each man must decide for himself the course he will follow.

The stories of past courage cannot supply courage itself. For this each man must look into his own soul.

I pray that I can have the courage to make the right decision. Whatever is decided, whatever the future holds for me, I hope that I shall be able to put this most recent tragedy behind me and make some further contribution to our State and mankind, whether it be in public or private life.

Thank you, and goodnight.

John F. Kennedy In Red Spain

It is well known that Ambassador Joseph Kennedy's sympathies during the Spanish Civil War were on the Nationalist side. However, according to an article by Ricardo de la Cierva appearing in the July 1968 issue of the Spanish magazine *Historia y Vida,* from which the following excerpts are translated, this was not the case with young John Kennedy, the future President of the United States. Indeed, the Ambassador's son seems to have paid a visit, in 1938, not — like Lady Austen Chamberlain, Charles Maurras, Jacques Doriot, Léon Degrelle, and other Western political personalities — to the Franco side of the conflict, but to the "Republican" or Communist side — like Clement Attlee, George Bernard Shaw, the Duchess of Athol, Ernest Hemingway, Jawaharlal Nehru, Indira Gandhi, Krishna Menon, and others of the "clenched fist" persuasion.

This is what de la Cierva writes, with photographic documentation to substantiate his assertions, under the heading:

JOHN KENNEDY ALIAS JOE DAVIDSON

The second diplomatic gambit that Alvarez del Vayo [Minister of State in the Republican Government] thrust upon the Anglo-Saxon world through the opportunity of that visit [a publicity stunt organized by the Government] was aimed specifically at the United States. The only American the anxious State Minister could find for his maneuver was a sculptor, Joe Davidson, who had been living in France since 1907, specializing in making busts of well-known personalities. His heads of President Wilson and Anatole France can be seen in the Luxembourg Museum in Paris . . . . The artist consented to announce publicly that he was going to Spain to reproduce the heads of the Heroes of the Revolution, for exhibit in New York according to his custom. But the Heroes of the Revolution were just then losing the war, and Davidson was interested only in conquerors. So the obscure American sculptor played no part in building the iconographic history of the Spanish Civil War, nor is he to be found in the pages of the 1938 news.

The Barcelona archivists did, however, write the name of Davidson under the picture of a young man listening very attentively to the explanations of Enrique Lister [one of the most celebrated of Communist mass murderers]. The young man, obviously an American, cannot be the sculptor Joe Davidson, who at that time was 54 years of age. Once more a photograph has been a fundamental source of information, not confirmed by other evidence, but not to be neglected for that reason. Is the American of our picture John Fitzgerald Kennedy? Several friends of the Kennedy family have confirmed the fact to us. We know that John Kennedy, who was born in 1917, was, in the summer of 1935, at the London School of Economics. He made two visits to Europe during the Spanish Civil War, besides other shorter trips . . . . During those visits, John F. Kennedy was in contact with United States embassies, and he talked with newspapermen, political leaders, and diplomats. Several times he interested himself in a Hindu politician whom his intuition showed to be a man of the future: Nehru . . . . John F. Kennedy's visiting Republican Spain at the same time as Nehru is, therefore, perfectly possible . . . .

Nehru and Davidson delivered the inevitable declarations of sympathy with the Republican cause. But the young gods of the new age, Indira Gandhi and Jack Kennedy, contented themselves with observing and taking notes . . . . It seems that the eldest of the Kennedy brothers, Joe Jr., who was at that time destined by his father for the highest possible aims, also visited embattled Spain. The photograph we publish of the two brothers in uniform in 1941 seems to confirm that the visitor to Barcelona was John. His presence in Barcelona in 1938 is no proof of a political adherence to the Republican cause. Alvarez del Vayo would not have failed to stress it [if such had been the case].

The *Boston Record American* of May 13, 1965, informs us that Joseph Kennedy Jr. spent six weeks in Red Spain during the Civil War. For that reason we cannot agree with Señor de la Cierva that those visits of the young Kennedys to the Communist side of the conflict did not correspond with the sympathies and inclinations of the two brothers.